# WITHIN CONTEXT

## Essays on Jews and Judaism in the New Testament

Mary C. Boys, S.N.J.M.
Anthony J. Saldarini
Philip A. Cunningham
Urban C. von Wahlde
David P. Efroymson
Eugene J. Fisher
Terrance Callan

*edited by*
David P. Efroymson
Eugene J. Fisher
Leon Klenicki

*forewords by*
Irwin J. Borowsky
Leon Klenicki

A Michael Glazier Book
THE LITURGICAL PRESS
Collegeville, Minnesota

A Michael Glazier Book published by The Liturgical Press

Cover design by David Manahan, O.S.B.

Cover: Ms Opp. 154, folio 23 verso, Bodleian Library, Oxford.

1    2    3    4    5    6    7    8    9

**Library of Congress Cataloging-in-Publication Data**

Within context : essays on Jews and Judaism in the New Testament /
    Mary C. Boys ... [et al.] ; edited by David P. Efroymson.
        p.    cm.
    "A Michael Glazier book."
    Includes bibliographical references.
    ISBN 0-8146-5033-3
    1. Jews in the New Testament.  2. Judaism—History—To 70 A.D.
3. Christianity and other religions—Judaism.  4. Judaism-
-Relations—Christianity.  5. Catechetics—Catholic Church.
I. Boys, Mary C.     II. Efroymson, David P. (David Patrick), 1931–
BS2545.J44W579   1993
225.8'296—dc20                                              92-34914
                                                              CIP

# Contents

# Forewords

We salute the editors and contributors to *Within Context* . . . .
Their work will build strong bridges of understanding among Christians and Jews.

Words are, indeed, major tools for instilling trust or injecting poison. Unfortunately, there are words in the New Testament that have been invoked by bigots to foment prejudice and distrust; to accuse and abuse.

As a result of these words, a tradition has developed wherein Jews are blamed for the death of Jesus. Jews from ancient times to this very day are damned in New Testament prose that defames all Jews. For centuries, these references have provided the warrant for hostility and the murder of those whose roots were from the same stock that nurtured Jesus.

There are millions of Christians of goodwill who are also fearful whenever anti-Semitism erupts. Many work diligently in interfaith programs and publish statements explaining that Christianity does not blame contemporary Jews for the death of Jesus. Churches have issued powerful statements affirming the ongoing and permanent nature of the Jews' covenant with God and they have rejected and condemned anti-Semitism. Yet, throughout the world, new converts to Christianity as well as those who are re-discovering their Christian faith, are exposed to the same language that has created anti-Jewish attitudes in the past.

As French scholar Paul Deman has noted, the Jews that Christians meet in their religious textbooks will be, for most, the first Jews they will ever know and perhaps the only Jews they will ever encounter. If that is true with textbooks, how much greater the impact when it is the Bible that depicts the Jews so negatively.

Cardinal Jan Willenbrands discusses this problem candidly in his new book titled "The Church and Jewish People." He points specifically to the Gospel of John where the Jews appear mostly, if not always, as the opposers of Jesus; as persecutors and murderers.

He writes, "It must be admitted that texts such as these have a long-lasting negative effect on the Christian view of Jews and Judaism. It must be admitted that they have horrendous anti-Semitic consequences."

If the gospel writers had known that the invective and anger they expressed in the context of an internal struggle within the Jewish community would be later used to justify hatred, violence and even murder of Jesus' people, they would not have allowed such language into the canon. They would have done what the contributors to this volume are working to accomplish.

Proper reconstruction of the New Testament requires the inclusion of the social and political environment of the first century and the clarification that Jesus was condemned by the Roman procurator and crucified by Roman soldiers.

Let us join together to extend our research and resources to Bible publishers. Let us help them understand that the use of the word "Jew" in the exclusive sense as the enemy of Jesus represents a misguided, incorrect and, ultimately, harmful calumny of an entire people.

Irvin J. Borowsky
Founder and Chairman
American Interfaith Institute

---

*Within Context* is the result of a dialogue of Christians and Jews committed to the interreligious relationship and aware of the problems involved in teaching and preaching about the other person as a person of faith. Much harm has come out of the teaching of contempt denigrating Judaism and its vocation in God's design.

The publication of *Within Context* marks a unique moment in the relationship of Christians and Jews, a time of hope and mutual recognition as part of God's people witnessing covenants and the promise of peace. *Within Context* is the attempt to bridge differences through education respectful of theological differences and religious commitments. Our joint effort was helped and inspired by Bob Born, president of the Born Foundation, which fosters interfaith work. We thank him for his friendship and help which funded the first stages of this educational project.

We hope that *Within Context* in its enlarged present form will inspire teachers and preachers in their presentation of Judaism and the

Jewish people. This task will allow all to be responsible for the other person of faith while entering into the realm of interpersonal sacredness so well described by the Jewish theologian Emmanuel Levinas:

> The existence of God is sacred history itself, the sacredness of man's relation to man through which God may pass.

*Within Context* is evidence of the new reality of friendship in the lives of Christians and Jews.

Rabbi Leon Klenicki
Director, Department of Interfaith Affairs
Anti-Defamation League of B'nai B'rith

# Introduction

The various writings which together make up what Christians call the New Testament have been treasured by these same Christians for their witness to Jesus, for their witness to the God of Israel whom Jesus called "Father," and for the light they throw on the "Church," the communities of Jews and then of Jews and Gentiles who had accepted Jesus. Inevitably then, and rightly, the New Testament, together with the older and larger collection of the Hebrew Scriptures, has been fundamental in every kind of Christian teaching and preaching. A generation or so ago this was not always the case for Catholics. But since Vatican Council II and the biblical, catechetical, liturgical, and theological revivals which led up to it and took sustenance from it, the New Testament has regained its place. Catholics are hearing it read in church, are reading it themselves, and are using it in discussion and prayer groups, as well as in teaching, from elementary school through adult education.

But there is an aspect of much of the New Testament which demands more attention than it sometimes receives in Catholic teaching and preaching. The person at its center was a first-century Jew, a person from a time and culture far removed from our own. Further, he was a Jew who tried to persuade other Jews of something; with many he succeeded, but many were not persuaded. Most of the world's Jews, of course, had never seen or heard of him. After his death, his Jewish followers, emboldened by their experience of his resurrection, argued the rightness of his—and their—position, against other Jews who had not been persuaded. To complicate matters further, his Jewish followers argued with each other over the conditions under which Gentiles might be admitted to the new movement. Finally, some of the Jewish communities within the Jesus movement (some now with Gentile members) found themselves further at odds with other Jews: over Torah-observance, over more elaborate claims being made for Jesus, over who or what was authentically "Jewish." And what has all this to do with the New Testament? Everything! All four Gospels, the Acts of the Apostles, and the most important of

Paul's letters not only bear witness to all this polemic. They are written largely to take part in and to take sides on these disputes.

The disputes were vigorous, serious, and sometimes bitter. But those who engaged in these arguments were mostly Jews, arguing with other Jews. Eventually, at different times in different places, the ways parted. Eventually there arose "Christianity" and "Judaism." But at the time they were written, the New Testament documents arose among Jews who followed Jesus (or their Gentile converts). When they argued— and these writings frequently argue—they argued either against other Jews who also followed Jesus (with *their* Gentile converts), or against Jews who did not. But the issues were nearly always Jewish issues.

The danger here is to read the polemical passages, or the polemical writings, as if they were "Christian" arguments against "Jews" or "Judaism." But this would be to read them *out of context;* it would be to mis-read them.

Mis-reading them in the framework of Christian teaching or preaching turns Christianity into a source, or at least a "carrier," of anti-Judaism, the "teaching of contempt" for Jews and Judaism. And it distorts Christianity itself. Thus it is essential that the New Testament be read "within context." It is to aid in this effort that the essays which follow were envisioned and written.

The original *Within Context* (included as an appendix at the end of this book) was a 12-page booklet presenting a set of "Guidelines for the Catechetical Presentation of Jews and Judaism in the New Testament." It was an attempt "to provide a practical and readable tool" which expanded on certain brief sections of the Holy See's *Notes on the Correct Way to Present the Jews and Judaism in Preaching and Catechesis of the Roman Catholic Church* (issued on June 24, 1985: USCC Publication No. 970). The relevant section of the *Notes* dealt with "the New Testament portrayal of Jews and Judaism, and with the origins of Christian liturgy in Second Temple Judaism." The booklet *Within Context* received wide distribution through Silver Burdett and Ginn, and was translated into German, French, Italian, and Polish. It served as a kind of agenda for several meetings in various dioceses throughout the country.

As useful as the original *Within Context* has proven to be, it became clear that something more was required. The lapidary sentences of the Vatican's *Notes* had become full paragraphs in *Within Context.* It was a solid but brief statement of a position, a stance, which teachers ought to take on the presentation of Jews and Judaism in Catholic teaching. What seemed to be needed was something full enough to treat the thornier issues more elaborately, but which still would be succinct and clear enough to be readable. We decided on a series of essays by competent scholars, written in a non-technical way for the literate but not fully biblically trained Catholic teacher. The essays do not deal with the question—itself legitimately debated—about whether parts of the New Testament might be "anti-Jewish" or "anti-Judaic." Rather, they attempt to "unpack" the most difficult issues, events, passages, or whole writings, in ways that the ordinary Catholic teacher, preacher, or discussion group participant is likely to find helpful.

Each essay stands on its own, but the order in which they appear is not random. Mary Boys' lead essay deals with the erroneous and dangerous claim, mistakenly held by many Christians until recently, that God had "replaced" Jews with Christians as his people, or that Judaism had been rejected by God and "superseded" by Christianity. She shows how the idea arose, what is wrong with it, and why such a position is untenable. She then provides an alternative vision, biblically and theologically more authentic, together with certain practical guidelines for teachers and preachers.

Anthony Saldarini sets the stage for the essays to follow with an up-to-date picture of the Judaism contemporary with Jesus. This Jewish context within which Jesus lived, taught, and sometimes argued is essential for understanding both Jesus and the Jewish origins of Christianity.

Chronologically one might first turn to an examination of the polemical aspects of Jesus' teaching and deeds. But practically our only sources of knowledge of Jesus are the four Gospels, so they are treated next. Philip Cunningham introduces the Gospels of Mark, Matthew, and Luke (the "Synoptic" Gospels) with a careful eye in the direction of those aspects which might appear antagonistic toward Jews and Judaism. He describes the origins of the gospel tradition in the early church and then each of the three Gospels separately, showing how important it is to be aware of the theological agenda of each, so they are not mis-read as "history," in the sense in which that word is frequently taken today, for example as transcripts of TV coverage of events.

The Gospel of John receives separate treatment by Urban von Wahlde, because of the peculiarly polemical passages in that work. The history of the community out of which that Gospel arose, and the history of the composition of the document itself, are essential if serious distortion is to be avoided.

Jesus, of course, is both at the beginning and center of the whole Christian venture. David Efroymson examines those aspects of Jesus' ministry and teaching which appear to have provoked opposition. What seem to have been the issues in dispute? How serious was the opposition? From which quarters is the opposition likely to have arisen? Oversimplified answers to such questions have caused a good deal of mischief in Christian history and theology.

The passion and the death of Jesus might be as difficult to handle as anything treated in this book. Eugene Fisher shows how distorted popular presentations frequently are, and how imperative it is to approach the trial narratives in the Gospels critically. We can reconstruct at least the principal historical facts, and those facts do not support the ugly claim that "the Jews" crucified Jesus.

Paul's letters are the subject of Terrance Callan's essay, which focuses on the troublesome issues of Paul's position on the Jewish Law and the Jewish people. Certain passages, especially in the letters to the Galatians and to the Romans, raise serious questions for Christianity today. Callan presents several ways of understanding these passages, and some healthy suggestions about how they are *not* to be understood.

We have added a set of reflection and discussion questions for each chapter and for the book as a whole. Philip Cunningham was asked to provide them because of his extensive experience with adult discussion groups and with the training of teachers.

This project was conceived by Rabbi Leon Klenicki and assisted by Bob Born, president of the Born Foundation, which funded its first stages.

The original *Within Context* has also been included as an appendix with the permission of Eugene Fisher and the National Conference of Catholic Bishops. Both its succinctness and its practical catechetical orientation should, we hope, prove useful to those teachers, preachers, and adult discussion group leaders and participants for whom this collection of essays is primarily intended.

The Editors

# A More Faithful Portrait of Judaism: An Imperative for Christian Educators

*Mary C. Boys,* S.N.J.M.

Christian educators teach about Jews and Judaism, whether they are aware of it or not.[1] In fact, there is simply no way to talk about Christianity without reference to Judaism. From Jewish tradition Christians learned the vocabulary and grammar of their own tradition. Judaism is the source of Christian proclamation of God as one, of its conviction that the merciful and gracious God is joined to them by covenant, of the concept "messiah" as an image of longing for divine justice, and of the heritage of prophetic critique. That Jesus of Nazareth was a Jew is not incidental to his mission and ministry; his deeds and words assume their full meaning only when understood in the context of first-century Palestinian Jewish life. The first disciples of Jesus were Jews, and many of the early Church's concerns and controversies centered around the relationship of the "Followers of the Way" to Judaism.[2] Christians in part share the Scriptures of the Jews, and their way of worship, most notably the Eucharist, emanates from Jewish modes of worship.[3] In short, Christian self-

---

[1] I use the phrase "Jews and Judaism" to emphasize that Judaism is a living tradition, and that what Christians teach affects how they understand a people. Hence, the desirability of engaging in conversation with Jews themselves, and not simply learning about Judaism from texts. Unfortunately, in many places of the world, the small number of Jews precludes the possibility of this engagement.

[2] Most likely the earliest designation for the emerging Christian community (see Acts 9:2; 19:9, 23; 24:22).

[3] The Jewish Scripture, the Tanakh—an acronym formed from the Hebrew words for *the Five Books of Moses* (*Torah*), Prophets (*Nevi'im*) and Wisdom (*Ketuvim*)—is not identical with the books included in the Catholic "Old" (or First) Testament. Catholics have a more extensive canon of 46 books (as do the Eastern Orthodox in general), whereas the Jewish canon has 39 books. The Protestant canon also has 39 books, although arranged differently. See Raymond E. Brown, "Canonicity [#s 20–47]," in R. E. Brown, Joseph Fitzmyer, and Roland E. Murphy, eds., *The New Jerome Biblical Commentary* (Englewood Cliffs: Prentice Hall, 1990) 1037–1043. On the connection between Jewish and Christian worship, see R. Beckwith, "The Jewish Background to Christian Worship," in *The Study of Liturgy*, A. Jones, G. Wainwright, and E. Yarnold,

understanding is inextricably linked to Judaism.[4]

Precisely because of Judaism's centrality to Christianity, Christian teachers and preachers have long been preoccupied with defining the relationship. The explanation that enjoyed dominance for nearly two thousand years is that Judaism had been supplanted by Christianity. Judaism represented the old covenant, and Christianity the new. Judaism's rule of law contrasted with the sovereignty of love preached by Jesus. In the words of the venerable hymn, the Pange Lingua, "Lo! o'er ancient forms departing, newer rites of grace prevail."[5]

Visually, this replacement was popularly reflected in the medieval imagery of Church and Synagogue. Two sculptures, for instance, appear in the facade of the Strassbourg Cathedral, constructed in the thirteenth century. The figure of the Church stands erect, with head crowned and a staff in the form of a cross grasped firmly in one hand and a chalice in the other. Far less triumphant is the second figure, Synagogue, with head turned toward the earth, eyes blindfolded, and staff broken. Similarly, in the cathedral of Breme (late fourteenth–early fifteenth century) the same figures appear, carved in wood. The figure of the Church holds a banner reading, "Be faithful unto death and I will give you the crown of life." In contrast, Synagogue's banner says, "Ah, the crown of my head has fallen and our glory."[6]

This is precisely what the rather daunting term *supersessionism* (from the Latin *supersedere*, to sit upon, to preside over, to forbear, to refrain) means. Supersessionism, a word that has little currency outside theological circles, denotes the longstanding point of view of Christians that they have replaced the Jews as God's people because of the Jews' rejection of Jesus Christ. The bedrock of supersessionism is the argument that the Church has made Judaism obsolete.

eds., *The Study of Liturgy* (New York: Oxford University Press, 1978) 39–51; Jacob Petuchowski and Michael Brocke, eds., *The Lord's Prayer and Jewish Liturgy* (New York: Seabury, 1978); and Eugene J. Fisher and Daniel Polish, eds., *Liturgical Foundations for Social Policy in the Catholic and Jewish Traditions* (South Bend: University of Notre Dame Press, 1983).

[4] This axiom, however, cannot be reversed, because Jewish self-understanding at a fundamental level is not connected to Christianity. Christianity and Judaism are not symmetrical traditions, so one must take great care in drawing parallels.

[5] From the fifth verse, here in full: *Tantum ergo Sacramentum Veneremur cernui/Et antiquum documentum Novo cedat ritui/Praestet fides supplementum Sensuum defectui* (Down in adoration falling, Lo! the sacred Host we hail/Lo! o'er ancient forms departing, newer rites of grace prevail/Faith for all defects supplying where the feeble senses fail) *Worship II: A Hymnal for Roman Catholic Parishes* [Chicago: G.I.A. Publications, 1975, #225]. Though sung far less often now, this hymn was in pre-Vatican II days part of the fundamental repertoire of Catholic hymnody.

[6] See Bernhard Blumenkranz, *Le juif medieval au miroir de l'art chretien* (Paris: Etudes Augustiniennes, 1966), p. 64. The Latin original of each banner: *"Esto fidlis usque ad mortem et dabo tibi coronam uite." "Heu cecidit cornona capitis mei et g(lo)r(i)a n(os)tra."*

Two problems, however, arise from this premise: (1) whether current biblical and theological thought can any longer justify supersessionism and (2) whether argumentation is the most appropriate model for the Church to adopt in relationship to Judaism.[7]

My twofold thesis follows directly from these problems. First, I believe that both biblical and theological studies of the late twentieth century offer persuasive grounds for rejecting supersessionism. Jesus did not make Judaism obsolete, and its survival over subsequent centuries—despite hostility, persecution and holocaust—testifies to its vitality. Second, I believe that argumentation is an inadequate method for the way the Church should relate with Jews and Judaism. Disputation indeed prevailed for centuries, but a Church which now speaks of "the bond which joins us as a Church to the Jews and Judaism," must reject supersessionism as incompatible with dialogue.[8] Rather, the Church must develop more adequate ways of expressing its relationship with Judaism so that its self-identity will rest on a more truthful foundation:

> To enter into dialogue with another religious tradition is to come to see the world through other eyes. One comes to understand what their categories are, how they relate to each other, how they relate to the world. One even becomes able to anticipate how a member of another tradition will respond in certain circumstances. One begins to be able to use the concepts and categories of the other tradition for oneself. *Most significantly, one is able to look at one's own faith and its categories through the eyes of the other. When that happens, we see things about ourselves and our faith that we had not seen before.* In all of that, we do not cease to be committed and faithful members of our own tradition. We are on the way to becoming religiously bilingual.[9]

A Church which seeks deeper self-understanding must engage in dialogue. If it is to honor its bond with Judaism, the Church must

[7] For a superb analysis of the weakness of argument vis-a-vis conversation, see Margret Buchmann, "Improving Education by Talking: Argument or Conversation," *Teachers College Record* 86/3 (1985) 441–453.

[8] Commission for Religious Relations with the Jews, "Notes on the Correct Way to Present the Jews and Judaism in Preaching and Catechesis in the Roman Catholic Church," in Helga Croner, ed., *Further Stepping Stones in Jewish-Christian Relations* (New York: Paulist, 1985) #8. This echoes the earlier statement (1965) from *Nostra Aetate* #4: "As this sacred Synod [Vatican II] searches into the mystery of the Church it recalls the spiritual bond linking the people of the new covenant with Abraham's stock." The text of *Nostra Aetate* is available in Austin Flannery, ed., *Vatican Council II: The Conciliar and Post Conciliar Documents,* vol. 1, new rev. ed. (Collegeville: The Liturgical Press, 1984).

[9] David Lochhead, *The Dialogical Imperative: A Christian Reflection on Interfaith Encounter* (Maryknoll: Orbis, 1988) 69–70. Emphasis added.

enter into conversation with Jews. This is not a peripheral matter, an option for those few people engaged in formal interreligious dialogue. In particular, Christian educators must, at minimum, avail themselves of the major findings of the Jewish-Christian dialogue if they are to replace supersessionist notions that block the development of a mature Christianity.[10]

I will develop my thesis by means of a four-part structure. In the initial part, I will explicate the elements of supersessionism, and demonstrate in the second section that biblical and theological developments have undermined each element. In the third and fourth sections, respectively, I will propose an alternative schema and suggest some guidelines for teaching that might serve to enhance and complement *Within Context.*

## I. The Tenets of Supersessionism (see fig. 1)

The fundamental axiom of supersessionism is that God's revelation in Jesus Christ supersedes the revelation to Israel. God had indeed spoken on Sinai, but Christ's death on Calvary manifested the definitive word of salvation. Thus the prior word was mere preparation, an anticipation of Jesus the *Logos.*

From this flow three pivotal, interrelated claims: (1) The New Testament fulfills the Old Testament;[11] (2) The Church replaces the Jews as God's people; and (3) Judaism is obsolete, its covenant abrogated.

Crucial to understanding these claims is the context in which they developed. After the destruction of Jerusalem in 70 C.E., the Followers of the Way increasingly defined themselves *against* the other major surviving group of Jews, Pharisaic Judaism. Theirs was a sibling rivalry, to which the New Testament bears witness, especially in later texts such as the Gospel of Matthew (e.g., Jesus' excoriation of the Pharisees in chapter 23; the blood curse in 27:24-25), the Acts of the Apostles (e.g., the accusation that the Jews had killed Jesus; see Acts 4:10; 5:30; 7:52) and the Gospel of John (e.g., the emphasis on the culpability of "the Jews" in the crucifixion of Jesus).

Because of the conflict between the siblings, the two traditions moved into the second and third century with hostility. Much Chris-

---

[10] See Norman A. Beck, *Mature Christianity: The Recognition and Repudiation of the Anti-Jewish Polemic of the New Testament* (Selinsgrove: Susquehanna University Press, and London and Toronto: Associated University Presses, 1985). Beck's thesis is that responsible self-criticism is an indication that a religious community has attained a significant level of maturity (see 11–13).

[11] This is most succinctly expressed by a formula of Augustine that had enormous influence: "In the Old Testament, the New Testament lies hid; in the New Testament, the Old Testament becomes clear" (*Questions on the Heptateuch,* 2.73).

**Fig. 1**

| |
|---|
| THEOLOGICAL TENETS OF SUPERSESSIONISM |

| |
|---|
| God's revelation in Jesus Christ supersedes the revelation to Israel. |

Therefore:

| |
|---|
| The New Testament fulfills the Old Testament. |

"In the Old Testament, the New Testament lies hid;
in the New Testament, the Old Testament becomes clear."
Augustine (d. 430)

| |
|---|
| The Church replaces the Jews as God's people. |

| |
|---|
| Judaism is obsolete, its covenant abrogated. |

Related Claims:

| |
|---|
| Post-exilic Judaism was legalistic. |

The Pharisees represented the apotheosis of legalism.

| |
|---|
| The Jews did not heed the warning of the prophets. |

| |
|---|
| The Jews did not understand the prophecies about Jesus. |

The Jews rejected Jesus because their hearts were hardened.

The Jews did not accept Jesus as Messiah because they expected a royal, glorious messianic figure.

| |
|---|
| The Jews were Christ-killers. |

Therefore "God has been murdered." (Melito of Sardis, d. ca. 190)

Because they have rejected Jesus, they must wander in exile, though they must not be killed. (Augustine) tian literature in the second and third centuries was preoccupied with apologetics, i.e., with explaining and justifying the belief in Christ. Christians had to justify their choice to retain the Hebrew Scriptures (against Marcion, who had proposed it be jettisoned) even as they proclaimed the radical newness of Christianity. So teachers such as the author of *The Epistle of Barnabas* (ca. 97 C.E.), Justin Martyr (ca. 100–165), Tertullian (ca. 160–ca. 225), and Origen (ca. 185–254) argued, often vehemently, that the Jews misinterpreted the Scriptures. Only Christians rightly read the prophecies, only Christians worshipped in true ways. The Jews, blind to God's ways and lacking faith, were mired in the law.[12] All of the "related claims" (see chart) surface in these writings, and constitute a heritage that has shaped Christian self-identity.

Moreover, in the fourth and fifth centuries the work of influential teachers and preachers such as Augustine (354–430), John Chrysostom (347–407), and Cyril of Alexandria (d. 444) exacerbated the rift. Augustine, in an allegorical exposition of the story of Cain and Abel (Genesis 4:1-15), argued that because the Jews had rejected Jesus, they must wander in exile, though they must not be killed: "Abel, the younger brother, is killed by the elder brother; Christ, the head of the younger people, is killed by the elder people of the Jews. Abel dies in the field; Christ dies on Calvary." Augustine maintains, therefore, that the Jews are cursed:

> That is, the Church admits and avows the Jewish people to be cursed, because after killing Christ they continue to till the ground of an earthly circumcision, an earthly Sabbath, an earthly Passover . . . . In this way the Jewish people, like Cain, continue tilling the ground, in the carnal observance of the law, which does not yield to them its strength because they do not perceive in it the grace of Christ.[13]

---

[12] See especially "The Epistle of Barnabas," in Kirsopp Lake, ed. and trans., *The Apostolic Fathers,* vol. 1 (Cambridge, Mass.: Harvard University Press; and London: W. Heinemann, 1952); R.P.C. Hanson, ed. and trans., *Selections from Justin Martyr's Dialogue with Trypho, a Jew* (London: Lutterworth Press, 1963); and Ernest Evans, ed., *Tertullian: Adversus Marcionem,* 2 vols. (Oxford: Clarendon Press, 1972). For the most pertinent secondary literature, see David P. Efroymson, "The Patristic Connection," in Alan Davies, ed., *AntiSemitism and the Foundations of Christianity* (New York: Paulist, 1979) 98–117; Nicholas de Lange, *Origen and the Jews* (Cambridge: Cambridge University Press, 1976); Stephen G. Wilson, ed., *Anti-Judaism in Early Christianity:* Separation and Polemic, Studies in Christianity and Judaism, No. 2 (Waterloo, Ontario: Wilfrid Laurier Press, 1986); and Theodore G. Stylianopoulos, *Justin Martyr and the Mosaic Law* (Missoula, Mont.: Society of Biblical Literature and Scholars Press, 1975).

[13] Augustine, "Reply to Faustus the Manichean" (Book 12, #s 9–13) in Frank Talmage, ed., *Disputation and Dialogue* (New York: KTAV and the Anti-Defamation League of B'nai B'rith, 1975) 29–30. Marc Saperstein contends that Augustine's theory about Jewish existence became the foundation of official church doctrine through the Middle Ages.

In the preaching of the presbyter John Chrysostom in late fourth-century Antioch, supersessionism received its most eloquent and forceful expression. In the contentious atmosphere of the day, John used his considerable powers of persuasion to inveigh against those he alleged to be enemies of orthodox Christianity.[14] Among those he attacked were the "Judaizers," Christians attracted to the celebration of Jewish festivals and to the observance of Jewish customs. By adopting the Jewish ways, the Judaizers seemed to call into question the truth of Christianity. As Robert Wilken observes, "If Christians were going around the corner to attend the synagogue, this meant that the divine was more tangibly present in the synagogue than in the churches. If the churches were empty because the Jews were celebrating their high holy days, this suggested that the Jewish way was more authentic."[15] In short, John sought to persuade the Judaizing Christians that Christian rites were more effective. The Hellenistic rhetorical form he employed, invective (*psogos*), meant that he held Judaism up to derision; invective was used to villify and defame.[16] Thus, in a sermon preached in 386 he railed against those "who are sick with Judaism":

> Do not be surprised if I have called the Jews wretched. They are truly wretched and miserable for they have received many good things from God yet they have spurned them and violently cast them away. The sun of righteousness rose on them first, but they turned their back on its beams and sat in darkness. But we, who were nurtured in darkness, welcomed the light and we were freed from the yoke of error. The Jews were branches of the holy root, but they were lopped off. We were not part of the root, yet we have produced the fruits of piety. They read the prophets from ancient times, yet they crucified the one spoken of by the prophets. . . . They were called to sonship, but they degenerated to the level of dogs.[17]

Augustine's theory had a double-sided character. On the one hand, it maintained that Jews not be harmed or killed. On the other, it meant that Jews should live in such a way that would give evidence of their "reprobate character and attest to their status of being accursed" (*Moments of Crisis in Jewish-Christian Relations* [London: SCM, and Philadelphia: Trinity Press International, 1989] 10–11.)

[14] This was a time in which Christology sparked vigorous and trenchant debates, with various alliances adhering to the teaching of Arius or Apollinarius (or Apollinaris) rather than following the decrees of the Council of Nicea (325). John Chrysostom villified the Christians whom he judged to be heretical as much as he did Jews and Judaizers.

[15] Robert L. Wilken, *John Chrysostom and the Jews: Rhetoric and Reality in the Late Fourth Century.* (Berkeley: University of California, 1983) 78.

[16] See Wilken, *John Chrysostom and the Jews,* 113.

[17] John Chrysostom, "Homily One Against the Jews," in Robert Wilken and Wayne Meeks, eds., *Jews and Christians in Antioch* (Missoula: Scholars Press, 1978) 87.

In the same sermon, he continued his indictment against the Jews, now charging his fourth-century Jewish contemporaries with the death of Christ:

> What sort of folly, what kind of madness, to participate in the festivals of those who are dishonored, abandoned by God, and provoked the Lord. . . . They killed the son of your Lord, and you dare to gather them in the same place? When the one who was killed by them honors you by making you a brother and fellow heir, you dishonor him by revering his murderers, those who crucified him, and by attending their festival assemblies? You enter their defiled synagogues, you pass through impure gates, and you share in the table of demons. That is what I am persuaded to call the Jewish fast after the God-slaying. What else can one call those who set themselves against God than worshippers of demons?[18]

Augustine's conviction that the Jews must wander in exile, and Chrysostom's "rhetoric of abuse" were echoed in Cyril's bitter diatribes against the Jews for their failure to recognize Christ. The Jews lacked the spirit to properly grasp the Scriptures: "in the arrogant obtuseness of the letter of the law, you still think that you can honor God through this [sacrifices], and you shake off the more accurate perception of the law as if you had entire knowledge of what was written when you have only perceived trash."[19] The three shared a common conviction, born out of supersessionism:

> The fathers thought Judaism was dying, that the victory of the Church signified the demise of Judaism. They created a caricature to meet their expectations and refused to look at Judaism for what it really was. But the problem of Judaism arose as a theological issue because Judaism had not died. It had not come to an end in Jesus, and it was still a force to be reckoned with in the Roman empire.[20]

Supersessionism caricatures Judaism. Having developed in a disputatious age, it is inappropriate in a dialogical one.

## II. Supersessionism Reexamined: A Biblical and Theological Assessment

Supersessionism is by no means extinct in the Church of the late twentieth century. After all, the New Testament continues to be proclaimed, and those same texts—the denunciation of the Pharisees

[18] Homily One Against the Jews, 100.
[19] Cyril of Alexandria in J. P. Migne, ed., *Patrologiae cursus completus* 77: 513d–516b, cited in Robert L. Wilken, *Judaism and the Early Christian Mind* (New Haven and London: Yale University Press, 1971) 75.
[20] Wilken, *Judaism and the Early Christian Mind,* 229.

and the "blood curse" in Matthew, the culpability for the death of Jesus assigned to "the Jews" in John—are regularly heard by church-goers. Unless the homilist places texts such as these in context, or one has learned an alternative interpretation, an attentive hearer cannot but pick up a negative view of Judaism. Moreover, the writings of the early Christian teachers influenced generations of theologians; their legacy cannot merely be tossed aside.

Despite supersessionism's tenacious grip on Christian preaching, teaching and liturgy, biblical and theological developments have made it obsolete. Not one element can withstand the weight of knowledge gained in recent times. Though simplistic enough for polemics, the tenets cannot sustain the complexities of modern scholarship. Those who teach an understanding of Christianity grounded in supersessionism are, therefore, promulgating a distorted view of the tradition. A faithful portrait of Christian life cannot be based on a caricature of Jewish life.

## A. Biblical Studies and the Obsolescence of Supersessionism

Two principal factors have contributed to the obsolescence of supersessionism. One is the explosion of knowledge in biblical studies, which has in turn influenced systematic theological reflection. Archaeological discoveries, facility in Near Eastern languages and literature, and highly refined methods for studying both biblical and extra-biblical texts have revolutionized scholarship. Because each of the essays in this volume testifies to the breadth and depth of such research, it is appropriate here simply to take general note of three critical areas of study that necessitate a rejection of supersessionism: the pluralism of "Early" Judaism, the Jewishness of Jesus, and the painstaking analysis of complex issues such as the trial of Jesus and the concept of messiah.

The adjective "early" applied to Judaism bears considerable significance because it points to the diverse and lively views evident in Jewish life from ca. 250 B.C.E. to 200 C.E. Moreover, it reflects a complete turn from what had been the dominant view of Christian scholars of previous eras, namely, that Judaism after the exile (587 B.C.E.) had degenerated into legalism and was "late" or, in other words, past its prime. "Early Judaism" has become a technical term referring to the pluralistic character of pre-70 Judaism when many groups vied for their interpretation of *Torah* and no single viewpoint was regarded as normative.[21] Among those groups was the "Palestinian Jesus Move-

---

[21] See especially Anthony J. Saldarini, *Pharisees, Scribes and Sadducees in Palestinian Society: A Sociological Approach* (Wilmington: Michael Glazier, 1988).

ment," based in Jerusalem, loyal to Jesus of Nazareth, and developing boundaries that clarified how and why its understanding of Torah was appreciably different from all the other Jewish groups.[22]

After the destruction of the Temple and Jerusalem in 70, only two of the groups survived: Pharisaic Judaism, which became Rabbinic Judaism; and the Palestinian Jesus Movement, which became Early Christianity. So the two are siblings. Modern Judaism and Christianity have the same "mother," Early Judaism. To say that the latter has made the former obsolete falsifies the origins.

Given this genesis, it is obvious that researchers should pursue the implications of the Jewishness of Jesus. Scholars here are moving on several fronts at once. One direction involves speculation on the most appropriate category for understanding Jesus the Jew. As charismatic miracle worker? As the one bringing the restoration of Israel? As Pharisee? As eschatological prophet?[23] A second direction in which scholars are proceeding is fuller identification of the Jewish context of the New Testament writings, that is, showing how Jesus' teachings come out of the world of Early Judaism and how Rabbinic Judaism handed on many of those same teachings.[24]

The enormous amount of data available to contemporary scholars and the painstaking methods of analysis they employ has enabled dispassionate reconsideration of once contentious issues. Two complex topics in particular reflect scholarly efforts: the passion and death of Jesus and the concept of the messiah. The first of these obviously includes the question of who and what killed Jesus—a question that previous ages had grossly oversimplified.[25] The second topic involves sorting out the strands of messianic imagery not simply in the First Testament, but also in the way both Judaism and Christianity have

[22] James H. Charlesworth, "Exploring Opportunities for Rethinking Relations among Jews and Christians," in J. H. Charlesworth, Frank X. Blisard and Jeffrey S. Siker, eds., *Jews and Christians: Exploring the Past, Present, and Future* (New York: Crossroad, 1990) 38.

[23] For two synoptic studies, see Daniel Harrington, "The Jewishness of Jesus," *The Catholic Biblical Quarterly* 49/1 (January 1987) 1–13; and James H. Charlesworth, *Jesus within Judaism* (Garden City: Doubleday, 1988).

[24] See, e.g., Samuel Tobias Lachs, *A Rabbinic Commentary on the New Testament: The Gospels of Matthew, Mark and Luke* (Hoboken: KTAV, and New York: Anti-Defamation League of B'nai B'rith, 1987); Pinchas Lapide, *The Sermon on the Mount: Utopia or Program for Action?* (Maryknoll: Orbis Books, 1986); Clemens Thoma and Michael Wyschogrod, eds., *Parable and Story in Judaism and Christianity* (New York: Paulist, 1989); and Brad Young, *Jesus and His Jewish Parables: Rediscovering the Roots of Jesus' Teaching* (New York: Paulist Press, 1989).

[25] See Paul Winter, *On the Trial of Jesus* 2nd. ed. rev. and ed. by T. A. Burkill and Geza Vermes (Berlin and New York: De Gruyter, 1974); Martin Hengel, *Crucifixion* (Philadelphia: Fortress, 1977); David R. Catchpole, *The Trial of Jesus* (Leiden: Brill, 1971); Gerard Sloyan, *Jesus on Trial* (Philadelphia: Fortress, 1973).

differently appropriated the term.[26] As Clemens Thoma has succinctly expressed it: "Christians perceive in Christ far more than a Jewish messiah."[27]

The import of these studies requires teachers to be wary of the many oversimplifications and distortions that Christian teaching has passed on for centuries. A document such as *Within Context* provides a condensed, readable survey of the developments specified above. But let the reader beware: the demands it makes on the teacher are considerable. Especially in cases where one's fundamental understanding of Christianity has been derived from a primitive grasp of Judaism, an entire new foundation must be constructed.

## B. The Holocaust and the Obsolescence of Supersessionism

This constructive task involves consideration of another factor contributing to the obsolescence of supersessionism: the impact of the Holocaust.[28] One major issue that Christian educators must confront is the extent to which the teaching of supersessionism played into Nazi hands. If Christians were too often "silent bystanders," was the caricature of Judaism they had inherited a contributing factor to their apathy?

Moreover, if Jews have not simply survived the Holocaust, but risen from its ashes to recreate a vibrant people, then what might theologians deduce? To Catholic theologian Michael McGarry, Jewish survival is a sign that God does not want a world without Jews. There-

[26] Appropriate terminology is a problem. Too often when Christians speak of the "Old Testament," they imply that it is outmoded. Alternatively, one might speak of the "Hebrew Scriptures" or, as I prefer, the "First Testament." This follows the editorial board of the *Biblical Theology Bulletin;* see especially James A. Sanders, "First Testament and Second," *Biblical Theology Bulletin* 17 (1987) 47–49. For a superb analysis of the question of terminology, see Roger Brooks and John J. Collins, eds., *Hebrew Bible or Old Testament? Studying the Bible in Judaism and Christianity,* Christianity and Judaism in Antiquity, No. 5 (Notre Dame: University of Notre Dame Press, 1990).

[27] Clemens Thoma, *A Christian Theology of Judaism,* Stimulus Books (New York: Paulist, 1980) 135. See especially Donald Juel, *Messianic Exegesis: Christological Interpretation of the Old Testament in Early Christianity* (Philadelphia: Fortress, 1988). Cf. Jacob Neusner, *Messiah in Context: Israel's History and Destiny in Formative Judaism* (Philadelphia: Fortress, 1984).

[28] Because biblically a holocaust is a burnt or entirely consumed offering, the appropriateness of this term to refer to the victims of the Nazi *die Endlösung der Judenfrage in Europa* ("The final solution of the Jewish question in Europe") is questionable. One alternative is the Hebrew term *Shoah,* whirlwind, destruction, catastrophe. See Alice L. Eckardt and A. Roy Eckardt, "Studying the Holocaust's Impact Today: Some Dilemma of Language and Method," in Alan Rosenberg and Gerald E. Myers. eds., *Echoes from the Holocaust: Philosophical Reflections on a Dark Time* (Philadelphia: Temple University Press, 1988) 432–442.

fore, he argues, Christians are not to eliminate Jews. Specifically, they are not to proselytize them, not to attempt to convert them:

> Christians believe, with all their heart, that Jesus stands for them as the forever valid sacrament and sign of God's saving action. That they are called as individuals to respond in community is the particular privilege and vocation of the Church, which stands as the sacrament of this belief. But as believers of both Testaments know and proclaim, God calls people not only as individuals, but also as communities. YHWH's call in and through community is as irrevocable and unavailable to renegotiation as God's call to each heart is. Thus, this former part of the Christian belief requires a sign and a sacrament to be real to and for the world.
>
> The Jewish people, I submit, stand as the necessary sacrament and sign of this fuller message. God's election, given through Moses, does not end, even with the definitive coming of salvation which Christians recognize in the Jew Jesus. If Christians focus their energy on converting the Jews, they are systematically attempting to eliminate the sacrament and sign that YHWH calls humans as community as well as individuals, thereby undermining their very own faith.[29]

The biblical and theological reevaluation places an enormous responsibility on Christian educators. It is not sufficient to set aside supersessionist notions. Teachers need access to an alternative schema. What follows is one possibility.

### III. Tenets for a Church in Conversation with Jews and Judaism (see fig. 2)

The fundamental axiom of a Church in conversation with Jews and Judaism is that the one God is truly revealed in both the Jewish people and in the followers of Jesus Christ. Jews and Christians worship the same God, the One who is over all and in all, the One who is gracious and merciful. The manifestation of the Holy One in the life, death and resurrection of Jesus of Nazareth neither negates nor limits the divine presence with the Jewish people.

In Paul's metaphor, the Church is a wild olive shoot grafted onto the root (Romans 11:17).[30] Perhaps one might add, in light of what

---

[29] Michael B. McGarry, "A Question of Motive: A Conversation on Mission and Contemporary Jewish-Catholic Relations," (Paper presented to the Christian Study Group on Jews and Judaism, Baltimore, 7 October 1989) 21. I have used the Tetragrammaton rather than follow McGarry's spelling of the Divine Name. Cf. M. B. McGarry, "Contemporary Roman Catholic Understandings of Mission," in Martin A. Cohen and Helga Croner, eds., *Christian Mission-Jewish Mission,* Stimulus Books (New York: Paulist, 1982) 119–146.

[30] Pope John Paul II has spoken of the Church as the "new branch from the common root" (Eugene J. Fisher and Leon Klenicki, eds., *Pope John Paul II on Jews and Judaism*

Fig. 2

| THEOLOGICAL TENETS FOR A CHURCH IN CONVERSATION WITH JEWS AND JUDAISM |
| --- |

| God is truly revealed in both Israel and in Jesus Christ |
| --- |

Therefore:

| The Church has been "grafted" onto God's people. |
| --- |

| Both the Jews and the Church are faithful witnesses to the one God. |
| --- |

| The New Testament (Second Testament) is a normative commentary on the Old (First) Testament for the Christian community, but it is not the only commentary on the Prime Testament. |
| --- |

Related Claims:

| Early Judaism was pluralistic, with numerous groups contending for the legitimacy of its interpretation of *Torah*. Among these groups was what might be called "Jesus' Movement." |
| --- |

| Jesus, therefore, must be understood in his context as a Palestinian Jew of the first century. |
| --- |

| Certain Gospel texts, such as the portrait of the Scribes and Pharisees in Matthew and the depiction of "the Jews" in John, reflect a polemical rather than an historical perspective. |
| --- |

| The prophetic writings reflect Jewish self-criticism, and should be used in a similar way by Christians. |
| --- |

| Teaching and preaching on, and liturgical enactment of, the passion and death of Jesus must take account of the longstanding accusation that the Jews are "Christ killers." The passion and death of Jesus must be handled with sensitivity to the historical context and with repentance for the Church's charges of deicide. |
| --- |

| The claim that Jesus is the messiah of Israel reflects distinctively Christian assumptions. Thus it must be understood in the context of a confession of faith and not merely as a fulfillment of predictive prophecies. It should be taught in such a way that Christians understand their link with Jewish longing for the messianic era. |
| --- |

| Christians desirous of deepening their understanding of the tradition must study Judaism and the history of Jewish-Christian relations. |
| --- |

13

we now know about Early Judaism, that both Rabbinic Judaism and Early Christianity are branches growing from the same olive tree.[31] Each has now grown in quite distinct ways, but the fundamental relationship remains. The two communities, as Pope John Paul II has said, "are connected and closely related at the very level of their religious identities."[32]

Such comments represent nothing less than a conversion of the Church—a rejection of the supersessionist line of argument that so long had Christians in its grip. Recent ecclesial documents speak of the Jews as remaining "most dear" to God (*Nostra Aetate* #4); of the "great spiritual patrimony" common to Jews and Christians (*Nosta Aetate* #4); of the Jews as bound to God in an "irrevocable covenant," a "covenant which has never been revoked by God" (Pope John Paul II in Mainz, Germany [1980]). Both the Jews and the Church are faithful witnesses to the one God.

Clearly, such language requires a new way of formulating the relationship between the Testaments. No longer can Christians regard the Old Testament as mere preparation for the New.[33] The Old Testament—or First Testament—needs first and foremost to be read in its literary and historical context. Then the layers of the interpretative process need to be featured so that moderns can gain a glimpse into the fascinating dynamic by which the various groups of Early Judaism drew upon the Scriptures to express their own identity. These groups shared common methodologies for reading texts, but differed in their assumptions. Thus, for instance, the Followers of the Way, although following standard Jewish exegetical techniques of the first century, differed from the ways that the Essenes interpreted texts; they read the texts through the lens of their belief that Jesus was God's

---

*1979–1986* [Washington: NCCB Committee for Ecumenical and Interreligious Affairs, and New York: Anti-Defamation League of B'nai B'rith, 1987] 38).

[31] For a clear exposition of this, see Leon Klenicki and Eugene J. Fisher, *Root and Branches: Biblical Judaism, Rabbinic Judaism, and Early Christianity* (Winona, Minn.: Saint Mary's Press, 1987).

[32] In *John Paul On Jews and Judaism,* 37.

[33] The Catholic bishops of the United States write: "In the second century, Marcion carried it [a de-Judaizing process] to its absurd extreme, teaching a complete opposition between the Hebrew and Christian Scriptures and declaring that different Gods had inspired the two Testaments. Despite the Church's condemnation of Marcion's teachings, some Christians over the centuries continued to dichotomize the Bible into two mutually contradictory parts. They argued, for example, that the New Covenant 'abrogated' or 'superseded' the Old, and that the Sinai Covenant was discarded by God and replaced with another. The Second Vatican Council, in *Dei Verbum* and *Nostra Aetate,* rejected these theories of the relationship between the Scriptures" (*God's Mercy Endures Forever: Guidelines on the Presentation of Jews and Judaism in Catholic Preaching* [Washington: Bishops' Committee on the Liturgy, National Conference of Catholic Bishops, 1988), #6]. See also n. 26 above.

messiah. Hence, the New Testament—or Second Testament—reveals a quite different appropriation of the Scriptures than do the Dead Sea Scrolls. For Christians the Second Testament has become a normative commentary, as it were, on the First Testament. For Jews, commentary has continued in the Mishnah and Talmud. And for both communities, the traditions of liturgy, prayer, homiletics, and mystical or spiritual writings also constitute a body of commentary on the First Testament and on the Second Testament (for Christians) and on the Midrash and Talmud (for Jews).[34] In Christianity, the creeds and doctrines also continue the commentary on sacred texts, although the status assigned these differs in the Roman, Orthodox and Protestant communions.

As one enters into the dynamic of the interpretative process, it becomes much more possible to situate Jesus in the environment of first-century Palestinian Judaism and the Church in its emergence from Early Judaism. Moreover, it becomes evident that the sibling rivalry experienced after the destruction of Jerusalem shaped Early Christianity's portrayal of its "rival" interpreter, Pharisaic Judaism. Thus, the polemics of the New Testament can be properly placed in context. Similarly, the strident critique of the prophets can be seen for what it was: a community's self-criticism. And then it can be re-used for precisely that purpose: a community's self-criticism. The Church reads the prophets for the sake of judging its own fidelity to God, not for looking over the shoulder of the Jewish community.

Likewise, the Church reads the passion of Jesus Christ so as to remember the extent of his love—even to the point of laying down his life—not for assigning blame for his death. Recent historical and biblical studies have demonstrated how the threat of Roman persecution influenced the New Testament writers in their accounts of the passion and death of Jesus. Thus, they exculpated the Roman authorities and exaggerated Jewish responsibility. Moreover, in the last quarter century, the Church has at long last acknowledged that Jews should not be blamed for the death of Jesus.

However, the emotion-laden accusation of "Christ-killers" with which Christians raged against Jews for nearly two-thousand years has not been laid to rest simply because a host of ecclesial documents since *Nostra Aetate* #4 refutes the charge of deicide. Teaching and preaching on the passion must be sensitive to the tragic effects that accusation had on Judaism, and must seek to compensate. The U.S. Bishops' Committee on Ecumenical and Interreligious Affairs advises

[34] See Barry W. Holtz, ed., *Back to the Sources: Reading the Classic Jewish Text* (New York: Summit, 1984).

that great caution must be taken in drawing upon passages from the New Testament that seem to show Jews in an unfavorable light. They recommend:

> A general principle, might, therefore, be suggested that if one cannot show beyond reasonable doubt that the particular gospel element selected or paraphrased will not be offensive or have the potential for negative influence on the audience for whom the presentation is intended, that element cannot, in good conscience, be used.[35]

It is vital, then, that Christian educators contemplate the accounts of the passion in light of recent biblical scholarship and with sensitivity to the history of Jewish-Christian relations.

Another topic that makes demands on educators is the concept of the messiah. Again, the history of the Church's usage makes it necessary to revise previous understandings. Not only has the Church wrongly taken the prophets out of context in order to draw a contrast between the infidelity of the people of the old covenant and the fidelity of the people of the new covenant, but it has wrenched messianic imagery from its matrix in Early Judaism.

Under the umbrella of supersessionism lived a simplistic notion of messiah linked with a one-dimensional understanding of prophecy as prediction. In fact, the term "messiah" is notoriously difficult to define with precision. It is more accurate to speak of "messianic expectations": the intense hope that developed in Early Judaism that the faithful God would act definitively to overthrow evil and establish divine rule. Messianism might be thought of as a kind of magnet to which one's hopes were ineluctably drawn; alternatively, it might be thought of as a prism refracting peoples' longings for deliverance from evil.

Given the diversity characteristic of Early Judaism, no consensus existed about how God's deliverance would take place, or under whose agency it would happen. Specific understandings of the identity of God's anointed varied considerably: Israel would have, at long last, a *true* high priest, and/or a *true* king, and/or a *true* prophet. Clemens Thoma speaks of these as the "palette of messianic ideas."[36] The constant was the belief that God would act to change the history of Is-

---

[35] *Criteria for the Evaluation of Dramatizations of the Passion* (Washington: Bishops' Committee for Ecumenical and Interreligious Affairs, National Conference of Catholic Bishops, 1988). A superb resource for teachers, liturgists, and preachers is John T. Townsend, *A Liturgical Interpretation in Narrative Form of the Passion of Jesus Christ* (New York: The National Conference of Christians and Jews, 1985).

[36] Thoma, *A Christian Theology of Judaism*, 60.

rael, that God would intervene through spirit-filled figure(s) to bring justice.

When the disciples of Jesus confessed him to be God's messiah, they were not rejecting Jewish messianism. They were, rather, drawing from one of its streams. Moreover, their appropriation of the term did not fit precisely any of the images in the First Testament, but reflected a new dimension. As Donald Juel suggests, it resulted from "creative reflection" on the historical ministry of Jesus and particularly on his death on the cross and his vindication in the resurrection.[37]

Fitting, then, are the careful distinctions the United States Catholic Bishops' Committee on Liturgy has made in their monograph *God's Mercy Endures Forever*. They note that the messianic prophecies in the Hebrew Scriptures are not merely *temporal predictions,* but "profound expressions of eschatological hope." Thus, by "fulfillment" the bishops mean something quite different from a "checklist" of correspondences. They write that the biblical prophecies are fulfilled insofar as they have been "irreversibly inaugurated in Christ's coming." That is, the Christian confession that Jesus "fulfills" the promise of the messiah does not mean that fulfillment is completely worked out in each person's life or perfected in the world at large. The Church awaits the completion of the messianic era. It is the mission of the Church and of the Jewish people to proclaim and prepare the world for the full flowering of God's reign.[38]

In a similar vein, the 1985 Vatican document *Notes on the Way To Present Jews and Judaism in the Catholic Church* includes this eloquent section:

> It is more clearly understood that the person of the Messiah is not only a point of division for the people of God but also a point of convergence . . . . Thus, it can be said that Jews and Christians meet in a comparable hope, founded on the same promise made to Abraham (cf. Gen 12:1-3; Heb 6:13-18).
>
> Attentive to the same God who has spoken, hanging on the same word, we have to witness to one same memory and one common hope in him who is the master of history. We must also accept our responsibility to prepare the world for the coming of the Messiah by working together for social justice, respect for the rights of persons and nations and for social and international reconciliation. To this we are driven,

---

[37] Juel, *Messianic Exegesis*, p. 175. See Raymond E. Brown's succinct exposition of the concept messiah in "Aspects of Old Testament Thought [#152–163]," in *The Jerome Biblical Commentary*, 1310–1312.

[38] *God's Mercy Endures Forever*, #11.

Jews and Christians, by the command to love our neighbor, by a common hope for the kingdom of God and by the great heritage of the prophets.[39]

## IV. Some Guidelines for Teachers

If a faithful presentation of Christianity rests in large part on an adequate understanding of Judaism, then Christian educators must place this formidable yet energizing task high on their agenda. Difficult as it is in view of the many demands on their energies, they must search for resources, seek conversation partners and set aside time for study. Jewish-Christian dialogue cannot be a peripheral issue for Christian educators: it involves their very self-identity.

This task of rethinking their heritage will be made easier if some general guidelines are observed. Let me suggest three in regard to attitudes, inquiry, and pedagogy:

1. *Attitudes.* Humility is an essential component of the educational process; learning demands a willingness to change in the light of new knowledge, receptivity to other points of view, and a respect for the complexity of truth. The Vatican's Commission for Religious Relations with the Jews has pointed out that "there is evident in particular a painful ignorance of the history and traditions of Judaism, of which only negative aspects and often caricature seem to form part of the stock ideas of many Christians."[40] Thus, Christian educators engaged in dialogue with Jews and Judaism will face the necessity of revising once-comfortable formulas, and of learning new concepts. They will also encounter the shadow side of the Christian tradition, which, however painful to confront, chastens triumphalism.

2. *Inquiry.* The fruitfulness of study often depends upon the quality of the question one is pursuing. It is vital that Christians approach their study of Judaism with questions that disclose and illumine. For instance, too often Christians begin their questioning with "Why don't Jews_____?" (e.g., believe in the messiah, believe that Jesus is God). But such questions immediately frame Judaism in Christian terms, and do not elicit the fuller context in which Jews understand their tradition. Christianity and Judaism are not symmetrical; categories and terms essential to the one may have no parallel in the other, or may be understood differently. For instance, Michael Rosenak proposes that there are five key terms of the Jewish religious tradition through which the notion of covenant takes on meaning: *Torah,* messianism, *Am Yisrael* (the people of Israel), the God of Israel, and *Eretz Yisrael* (the land of

---

[39] *Notes,* #s 10–11.
[40] *Notes,* #27.

Israel).[41] Christians also hold *Torah* of central importance, but *Torah* does not suggest the national and cultural characteristics it does in Judaism. Christian messianism has developed out of some dimensions of Jewish messianism, but obviously holds a different status. When Christians speak of themselves as a "people of God," they are using language analogous to *Am Yisrael*. Yet there is a major difference, since there is an ethnic dimension to the Jewish people that does not exist in Christianity. Christians, of course, worship the God of Israel, but their monotheistic confession of faith is imaged in trinitarian terms. Nothing in Christianity corresponds to the role of land in Jewish life.

Those who inquire into Judaism will need to stretch their categories and try on new ways of thought. Thus, the importance of asking probing questions and of being willing to pursue a tradition on its own terms.

3. *Pedagogy.* One of the most serious problems Christian educators confront is that it is far easier to teach supersessionism than its alternative. Precisely because the tenets of supersessionism are simplistic, they provide teachers with a more straightforward task. It is far easier to draw sharp contrasts—e.g., "The Jews believed in a royal, kingly messiah, but the followers of Jesus believed in a suffering messiah"—than it is to lay out the complexities of a term such as messiah. The more one learns about Early Judaism, the more difficult it becomes to make simple assertions that draw firm distinctions between the early Christians and Jews. This poses quite a challenge to teachers, particularly those who work with children. As the scholarship of the Jewish-Christian dialogue is taken into textbooks and other resource materials, teachers will have less difficulty. Until that time, however, teachers should adopt one pedagogical principle: never teach Christianity by denigrating Judaism.

Supersessionism ultimately rests on an impoverished notion of God, because it implies that the Holy One is capable only of one way of revelation. But an understanding of Christian life drawn from a conversation with Jews and Judaism enlarges our image of God. It reminds us that the Creator's resourcefulness is not exhausted, that God is continually about doing something new. And what could be more faithful to the teaching of Jesus Christ than that realization?

---

[41] Michael Rosenak, *Commandments and Concerns: Jewish Religious Education in Secular Society* (Philadelphia: Jewish Publication Society, 1987) 100–101. John Pawlikowski claims that "after the Incarnation the theological significance of the land of Israel remains the second most important difference between Judaism and Christianity" ("Reflections on 'Notes on the Correct Way to Present Jews and Judaism in Preaching and Catechesis in the Roman Catholic Church,' " manuscript (23 July 1985) 12.

## Questions for Reflection and Discussion

1. Describe the basic elements of a theology of supersessionism. Why did this view dominate Christian thinking about Jews and Judaism for so long? Why has the Church repudiated these ideas in the twentieth century?

2. What social factors in the second through fifth centuries prompted Christian preachers to speak of Judaism in hostile ways? Why is it important to be aware of these societal circumstances?

3. What elements of supersessionism does modern biblical scholarship throw into question? In what ways does reflection on the *Shoah* undermine supersessionism?

4. What New Testament topics concerning Jews and Judaism must religious educators be especially careful in presenting? What practices can teachers employ in order to convey accurate, non-supersessionist understandings of Jews and Judaism?

# Within Context:
# The Judaism Contemporary With Jesus

*Anthony J. Saldarini*

Modern Christians spontaneously think of Jesus first as the son of God, a savior from sin and the divinely sent founder of Christianity. They often lose sight of the human Jesus who was the son of a Galilean carpenter and a popular Jewish teacher and reformer. When they do, they often fall into anti-semitism because they assume that all first-century Jews should have recognized and accepted this divine figure and attribute Jesus' execution to culpable rejection and ill-will on the part of Jews. Detaching Jesus from his people, Israel, and from his historical place in first-century Judaism allows some Christians effectively to deny Jesus' Jewishness and to label Jews as evil or deviant. Thus, the way Christians imagine Jesus to have lived greatly influences their attitudes toward Jews and theology of Judaism.

That Jesus was a Galilean Jew in the first century is neither an insignificant accident of history nor a cultural veil masking his divine nature. When Christians affirm that Jesus is Christ they affirm his membership in first-century Israel, his rootedness in the Israelite and Jewish tradition and his fidelity to the God of Abraham, Isaac, and Jacob, the God of all Israel at all times. Jesus' activities and teachings along with most of the New Testament claims made about him can only be understood within the context of first-century Jewish society and the on-going tradition of Israel.

In the Mediterranean world of late antiquity, into which Jesus was born, to be the member of a people was to be part of a unified network of political, economic, social, intellectual and religious relationships. Judaism was not just a religion in the modern sense, separate from political and social life, but a total way of life which involved daily speech, tasks, economic relationships, rituals, cultural symbols and fundamental outlooks on life. The Jewish people were not just a group of people who happened to live in the Roman empire, but a national group which stretched back over the centuries to their kings

and founders, like David, Moses and Abraham, and looked forward
to the day of the Lord, when Israel would once more live in peace
under God's direct rule. They also stretched outward geographically
throughout the Roman empire and the Middle East. The community
in Babylon, which originated in the forced exile of 597 and 587 B.C.E.,
remained strong. Other Jews had subsequently travelled to Egypt,
North Africa, Asia Minor, Greece, Italy and beyond. Despite their dis-
persion in place and time and the varieties of their practice of Judaism, to be a Jew was to be different from a Roman, or a citizen of
Antioch in Syria, or a Galatian farmer in Asia Minor. And to be a Jewish carpenter in Nazareth, lower Galilee, who became a popular
preacher was to be a certain kind of Jew in the first century. What,
then, was Jesus' way of life and what was the context within which
he lived it? This will become clear through a brief overview of Jesus
as a member of Israel and then a detailed and careful look at the first-
century Jewish communities in Galilee, Judea and Jerusalem, all in
their context within the Roman empire. Special attention will be given
to the social relationships which bound these communities together
and to the prayers and customs of ordinary Jews in the villages that
are parts of the rich and varied Jewish heritage of the first century.
The Temple worship at the center of the Jewish world and the dozens
of communities throughout the ancient world formed the complex
whole we call Judaism.

## Jesus within Israel

Jesus was a popular teacher and preacher in northeastern lower
Galilee during the first half of the first century. He was a reformer
who taught many things drawn from the common fund of Jewish
tradition. He sought, as did others, to increase his fellow Jews' adherence to their traditions and to enliven their relationship with God.
The central symbol for his reform was the political image of the kingdom of God, a symbol which connotes God's rule over Israel in the
present and God's eventual triumph over all evil powers, including
the oppressive Roman empire. The norms which governed this renewed Israel were drawn from the Biblical tradition and given a particular emphasis and application for the Galilean community. Some
of the themes which appear often are care for the poor and needy,
reliance on God, deemphasis on honor and human authority, and
just social relations. Jesus' program offered healing for the sinfulness
and weakness of humans and hope for the Galilean peasants who had
no control over their government or life. His program was based on

faith in God's active presence as protector of Israel. As such, his teaching was quintessentially Jewish.

Though such a program can be couched in apparently innocuous Biblical and spiritual terminology, the emphasis on God's rule implies that the current human rulers are illegitimate or seriously deficient. Thus Jesus' religious program was profoundly political and social. Jewish writings of the period, especially apocalypses, are filled with criticism against Israel's leaders for corrupting and misleading the people and with protest against violent and oppressive imperial powers from Babylon through the Romans. Since religion is integral to daily social relationships, economic ties and political arrangements, Jesus' teachings concerning God's will for Israel involved major changes in social and political relations, changes which threatened the wealth, power and influence of the governing class, both Jewish and Roman. Thus, Jesus was an implicit challenge to the local Jewish authorities, especially Herod Antipas, the tetrarch of Galilee, whose duty was to keep order, collect taxes and see that the living of Judaism was consistent with Roman imperial policy. The scribes, who were the local officials charged with keeping records, administering justice and educating the people came into conflict with Jesus' growing popular influence and authority. In Jerusalem the priests, who sought to bolster the people's loyalty to the Temple, its worship, sacrifices and tithes, also saw Jesus as a threat to political stability and the traditional way of life. The Pharisees were, like Jesus, Jewish reformers. They promoted a different program for the reform of Jewish life and the reinvigoration of the covenant with God in society. They sought to establish and protect Israel as a people holy to God through faithful observance of the ritual purity regulations reserved by the Bible for the priests in the Temple. They also stressed tithing produce and Sabbath observance as central to covenant fidelity. During the Hasmonean and Herodian periods they had come into political conflict with the authorities and been persecuted and executed on occasion. During Jesus' lifetime they were a politically and socially active group, greatly respected in Israel, and so, despite substantial areas of agreement, Jesus inevitably came into conflict with them over how Jewish life was best lived.

Jesus was not a revolutionary, even though his presence was sometimes disruptive in first-century Palestinian society. His influence and authority among the people were popularly granted, not officially recognized by political and religious powers. Some of the Jewish people recognized Jesus, who was one of a number of prophetic or messianic holy men, as an intermediary between God and his people, as someone who could help renew Israel's covenant with God and as a guide to rectifying strained and unjust relationships with the Roman and Jewish governments. Jesus' program for the renewal of society through a reinvigorated commitment to God's kingdom and renewed bonds among humans appealed strongly to the outcasts, poor and powerless who were not incorporated fully into the social and sacred system of Judaism. Jesus' popularity with the crowds, their eagerness to hear him and experience his power, and the opposition of the authorities all fit within the context of Galilean Jews who had been conquered by Rome, were sternly ruled by a Jewish proxy of Rome and suffered heavy taxes with no avenue of appeal or control over their own society.

### Galilee

Galilee, the northern region of Israel, is divided into a northern, mountainous part and a southern valley called the Esdraelon or Jezreel. Jesus' home village, Nazareth, was situated on a slope in the central part of the Esdraelon but when he began to teach he moved to Capernaum in the northeastern corner of the valley (Mark 2:1; Matt 9:1), on the shore of the Sea of Galilee. Life in Galilee centered on agriculture and fishing. Galilee was densely settled, with small farming villages and hamlets every mile or two, surrounded by fertile fields. The valley which made up most of lower Galilee was relatively small, only twenty-five miles west to east from the Mediterranean to the Sea of Galilee and fifteen miles south to north from the mountains of Samaria to the mountains of upper Galilee. Thus when people came to hear Jesus or Jesus went out to them, they did not travel far and in most cases could walk home in the evening.

Probably only a small percentage of the population was literate and had immediate interests beyond the village or town. However, Galilee was not a rural backwater, unaffected by Greco-Roman culture. The Esdraelon valley was a major trade route because it was a level passage through the mountains which separated the coast of the Mediterranean Sea from inland Syria and the caravan routes to Mesopotamia. Physical evidence recovered by archaeologists shows that trade with the rest of the Roman empire was lively and constant. Galilee exported wine and olive oil to other parts of the empire and imported luxury goods for the rich and other fine wares.

Galilee had two large cities (20,000 to 40,000 inhabitants), Sepphoris and Tiberias, and several smaller ones ( 10,000 to 20,000), such as Bethsaida and Capernaum. The cities were closely linked to the villages and countryside economically and socially. Sepphoris was only three miles north of Nazareth so presumably Jesus was familiar with it. The city had been destroyed when it revolted against the Romans after Herod's death (4 B.C.E.). Herod Antipas, ruler of Galilee and son of Herod the Great, rebuilt Sepphoris as the capital of Galilee and a major fortress in the early first century, C.E., when Jesus was growing up. Its new population was probably a mixture of Jews and non-Jews involved with the government and commerce. In the revolt against Rome (66 C.E.) Sepphoris remained loyal to Rome and survived the war. Tiberias on the west coast of the Sea of Galilee was also built by Herod Antipas as a new capital for himself. Antipas settled it with foreigners and landless poor. Its mixed population, its site on a graveyard and its Hellenistic public buildings, complete with images, made it offensive to many Jews.

Herod Antipas ruled Galilee and Perea, across the Jordan, for the Romans from 4 B.C.E. until he was removed from office under suspicion of sedition in 39 C.E. As a member of the imperial governing class, he travelled frequently, maintained complex personal and political relations with the emperors and their court and lived a life far removed from that of the ordinary farmer. Antipas, who is mentioned a number of times in the Gospels and Acts, was a typical native ruler, accommodating himself to Roman customs and practices outside his own country and for the most part fulfilling his obligations toward Judaism at home. He engaged in large building projects and cultivated patrons in Rome. He divorced his wife and married his niece with the ease of an upper class Roman. As the ruler responsible for keeping the peace, he was apprehensive about the growing reputation of Jesus, as he had been about John the Baptist whom he executed for criticizing his biblically illicit marriage (Mark 6:14, Luke 13:31; cf. also 23:7-12). The Herodians mentioned in the Gospels (Mark 3:6; 12:13) were the officials and upper class supporters of Herod Antipas who sought to blunt the influence of Jesus whom they saw as a dangerous new political force and threat to their control.

In the villages and small cities Jesus came into contact and sometimes conflict with local community officials, not with the leaders of society. The centurions who appear from time to time were low level Roman officials stationed at key points such as Capernaum (Mark 5:22). The Pharisees and scribes, who are mentioned often, were probably subordinate officials and functionaries of either the government or Jewish community, as was Jairus, the ruler of the synagogue (Mark 5:22). These officials were subordinate to the small percentage of the wealthy and powerful families and officials who ruled the Roman empire and Judea and Galilee. Yet they, along with the wealthy and powerful, were separated from the majority of the population who were farmers, artisans or landless. The governing classes were generally literate, had access to tax revenues to support themselves and were not compelled to put most of their efforts into manual labor. Consequently, they formed an independent social network far removed by fixed social position and wealth from that of the village and town.

The Gospels have no record of Jesus teaching in either Sepphoris or Tiberias. He was not a member of the governing class nor part of the groups who aided the rulers in administering the country. He found a following among traditional Jewish farmers and artisans in smaller cities such as Capernaum or Bethsaida and in the villages of the plain. The network of relationships which he developed and the influence which he gained through his teaching and powerful deeds spread among people like himself who subsisted off the produce of the land and were intermittently threatened by natural and political forces beyond their control.

Some romantic portraits of Jesus have pictured him as the gentle preacher in an idyllic countryside or as a fiery revolutionary rising up against poverty and oppression. Neither interpretation does justice to the Jewish community in Galilee in the first century. As in all ancient society, about 90 percent of the people were farmers who lived in small towns or villages and walked out to their fields daily. Since the Esdraelon valley was fertile, the farmers there were reasonably prosperous. However, prosperity for ancient farmers meant subsistence living with no opportunity for most to improve their station or build up a reserve for times of want. The government which collected taxes from the small landholder or the landlord who collected rent and paid the government in turn (anywhere from 30 percent to 70 percent of the crop) had the small farmer under their control. Farmers often fell into debt in bad years when they borrowed money to pay their taxes and rent; a series of bad years could lead to loss of land or tenancy and thus landlessness. (Since Joseph was a landless artisan, Jesus' family had experienced this process at some point.) In addition, Galilee like other parts of the Middle East, had known invasion and war from time to time. The Romans conquered and reorganized Galilee in the sixties and fifties, B.C.E. and the Persians invaded in 40 B.C., only to be driven out by the Romans. Herod did battle with bandits or brigands, that is, landless and homeless families who lived in caves and unsettled parts of the hills and supported themselves by stealing from the rich. Historical accounts from this period testify to a succession of disorders and revolutionary leaders who protested governmental and economic conditions and sought to reestablish a more just Jewish commonwealth under God. On the other hand, most of the people lived quietly and went about their business, hoping to be spared the sufferings of want and war.

## Jewish Life in Galilee

In the first centuries B.C.E. and C.E. Jews in Galilee shared a strong core of practices and beliefs with Judeans and Jews elsewhere in the Roman empire. For a time they had the same ruler, Herod the Great. After his death the rule of Judea and Galilee was split, so that the Galilean and Judean Jews belonged to different provinces of the empire. However, the traditional loyalty to the Temple continued. Attempts by some scholars to demonstrate hostility toward the Temple, rejection of Jewish customs or widespread assimilation to non-Jewish ways are not convincing. Though Galileans had their own distinctive, local customs, they journied to Jerusalem for the pilgrimage festivals (Passover, Pentecost, Tabernacles), sent tithes to the Temple (because they were collected by the authorities like all taxes) and kept alive common Jewish customs and rituals and community rules as they had for decades.

We do not have exact accounts of daily customs and observances in Galilean Jewish villages in the first century. Earlier biblical accounts and later stories and rules in Talmudic literature give us a sense of what Jewish life was like and of the continuity of custom and law which knit together the generations. Jews did not work on the sabbath. They prayed the biblical psalms as well as a rich variety of other psalms and blessings concerned with crops, family and health. It is likely that many Jews prayed some form of the blessings that later became known as the Amidah or Eighteen Benedictions. Though we do not have copies of these prayers as said in the first century, the first of these blessings as now prayed by Jews, will give their sense of God.

> Blessed are you, Lord our God and God of our Fathers,
>     God of Abraham, God of Isaac, God of Jacob,
> the greatest, mighty and revered God, the most high God,
>     who bestows loving kindnesses and possesses all things;
>     who remembers the pious deeds of the patriarchs
>     and in love will bring a redeemer
>     to their children's children for your name's sake.
> King, Helper, Savior and Shield,
>     Blessed are you, O Lord, the Shield of Abraham.

This and many similar blessings applied the biblical faith of Israel to the concrete needs and circumstances of the community. Israel also prayed the "Shema," a prayer composed of three biblical passages (Deut 6:4-9, 11:13-21; Num 15:37-41) which begins with the fundamental declaration of faith, "Hear, Israel! The Lord is our God, the Lord is One," continues with the command to love God and climaxes with the promise of blessings for obedience.

We know little about the institutions of worship in Israel during the first century. Synagogue buildings and their institutionalized leadership probably did not exist as such in most towns and villages of Israel until the third century. They were more common in the diaspora, though even there elaborate buildings became common only in the third century. Though a few synagogue buildings from the first century have been found in Israel, they are simple multipurpose meeting rooms without any iconography or specialized architecture. Elaborate synagogues emerged only in the third century, after the Jewish community had reorganized and developed its communal worship to compensate for the loss of the Temple. In Jesus' time people probably met to pray in the same place they met to conduct town business or settle disputes, that is, outdoors in the town square or in a public building, if there was one, or in the large courtyard and house of prominent citizen. The leaders of such an assembly would have been the elders of the community, the established and respected leaders of prominent families. If a village was large enough to own a Torah scroll and to have literate residents, they probably read from the scroll on the Sabbath and festivals. It is doubtful that most villages had a resident teacher or scribe who could give constant and expert instruction. (Rabbis did not yet exist as social and religious leaders.) Thus villages would have greeted with appreciation and even excitement a traveling scribe, or learned Pharisees, or a popular preacher such as Jesus.

Village life was structured by the agricultural seasons and tasks and the religious festivals followed the seasons. Passover, the spring festival, Pentecost, the harvest festival fifty days after Passover, and Booths, the fall harvest festival, were observed as agricultural celebrations and as memorials of events in Israel's history. The coming of the new moon each month provoked special prayers and observances. Irregular events such as drought and sickness were met with special blessings as were ordinary acts such as sleeping, dressing and eating. The welfare of crops, animals and humans was ensured by regular prayers and local rituals.

The boundaries of the village and town communities were maintained by traditional practices and relationships. Within the villages the elder male members of the most prominent or wealthy families would have been in charge because they had the most honorable positions and were the most respected members of the community. They saw to the settling of disputes, the planning of communal events and the maintenance of relations with outside governmental authorities. The arrival of a traveling teacher or of an official from Jerusalem or Herod Antipas could either enrich and support the ways of a village or upset them. The Gospel instructions concerning preaching in villages envision both acceptance and rejection (Mark 6:8-13). It is easy to imagine the elders of a village resenting or disagreeing with the teaching of a stranger such as Jesus or one of his followers, or of a Pharisee for that matter.

For the most part farmers' lives were bounded by their village and its immediate environs. Within a close-knit community of a few villages most people were born, married and buried. Males entered the social and religious community of Israel through circumcision. Children learned Jewish customs, rules, ethics, stories and rituals absorbed from their parents and neighbors. Young people married with the guidance and approval of their parents and family. When life ended, burial blessings and prayers as well as mourning rituals and customs cushioned the shock and reaffirmed the community bonds with each other and God.

### Jerusalem and Judea

Until the Temple and city of Jerusalem were destroyed at the end of the great war with Rome in 70 C.E. Jerusalem, the Temple and the chief priests were the religious and political center of Judaism. During the Roman period (after 63 B.C.E.) the high priest, the most influential priestly families, and the wealthy Jerusalem families who had traditionally ruled through a central council (the Bet Din or Sanhedrin) were dominated first by Herod the Great and his son Archelaus (37 B.C.E.–6 C.E.) and then by Roman governors appointed by the emperor. These Roman governors, prefects and later procurators, were subordinate to the Senatorial governor of Syria who was responsible for the security of the empire's eastern border. The governor of Palestine ruled Judea, Samaria, the Mediterranean coast, and Idumea. He had at his disposal non-Jewish auxiliary troops drawn from the area and he was responsible for keeping order, supervising tax collection, and judging major cases concerned with security. The misunderstandings, hostilities and conflicts created by this arrangement increasingly poisoned the atmosphere of Judea until a series of particularly venal governors in the 50s and 60s provoked a war with Rome in 66 C.E.

The Roman prefects left the local administration of justice to the traditional national authorities, the wealthy, hereditary community leaders. Because their social position and prosperity were subject to Roman power and dependent on an orderly society, the elites of all the provinces were coopted by the Romans to keep peace and collect taxes. The highest authorities in Jerusalem were the High Priest, the leading priestly families of Phiabi, Boethus, Camith, and Ananus (mentioned in John 18:13) and the wealthy families who had survived the reigns of the Hasmonean high priests and of Herod the Great. They exercised control through a supreme council in Jerusalem, and then through local councils, major administrative officers and a variety of lower officials, guards, courts and institutions. They had no direct power in Galilee, Herod Antipas's province, but the Temple collected taxes (tithes) from all Jews and through its control of ritual could influence Antipas and other Jews.

Because the Jerusalem supreme council ("Sanhedrin" in Hebraized Greek form) and the Roman prefect Pilate were involved in the condemnation of Jesus, according to the Gospel narratives, the exact nature of the supreme council and its powers has been often debated. A few things can be said with certainty. The institution of a supreme city council (*boule* or *synedrion*) is Greek. The powers and membership of the council varied during the Greco-Roman period according to the strength of the domestic or foreign ruler. Under Herod the Great the council was an advisory group of his family and friends; under the Roman prefects it was the major indigenous power in Judea, but firmly subordinated to the Roman governor. The Gospels, Acts and the Jewish historian Josephus testify that the council included high ranking priests, elders of leading families, scribes, and members of the Pharisaic and Sadducean parties.

The council's duties included anything pertaining to the overall welfare of the state, including politics, international relations, religious conflicts, the maintenance and administration of the Temple, the collection of taxes, the adjudication of important legal cases and the interpretation and legislation of law and custom. Since religious and political society and law were thoroughly integrated, any attempt to separate the council's religious and secular functions (or postulate the existence of two councils) is misguided. If the Gospels are accurate in reporting that action was initiated against Jesus by the Jerusalem authorities, the scenario was probably thus: faced suddenly, during the Passover festival, with a new religious, social reformer and leader of a popular movement (Jesus), the council in Jerusalem did what any city council would do. It investigated his activities, arrested

him to prevent trouble and finally recommended to the Roman governor that action be taken to keep the peace. Often the actions of the
Jewish leaders have been condemned by Christian polemic as ground-
less and corrupt. Granted that Jesus appeared as a threat to them, the
prudence of their policy is borne out by subsequent Jewish history.
When these leaders lost control of the people in 66 A.D., a revolt
against Rome broke out. No matter how justified the protest against
Rome, in human terms it was a disaster. The city was destroyed along
with its Temple and the people were killed or enslaved. If, on the
other hand, the Roman governor took the initiative against Jesus (and
the Gospels suppressed this for political reasons), then Pilate did what
any governor would have done. He gave the benefit of doubt to the
security of the empire, his first responsibility, and executed a local,
popular leader without a second thought.

## The Temple

The Temple in Jerusalem was the symbolic center of Judaism, even
for Jews who had never seen it. It was mandated, described and glori-
fied in the Bible and served as the focus of God's presence in Israel
and as a guarantee of God's choice of and love for Israel as his own
people. The morning and evening sacrifices of a lamb, flour, oil and
wine (Exod 29:38-42), offered daily for the nation, and the special
festival ceremonies were part of the divinely given order of Israel and
of the universe itself. Many sacrifices in thanksgiving for God's favor or in reparation for sin are prescribed in the Bible and were as-
siduously used by Jews from all over the empire. Three times a year
Jewish males in Palestine were expected to travel to the Temple to
celebrate the ancient agricultural festivals of Passover, Weeks and
Booths. The pilgrim to the Temple heard Levites singing and playing musical instruments and saw a richly symbolic public ritual in
the court before the Temple. Central moments in the Temple worship were announced by trumpet blasts and the sacrifices were accompanied by the singing of psalms. Public prayer and sacrifice in
the Temple required the labor of numerous priests and Levites. During the Greco-Roman period Levites were a lower class of priest en-
trusted with keeping order in the Temple, providing for physical
necessities and leading the singing with voice and instrument. They
and the priests labored daily to offer prescribed and voluntary
sacrifices.

During the day private sacrifices were brought by the people and
offered by the priests. When animals were offered, the fat of the animal and certain inner parts were burned on the altar, the hind quar-

ter and breast went to feed the priests and the rest of the animal went to the worshipers in a sacred meal eaten on the Temple property. The blood of the animals was thrown against the base of the altar because blood was considered a holy source of life. Various grains and vegetables were also offered, with a small portion burned on the altar and the balance dedicated to the support of the priests. In some sacrifices wine was poured out at the base of the altar. The individuals who offered the numerous sacrifices for sins or as a thanksgiving to God experienced the Temple not only as an awesome center of national worship but as a place of intimate relationship with God. The sacrifice affirmed the believers' reliance on God and the thanksgiving meal symbolized the close bonds that tied Israel to God. Thus the Temple was a communal sanctuary with an elaborate public worship and at the same time a religious center where the individual Jew could commune with God.

Ancient writings testify to the striking beauty of the Temple building and its surrounding compound, especially after its renovation by Herod. The Temple compound was a huge open space with the sacred Temple building in the center, surrounded by storage and utility buildings. The Temple was made of rare woods and decorated with precious metals; Herod had it covered with gold to increase its splendor (and his own reputation as well). The Temple equipment used in the daily sacrifices and purity rituals was made of gold. Around the perimeter of the Temple compound were colonnades and other administrative buildings and the sacred precincts were surrounded by a massive wall with several strong gates. The Temple mount could be entered from the south, up a massive stairway leading to a double gate and a triple gate, each of which led through underground passages up to the Temple platform. From the west the Temple could be entered from a monumental stairway at the southwest corner or over a bridge from the western hill of Jerusalem (now called Mount Zion). The overall impression made by the Temple fitted its role as unique sanctuary to God and center of the nation.

For modern Christians and Jews used to separation of Church and state, the military role of the Temple seems strange. Because it was on top of a hill and surrounded by high walls and gates, the Temple was the strongest fortification in Jerusalem and the last redoubt in time of siege. To neutralize its military potential the Romans maintained the Fortress Antonia at its northwest corner. Armories with weapons for the defense of the Temple and city in time of war and for maintaining civil peace were located on the Temple mount. Temple police and guards maintained order, especially during the feasts when thousands of Jewish pilgrims filled the city, for if civil unrest were threatening, festival time was a likely occasion for it to break out.

The buildings and colonnades surrounding the Temple compound were also the administrative, legislative, economic and judicial center of Judea and to some extent of worldwide Judaism. Here the half shekel tax to support the Temple was sent by all Jews in the Roman empire. The Temple buildings housed the national treasury and in various chambers the deposits of wealthy individuals were securely stored. The city council of Jerusalem (often called the Sanhedrin after one of the Greek words for council) also met in the Chamber of Hewn Stone. It was the highest legislative and judicial body of Jerusalem, with oversight of the government and Temple. It was composed of leading priests, wealthy, powerful citizens and high officials. Other subordinate courts and councils also met in various chambers of the buildings surrounding the Temple and the leaders of the nation often conferred there. The Temple was not just a house of religious worship but Judea and Judaism's central military, civic, and economic religious center.

The Temple and its priests were supported by agricultural tithes (taxes) mandated by the Bible and by a half shekel tax collected from every Jew in Israel and the diaspora. The rules for tithes (one tenth of the produce of a field, new fruit tree, wine, etc.) were complex and changed over time; complaints about non-payment of tithes testify to the natural human resistance to taxation, even when divinely sanctioned. Ideally, the first fruits of trees were brought to the Temple and the first born of animals were redeemed by money paid to the Temple. The agricultural tax was to be divided among the various levels of priests and Levites. Priests were further supported by the portions of sacrifices brought to the Temple which were reserved for them, and the Temple benefited from benefactions regularly bestowed upon it by Jewish and foreign rulers.

The Temple was the central governmental, social and religious institution in Israel. Public worship, administration of justice, legislative deliberations, the collection of taxes, the processes of the bureaucracy, the needs of national security and the teaching of Israel's traditions to a new generation of priests and scribes were all carried on together in the Temple area. In addition, Jerusalem and the Temple bore the burden and potential of Israel's history and tradition. Crucial historical events had happened in Jerusalem and Israel's cultural imagination was focussed on the holy city and God's house. The symbolic center and apocalyptic hopes, the stability of the social order and revolutionary potential of the people freed from Egypt long ago all rested on Jerusalem and in the Temple.

### Israel Among the Empires

The first century Jewish movements and groups and farmers in Israel carried with them the long history of Israel extending back to the Exodus and beyond to Abraham. The events and symbols associated with that history and its articulation in the sacred traditions of Israel are everpresent in the writings and prayers of the Greco-Roman period. However, more immediate historical happenings also had their effect on those in Israel. A series of wars, invasions, persecutions and changes in political administration had produced a relatively tense and volatile citizenry living in uneasy truce with the Roman imperial administration.

For reasons that are now obscure the Syrian ruler who controlled Israel in 167 B.C.E., Antiochus IV Epiphanes, sought to suppress the Jewish way of life by penalizing those who kept Jewish law and by initiating the worship of the Syrian gods in the Temple in Jerusalem. He forbade circumcision, the reading of Torah and other common practices. A three-year war led by Judas Maccabee of the Hasmonean priestly family resulted in the Temple being returned to the worship of the God of Israel (an event celebrated by the Feast of Hannukah). Judah's brothers, Jonathan and Simon, and Simon's son John and grandson Alexander ruled Israel, extricated it from Syrian control and enlarged its borders through frequent military campaigns. However, the little hellenistic kingdom they established was in constant conflict with its neighbors and was invaded numerous times. The Hasmoneans, who were not one of the traditional high priestly families, became high priests, much to the chagrin of the Essenes and others, and acted oppressively toward their opponents like any other hellenistic monarchy. Internal conflicts produced various reform movements and political parties and coalitions.

When Alexander Jannaeus' sons, Hyrcanus and Aristobulus, fought a civil war over the succession, the Roman army led by Pompey intervened and conquered Jerusalem (63 B.C.E.). Pompey violated the Temple and his successors set up various administrative districts which removed power from the traditional leaders and priests. A Parthian invasion (40 B.C.E.) was followed by the effective but authoritarian rule of Herod the Great. The successions at Herod's death (4 B.C.E.) and at the deposition of his son Archelaus as ruler of Judea (6 C.E.) were marked by revolt and bloodshed including the destruction of Sepphoris in Galilee and many other battles.

After Herod, his son Antipas ruled in Galilee and Roman prefects and procurators took over Judea, Samaria and on the coast. The most famous of these, Pilate (26–36 C.E.), was a typical governor who used his power cruelly to preserve Roman rule. He often acted arbitrarily, without sensitivity to Jewish customs and laws. He brought images into Jerusalem and provoked a riot in protest. He took money given for Temple sacrifices to build an aqueduct for Jerusalem. Eventually complaints against him resulted in his recall to Rome. After Pilate's rule, the Emperor Gaius Caligula, considered insane by some, attempted to place his own statue in the Temple. Before the statue could be shipped to Jerusalem, where it certainly would have provoked a revolt, Gaius died.

Because of Israel's history under Greek and Roman rule, first-century Palestine was rife with royal pretenders, messianic movements, prophetic figures and rebellious brigands, many of whom are mentioned in Josephus. Many of these bandits, that is, persons displaced from their land and without any place in society, fought the wealthy and the authorities with support from the subsistance level farmers of Judea and Galilee. The longing for an anointed leader (messiah), which appears in some Jewish literature of the period and comes from the old Israelite tradition of popular, anointed kingship, led to a number of rebellions against Rome. Athronges, a shepherd, and Simon, a servant of Herod, both claimed to be king and led armed groups of bandits until finally defeated and captured. (Note that the charge against Jesus was that he claimed to be king of the Jews.) In the first century a prophet named Theudas led followers toward the Jordan River, but Roman cavalry killed him and many of his followers. In such an atmosphere the Roman and Jewish authorities who wished to keep civil order could easily see the leader of a popular movement, such as Jesus, as a threat and take steps to remove the threat. Later in the first century coalitions of displaced peasants, bandits and rebels, called Zealots, did wrest control of Jerusalem from the priests and aristocrats and begin a disastrous war with Rome.

## Varieties of Jewish Belief and Practice

All Jews in the first century acknowledged the Temple as the central and unique shrine of Israel, but most were far removed from the Temple and saw it seldom if ever. Jews dispersed in the Roman Empire and Mesopotamia might journey once to Jerusalem for the festival but for the most part they lived their lives following local Jewish customs under the direction of indigenous community officials. The chief priests and other authorities in Jerusalem could exercise no direct authority over the hundreds of local communities of Jews. Their influence on communities as near as Galilee was limited because Galilee was ruled by its own tetrarch, Herod Antipas, and the cities, towns and villages there had their own rulers and elders independent of the priests and Jerusalem hierarchy. Talmudic Judaism, which developed during the second to sixth centuries and gradually dominated most Jewish communities in the Near East and Europe, did not yet exist. Local practice in all its variety was the norm.

In the first century the Hebrew Bible and its Greek translation, called the Septuagint, were accepted by all Jews as an authoritative repository of Israel's history and revelation from God. The laws, stories, prophecies and other teachings formed the core of Israel's self-conscious identity and communal laws. Jews were notable for their devotion to and education in the biblical laws and traditions which allowed them to retain their communal boundaries even when they were far from Israel for centuries. Persecution during the Maccabean period by Antiochus IV (see above) had crystalized adherence to several practices as the mark of a dedicated Jew. Worship of only the God of Israel was now normative after centuries of worship of Baal and Asherah along with the Lord of Israel in the monarchic period. Observance of Sabbath rest and certain rituals and prayers was widespread. Male children were circumcised on the eighth day and male adults wishing to join the Jewish community had also to submit to circumcision, a demand which was a formidable obstacle to conversion. Both these practices were remarked on by Greek and Roman commentators as characteristic of Jews. In addition Jews were noted for their strict sexual morality and for their adherence to the dietary laws of the Bible which forbade eating certain foods. Like any other ethnic community in antiquity Jewish communities in Judea, Galilee and elsewhere had their own marriage and inheritance laws, property and contractual statutes and detailed norms for communal behavior.

The Roman imperial authorities gave local communities, in the persons of their village elders or recognized officials, the authority to administer internal communal affairs and to punish lawbreakers through fines and physical punishments. In the diaspora the Jewish communities in cities were often recognized as political entities with their own quarter of the city and their own officials responsible for public order and tax collection. Jews belonged to synagogues (a Greek term for assemblies) in which they prayed on Sabbath, received education in Jewish tradition and through which they functioned as a public body in the larger Greco-Roman world. Such groups probably also met in the villages of Judea and Galilee, as was noted above. Dedicated synagogue buildings became common in subsequent centuries, but in the first century most synagogues probably met in large private houses. Whatever their precise form, Jewish communites were organized into private, voluntary associations similar to many others which had existed for centuries in the Greco-Roman world.

In the land of Israel a number of social movements with religious and political agendas and goals arose during the Greco-Roman period. From the Maccabean persecution on (mid-second century, B.C.E.) various groups hoped for divine intervention to free Israel from foreign rule and oppression. These apocalyptic movements, typified by the visions in the Book of Daniel, awaited the direct intervention of God to sweep away the evil powers. Using mythic, historical and prophetic traditions from the Bible, various authors reported visions of the heavenly world and future judgment of the wicked as protests against the political oppression of Israel by world empires and the corruption of Israel's leadership. Apocalyptic imagery, the emerging belief in life after death and traditional eschatological confidence in the triumph of God's justice reaffirmed the reality of the heavenly world. In the face of overwhelming oppression apocalypses encouraged confidence in God's power and justice.

In most apocalypses a human holy man is instructed by a vision, message or heavenly journey which is mediated or interpreted by an angel. The content of the message concerns the history of good and evil, the events of the end time and the ultimate destiny of humanity. Equally important are descriptions of the heavens and hell, various types of angels and the workings of the cosmos, stars and weather. All these future events and heavenly places, fantastic figures and even esoteric knowlege of the universe engendered confidence in the larger divine universe within which the immediately perceptible world is set. It especially promoted confidence in the divine will to enforce justice on behalf of the faithful. Clearly this stream of Jewish hope and religious expression influenced Jesus in his teaching of the kingdom of God and the early Christians in their teaching of the resurrection of Jesus and his second coming.

One of the groups which shared this apocalyptic outlook on the history of Israel and the world was the Jewish sect called the Essenes, especially the branch which had its center at Qumran near the Dead Sea. The Essenes considered the worship conducted at the Temple to be defective because the high priest was not from the proper family and the ritual was not conducted with adequate purity. Politically and socially they were in conflict with high priests and governmental administration over the nature of Israel and its role in the world. The compromises made by the Maccabees with the Seleucid kings in Syria in order to attain relative autonomy went too far for the Essenes. The infiltration of Hellenistic modes of social organization and cultural expression into the Jewish community were contrary to the strict adherence to biblical law advocated in Essene teachings. Devotion to prayer and study of Scripture, meals eaten in careful ritual purity, deep respect for elders and priests in the community and charitable attention to other members of the community marked the rules followed at Qumran. This way of life, which avoided all impropriety, contrasted sharply with the changeable and often brutal world of Hellenistic politics in Jerusalem. Wars of succession and civil unrest racked Israel during the last two centuries B.C.E. while at Qumran the Essenes awaited the coming of the Lord with his angels to destroy the human and demonic agents of evil and reestablish a pure Temple and just society. To prepare for these cosmic events the sectarians lived a monastic life centered on prayer and study. Other Essenes lived in the towns and cities of Judea and were more active politically in the conflicts which marked the Hasmonean and Herodian periods.

The Pharisees began as a religious, social movement in the mid-second century B.C.E. after the Hasmoneans gained power. They sought to reform Jewish society in order to bring it into closer conformity with biblical law as they interpreted it. Since their views of Jewish society had political implications, they became a political interest group, seeking to inf luence the governing class and ultimately seeking direct power over social laws and policies. Under John Hyrcanus (134–104 B.C.E.) they originally had great influence on how the law was enforced, but a dispute with a Sadducean court rival led to loss of influence and the ascendency of Sadducean laws and customs in the court. Under Alexander Jannaeus, noted for his cruelty and many wars, the Pharisees led the opposition. They suffered persecution and death, but gained influence with the people. Alexandra, the wife and successor of Alexander, made an alliance with the Pharisees in order to secure her own position as ruler. When the Pharisees gained direct power over domestic policy, they imposed their laws and punished their enemies. After Alexandra's death, they lost influence and their power was broken. Through the rest of the first century B.C.E. and C.E. the Pharisees strove continually to promote their policies and (unsuccessfully) to influence the succession after Herod died. Their conflicts with Jesus of Nazareth and his followers can be explained as part of their long term program to influence and reform Jewish society and to oppose those with different understandings of Israel.

The Pharisees sought to sanctify Israel, both the land and people, and thus to increase Israel's union with God in a time of great political and cultural challenge. They supported the Temple worship by insisting on a careful observance of the laws of tithing and extended the sanctity of the Temple and its priesthood to the people and daily life by observing biblical rules of ritual purity at home. Food was to be prepared and eaten in ritual purity and kept apart from all untithed and impure food. Sabbath was rigorously observed and the laws and traditions of Israel lovingly studied and interpreted. The Pharisees' demand for an intense level of commitment appealed to many who sought a way of adhering to Israel's traditions in new circumstances.

The Sadducees, too, were a reform group, though their program is less well understood than that of the Essenes and Pharisees. Sadducees were drawn from the high priests and wealthy leaders of society, though not all nor even a majority belonged to the Sadducees. They adhered to the traditional interpretation of the Bible, which means that they rejected the new belief in afterlife and apocalyptic scenarios for the end of the world. They were also disliked by the people because they were stern and rigorous in their interpretations of the law. As such they are typical of the ruling classes, holding onto their superior position in society, stressing this world in which they ruled rather than a coming, ideal world and seeing God at work in divine institutions which were controlled by them. Their emphasis on human free will and responsibility is consistent with their control over the government in Jerusalem. It is likely that their stress on Israel's traditions was a reaction against over hellenization by some of the ruling families and officials.

## Summary

During the first century when Jesus lived the people of Israel had a number of strategies for preserving their identity and adapting their traditions in changing and often hostile circumstances. The Temple priests, leading families and Sadducees negotiated with foreign governments, survived invasions and conquest and responded to the attractions of Hellenistic culture with a dogged determination to survive and continue the sacrificial rituals and national laws of Israel. The Essenes interpreted their policies and governance as a betrayal of God's will and established a pure priestly and lay community along the hot and barren shore of the Dead Sea in order to await divine intervention against both the Romans and Jerusalem leaders. The Pharisees sought to call Israel to greater fidelity to its covenant with God and stronger zeal in keeping the divine laws which guided Israel's life. The extension of priestly purity to the homes of ordinary Israelites sanctified people and land against the lure of Greek and Roman society and culture. Other popular leaders called the people to revolt, to expectation of the Messiah, to prophetic reform or to passive resistance. Jesus from the Galilean village of Nazareth was one of these Jewish reformers, calling his people to repent of their sins and reaffirm their commitment to God's rule (the kingdom of God). He was understood by his followers to be the Messiah, the anointed leader sent by God to save Israel from infidelity and injustice. In the decades after his death, Jesus' reform movement spread to Jews in surrounding countries and to Gentiles, became a Jewish sect, organized itself into assemblies (churches) and finally in the second century became a religion separate from Judaism. Though a religion separate from Judaism, Christianity remains profoundly Jewish in its worship of one God and acceptance of his revelation in the Bible.

## Questions for Reflection and Discussion

1. There was a great diversity of opinion on a wide variety of subjects among Jesus' Jewish contemporaries. Describe some of the different issues which were being debated among first-century Jews and how different Jewish groups approached these questions. How can teachers convey the variety and richness of first-century Galilean and Judean Judaism in their lessons?
2. What sorts of people, in terms of economic status and lifestyle, were most attracted to Jesus? Why? Who felt most threatened by his activities? Why?
3. Religion, politics, and social custom were inseparable in the time of Jesus. What implications does this have for your understanding of the ministry of Jesus?
4. The way Christians imagine Jesus to have lived greatly influences their attitudes toward Jews. Which aspects of Jesus' Galilean Jewish life, therefore, do you feel are the most important for religious educators to impart?

# The Synoptic Gospels and Their Presentation of Judaism

*Philip A. Cunningham*

## I. Introduction

The pivotal Vatican II declaration *Nostra Aetate* taught that "Jews should not be spoken of as rejected or accursed as if this followed from holy Scripture," and suggested that such preaching or teaching would not be "in accord with the truth of the Gospel message or the spirit of Christ."[1] This directive repudiated an ancient and fairly standard Christian practice of using the Gospels to portray Jews as a people cursed by God because of the crucifixion of Jesus.[2]

Such a custom has persisted in the Church until this century. Consider, for example, the pre-Vatican II American religion textbook which explained the parables in Matthew 21:33-43 and 22:1-14 by proposing that "[Jesus'] prophecy was partially fulfilled in the destruction of Jerusalem and more fully in the rejection by God of the chosen people." Another textbook in referring to Matthew 27:25 stated that "the chief priests took up a cry that put a curse on themselves and on the Jews for all time: 'His blood be upon us and our children.'" A third text opined that "since Pilate could not find anything wrong with Christ, he decided to disfigure his pure and beautiful body, so that even the bloodthirsty Jews would back down and say that Christ had had enough."[3]

---

[1] *Nostra Aetate*, 4. Austin Flannery, gen. ed., *Vatican Council II: The Conciliar and Post Conciliar Documents* (1981 edition; Northport, N.Y.: Costello Publishing Co., 1975) 741. Besides citing ecclesial documents and scholarly works, these notes will also suggest resources for further reading and study.

[2] See Edward H. Flannery, *The Anguish of the Jews* (revised ed.; New York/Mahwah: Paulist, 1985). This overview of the history of the Jewish-Christian relationship is required reading for teachers and preachers concerned with this subject.

[3] These three quotes come from a 1961 textbook study by Rose Thering, O.P. as presented in John T. Pawlikowski, *Catechetics and Prejudice: How Catholic Teaching Materials View Jews, Protestants, and Racial Minorities* (New York: Paulist, 1973) 81–83.

The Gospels clearly contain passages which have been used in the past to promote animosity toward Jews and Judaism. That potential still exists and needs to be reckoned with by religious educators.

However, there is another reason why Gospel references to Judaism must be carefully construed. Any distortion of the Jewish faith and tradition will inevitably result in a distorted picture of Christianity as well because, as Pope John Paul II has observed, "our two religious communities are connected and closely related at the very level of their respective religious identities."[4] The Vatican's 1985 "Notes" insist that this wholly unique bond which joins us as a Church to the Jews and Judaism" requires that a true knowledge of Judaism must be "organically integrated" into catechetical curricula and not be relegated to an "occasional or marginal" status.[5] Thus, accurate portrayals of Judaism are required not only because of legitimate concerns for justice and fairness, but also because this accuracy regarding Judaism is necessary for a proper understanding of Christianity.

This chapter will discuss how religious educators might pursue these goals when considering the Gospels of Mark, Matthew, and Luke. We begin with an important biblical principle which catechists should keep in mind when working with the Gospel texts.

## II. The Origins of the Gospel Tradition

In 1964 the Pontifical Biblical Commission issued an "Instruction on the Historical Truth of the Gospels" which outlined the findings of biblical scholarship concerning the origins of the Gospels.[6] It told modern readers to be aware that the Gospels contain materials which come from three different stages in the growth of the Christian movement.

*The first stage* or time period includes information dating from the actual ministry of Jesus in the early 30s of the first century of the Common Era.[7] For example, the tradition that Jesus had a reputation as a healer, or that he frequently participated in fellowship meals, or that he was crucified outside Jerusalem shortly before the feast of

---

[4] "Audience for Representatives of Jewish Organizations," March 12, 1979, in Eugene J. Fisher and Leon Klenicki, eds., *John Paul II on Jews and Judaism, 1979–1986* (Washington: U.S.C.C., 1987) 24.

[5] Vatican "Notes," I.2, 8.

[6] For the text of the Instruction and a commentary see Joseph A. Fitzmyer, *A Christological Catechism: New Testament Answers* (New York/Ramsey: Paulist, 1982) 97–142.

[7] The terms B.C.E. and C.E., respectively meaning Before the Common Era and the Common Era, are an alternative way of denoting the time before Christ and after Christ which is inoffensive to non-Christians.

Passover all date back to the time of Jesus' activities in Galilee and Judea.

*The second stage* comprises traditions which arose in the decades after his followers experienced Jesus as raised to transcendent new life. This period can thus be called the post-resurrectional preaching of the early apostles. It is characterized by the struggle to comprehend the significance for humanity of the life, death, and raising of Jesus and by the veneration of him as Christ, Lord, and Son of God. A 1984 instruction of the Pontifical Biblical Commission referred to the differences between stages one and two in this way:

> One must distinguish, on the one hand, the way Jesus *presented himself to his contemporaries and was able to be understood by them* (his family, opponents, disciples); on the other, the way those who came to believe in Jesus understood his life and his person *after the manifestations of him as one raised from the dead.*[8]

In other words, the resurrection-experience catalyzed ways of understanding Jesus which did not occur earlier during his ministry. The Gospel portrayals of Jesus' life, then, are permeated with resurrection-based insights about Jesus which are to some extent anachronistic in the context of the events being depicted. For instance, the demon in Mark 5:7 who exclaims that Jesus is the "Son of the Most High God," a cry, incidentally, which is apparently intended for the text's readers since none of the other persons in the narrative react to this startling identification, is expressing a post-resurrectional faith statement in the setting of Jesus' ministry. It is notable that no human character in Mark's Gospel is able to confess this of Jesus until the crucifixion (see Mark 15:39).[9]

*The third stage* of Gospel formation encompasses the events contemporaneous with the actual composition of the written Gospel texts. In the case of the synoptics, therefore, Mark's Gospel was influenced by the evangelist's concerns around the year 70 C.E., and Matthew and Luke by circumstances in the middle or late 80s.[10] The

---

[8] *The Bible and Christology*, 1.1.11.2a in Joseph A. Fitzmyer, *Scripture and Christology: A Statement of the Biblical Commision with a Commentary* (New York/Mahwah: Paulist, 1986) 21. Italics in the original.

[9] It might also be observed that the principle that Jesus' followers conceived of Jesus and his ministry in new ways as a result of the resurrection is explicitly recognized in John 2:2; 12:16; and 14:26.

[10] This dating of the synoptics is based on the all but unanimous scholarly understanding that Mark is the earliest Gospel and served as a source for Matthew and Luke. Those interested in the details of the debate about the relationships of the Gospels should see Frans Neirynck, "Synoptic Problem," in *The New Jerome Biblical Commen-*

issues and problems on the minds of the Gospel writers colored not only their presentations and conceptions of Jesus, but also affected their attitudes and depictions of Jews and Judaism.

As a further result of the three-layered nature of the Gospel's textual tradition, the evangelists' portraits of Jesus can sometimes be seen to be operating on more than one level. As shall be seen, a Gospel writer's concerns may occasionally prompt him to portray the "stage one" Jesus as dealing with what is really a "stage three" issue.[11]

## III. The Early Church

This all means that some awareness of the history of the first-century Church is needed for a thorough reading of the Gospels. This section will highlight some important features of that history.[12]

### A. The Jewishness of the Early Church

The Church as a distinct entity was born after the death and raising of Jesus, but it was one Jewish group amid many others. It is significant that some of the Church's earliest preaching, corresponding to stage two above, evolved in this context of debate with other Jewish groups. This intra-Jewish exchange operated according to contemporary cultural mores and customarily included fiery and abrasive language.

Echoes of this debate, which eventually were incorporated in the written Gospels, transposed an originally "in-house" exchange into the very different social context of later readers. Early disputes between Jews in the Church and other Jews took on a more dissonant tonality when later read by non-Jewish Gentiles. A Jewish-Jewish dynamic mutated into a Jewish-Gentile one which was susceptible to pagan anti-Jewish sentiment that had existed before the time of Jesus and was alien to the attitudes both of Jesus and of the originally Jewish Church.

### B. The Admission of Gentiles into the Church

One of the most crucial developments in the first-century Church was the admission of uncircumcised Gentiles into the community.

---

*tary,* ed. by Raymond E. Brown, Joseph A. Fitzmyer, and Roland E. Murphy (Englewood Cliffs: Prentice-Hall, 1990) 587–595. N.B. also 596, 631, 675–676.

[11] This principle has been recognized as pertinent for the Gospels' treatment of Judaism by the 1985 Vatican "Notes" [IV, 21, A] which explained that since "the Gospels are the outcome of long and complicated editorial work. . . . some references hostile or less than favorable to the Jews have their historical context in conflicts between the nascent Church and the Jewish community."

[12] For an excellent overview of the history of the New Testament Church see Paula Fredriksen, *From Jesus to Christ: The Origins of the New Testament Images of Jesus* (New Haven: Yale University Press, 1988).

This question was the source of major controversy in the Church's earliest decades, as the letters of Paul and the Acts of the Apostles make clear. The dispute indicates that Jesus was not remembered to have given any instructions on the topic, probably because his ministry addressed his fellow Jews.[13] The admission of Gentiles is yet another instance of the transformative effects of the resurrection experience as the Church passed from stage one into stage two.

There was a wide range of views about the admission of Gentiles among the Jews who formed the early Church. This diversity can be conveniently outlined by describing four basic opinions on the issue:[14]

> *Type One:* Christian Jews[15] and their Gentile converts who practiced full observance of the Mosaic Law, including circumcision, as necessary for receiving the fullness of salvation brought by Jesus Christ.

> *Type Two:* Christian Jews and their Gentile converts who did not deem circumcision to be salvific for Gentile Christians but did require them to keep some Jewish purity/kosher laws.

> *Type Three:* Christian Jews and their Gentile converts who did not deem cirucmcision to be salvific for Gentile Christians and did not require their observing Jewish purity laws in regard to food. This type did not entail a break with the cultic practices of Judaism (feasts, Temple), nor did it impel Jews in the Church to abandon circumcision and the Law.

> *Type Four:* Christian Jews and their Gentile converts who did not insist on circumcision and Jewish food laws and saw no abiding significance in Jewish feasts or the cult of the Jerusalem Temple, indeed eventually seeing these things as belonging to an abrogated and outmoded old covenant.[16]

The debates rebounding among these various types of Jews and Gentiles in the first-century Church are evident in the synoptic Gospels as will be seen below. Obviously, a person's attitudes toward

---

[13] See the 1985 Vatican "Notes," III, 12: "Jesus was and always remained a Jew, his ministry was deliberately limited 'to the lost sheep of the house of Israel' (Matt 15:24). Jesus is fully a man of his time and of his environment—the Jewish Palestinian one of the first century, the anxieties and hopes of which he shared."

[14] This model has been suggested by Raymond E. Brown in his joint work with John P. Meier, *Antioch and Rome* (New York/Ramsey: Paulist, 1983) 2–8.

[15] The term "Christian Jews" is employed herein instead of the more conventional "Jewish Christians" in order to emphasize that these earliest Church members did not consider themselves to have departed from their Jewish heritage. With the possible exception of late "Type Four" Christians, they were Jews "with a difference," not former Jews.

[16] Outline adapted from Raymond E. Brown, *Biblical Exegesis and Church Doctrine* (New York/Mahwah: Paulist, 1985) 133–134.

non-Christian Jews would be greatly affected by their place in this typology. Whether Jew or Gentile, a "Type One" Christian would be the most favorably disposed toward Judaism, whereas a "Type Four" Christian, again whether Jew or Gentile, would be the most hostile toward Judaism.

### C. The Jewish-Roman War of 66–72 C.E.

The outbreak of Jewish revolution against the Roman Empire, culminating in the Roman destruction of Jerusalem and the Temple in the year 70 C.E., was a major turning point in the histories of the Jewish people and of the early Church. It had different effects on each group.

Briefly, the military disaster triggered a process of consolidation in a Judaism now bereft of the focal Temple cult. The surviving Jewish religious leadership gathered in the last two decades of the century in the town of Yavneh (in Greek, Jamnia) and set the foundations for the spiritual richness of Rabbinic Judaism. As part of this redefinition process, boundaries between the slowly coalescing "mainstream" Judaism and various Jewish subgroups were clarified. Among the groups now being distanced from nascent Rabbinic Judaism was the Church, whose growing number of Gentile members called its Jewishness into question.[17]

The Church, on the other hand, was seeking to establish itself in the Roman Empire and to distinguish itself from those Jews who had rebelled against Rome. It was imperative for the Church to present itself as a peaceful, non-threatening assembly worthy of imperial recognition as a legal religion. Such legal status was especially important for the growing number of Gentile Christians who sought the exemption from having to worship Roman deities which Jews (including Christian Jews) had enjoyed for decades.

Thus, the post-70 context encouraged both Judaism and the Church to distance themselves from one another. It was in this climate that the Gospels of Matthew, Luke, and John were composed.

### D. Christian Jews in the Last Third of the First Century

The exact moment in which Christian Jews became the minority in the Church is impossible to determine, and, of course, the ratio of Jews to Gentiles in the Church varied from place to place. Whether or not these Jews were a minority by the time the Gospels were writ-

---

[17] For more on the origins of Rabbinic Judaism and its relations with the young Church see Hayim Goren Perelmuter, *Siblings: Rabbinic Judaism and Early Christianity at Their Beginnings* (New York/Mahwah: Paulist, 1989).

ten in the 70s, 80s, and 90s, they seem to have played a major, even if not dominant, role in the Church in the latter third of the century. The Gospels of Matthew and John were written by such Jews, and the Gospel of Luke was authored by one who held them in great reverence.

Yet they were in a very awkward position. The growing likelihood that the Church would become a completely Gentile assembly left them vulnerable to the charge that Christianity was just a heretical deviation from Judaism. As a result, the dwindling number of Christian Jews (and their Gentile associates) had two urgent priorities: (1) to insist that the Hebrew Bible be interpreted in light of the life, death, and raising of Jesus Christ; and (2) to defend the Church's mission to the Gentiles.[18]

## IV. The Gospel of Mark

### A. General Background

Having thus sketched some of the historical factors which form the backdrop for the writing of the Gospels, we turn now to examine the presentation of Jews and Judaism in each of the synoptic Gospels. This discussion will focus mostly on stage three of the Gospel tradition, the time of the evangelist, since other chapters in this volume treat such "stage one" issues as Jesus' contemporaries and the passion narratives. In other words, we won't be dealing directly with Jesus' ministry as much as with how and why an evangelist has framed his account of it.[19]

At the outset it should be stated that the Gospel of Mark is both the earliest and the shortest of the Gospels. It appears to have originated in a Church community which was faced with violence and chaos. Some suggest that it was written in Rome shortly after the persecutions under the emperor Nero (64–66 C.E.) and in the midst of the Jewish-Roman War (66–72 C.E.). The Gospel seems very concerned with suffering and forcefully asserts that true insight into the person of Jesus is possible only by reckoning with his suffering and death.

The Gospel can be neatly divided into two halves at the end of chapter 8, the scene known as "Peter's Confession." Prior to this point the

---

[18] See "The Mighty Minority" in Jacob Jervell, *The Unknown Paul: Essays on Luke-Acts and Early Christian History* (Minneapolis: Augsburg, 1984) 26–51.

[19] For an introduction to the perspectives of each of the synoptic evangelists and a treatment of the historical ministry of Jesus see Philip A. Cunningham, *Jesus and the Evangelists* (New York/Mahwah: Paulist, 1988).

Gospel has been dominated by Jesus' performance of miraculous feats, but both his words and actions produce only amazement and bewilderment (e.g, Mark 1:22, 27; 2:12; 4:41; 5:20, 42; 6:2, 6:51; 7:18, 37; 8:21). Demons repeatedly demonstrate a supernatural knowledge of Jesus' identity, but no other character in the narrative benefits from their exclamations (Mark 1:23-25, 34; 3:11-12; 5:7). While it might be thought that the early mention of Pharisees and Herodians planning to destroy Jesus could reflect an anti-Jewish sentiment by the evangelist (Mark 3:6), the fact of the matter is that the Gospel portrays a universal inability to comprehend Jesus. Scribes charge him with conspiring with Satan (3:22-30), his family arrives to apprehend Jesus because they've heard that he's beside himself (3:20-22, 31-34), the pig-herding Gerasenes request that he leave their region (5:17), his Nazarean townsfolk become angry with him (6:3), and his disciples are as befuddled as anyone else despite the private tutoring which they have received (e.g., 4:10-13, 33-34, 40-41; 6:35-52; 7:18; 8:4, 17-18, 21).

In the second half of the Gospel the tone is decidedly different. Following Peter's pivotal statement that Jesus is the Christ (8:29), Jesus begins a series of instructions that the Son of Man must suffer (8:31; 9:31; 10:33-34) and that those who would follow him must be prepared to suffer also (e.g., 8:34–9:1; 9:43-47; 10:29-31, 38-39; 13:9-13). The Gospel reaches its climactic moment as the crucified Jesus expires. "Now when the centurion, who stood facing him, saw that in this way he breathed his last, he said, 'Truly this man was God's Son!' " (15:39). This outcry marks the first time that a human being has been able to confess faith in Jesus as Son of God. The evangelist thereby asserts that such faith is possible only by standing at the foot of Jesus' cross and experiencing his suffering. Miraculous wonders, authoritative sermons, and private instruction all fail to provide true insight. For Mark, only the cross leads to authentic faith. This perspective is especially important for a church community which is itself in pain and misery.

Lastly, Mark understands his church's present troubles to be the final acts in the drama of salvation. He feels that his "generation will not pass away" before "they will see the Son of Man coming in clouds with great power and glory. . . [to] gather his elect from the four winds" (Mark 13:30, 26-27). Mark is not writing his Gospel for the sake of posterity because for him history is foreshortened. His aim is to narrate a "life of Christ" which will directly address the current needs of his community.

## B. Mark and Judaism

Even though relating the suffering of his community to Christ's passion and death is Mark's prime concern, there are portions of the Gospel which disclose the evangelist's understanding of Judaism. Of special note are three passages which discuss sabbath observance (Mark 2:23-28), purity (7:1-8), and kosher foods (7:18-19). In all three, Jewish norms are downgraded or eliminated. The Son of Man is said to be master of the sabbath (2:28), purity practices are characterized as mere "human precepts" (7:7), and all foods are declared to be clean (7:19).

There are a number of reasons for believing that the topics addressed in these verses owe more to the evangelist's concerns around the year 70 C.E. than to problems arising during the ministry of Jesus in the early 30s C.E. For instance, there is no evidence that either Jesus, his disciples, or any of their Jewish contemporaries seriously questioned the propriety of observing the sabbath or of eating kosher foods. Jews certainly debated what proper sabbath and dietary observances entailed, but there was no question of abandoning what is explicitly commanded in the Torah (e.g. Exod 20:8-11; Deut 14; Lev 11). The finality with which the Marcan Jesus devalues key Torah concepts seems incongruous with the Jewish setting of Jesus of Nazareth.

On the other hand, along with circumcision, the issues of kosher foods and of conformity to the sabbath were definitely controversial topics in the early Church (e.g. Gal 2:11-14, 4:10; Rom 14:1-6; Acts 10:9-16, 15:19-29, 21:17-26). The very existence of such debates indicates that Jesus himself spoke no definitive word on these matters despite what these Marcan passages might suggest. If Jesus had indeed declared all foods clean, why was there even a doubt about it later?

The question of the ongoing legitimacy of these customary Jewish practices seems to have arisen only after non-Jews were being admitted into the Church. It was the Church's new context which provoked debate as to whether Jewish norms had any meaning in an increasingly Gentile community. The fact that in these passages it is the disciples of Jesus and not Jesus himself who receive criticism suggests that it is followers of Jesus in Mark's day who are being criticized for their un-Jewish behavior.

This does not mean that the evangelist has created these scenes of Jesus disputing proper Torah observance out of thin air. Instead, it appears that Mark has taken traditions that Jesus engaged in typically Jewish debates about the interpretation of the Torah and has rendered them according to his understanding that his church community need not observe sabbath or kosher norms at all.

Further evidence of the influence of the evangelist's situation is seen in Mark's distant and not fully accurate editorial explanation of Jewish purity customs (7:3-4). The need of any explanation at all shows that Mark's intended readership is predominantly Gentile. As a matter of fact, all Jews did not observe these Pharisaic purity practices, nor does it appear that Pharisees demanded that their fellow Jews do so or think of them as sinners if they did not. In addition, the presentation of the Pharisees is somewhat stylized, reflecting a stage two or three context. Pharisees did not regularly patrol grainfields on the sabbath hoping to catch people plucking grain, nor did they inspect the cleanliness of the hands of non-Pharisees.[20]

All of these items, especially Mark's editorial assertion that "thus he declared all foods clean" (7:19), betray the perspectives of a largely Gentile church which sees itself as not bound by kosher, sabbath, or Pharisaic purity customs. In this, Mark differs from both Matthew and Luke. For example, Matthew omits the Marcan contention that Jesus declared all foods clean (Matt 15:10-20), while Luke has deleted the entire scene. Furthermore, Luke depicts the Apostolic Council in Jerusalem as requiring Gentile converts to observe some dietary restrictions (Acts 15:19-29), and Matthew may have the same idea in mind in his addition to the Parable of the Guests Invited to a Feast (Matt 22:11-14).

Mark's attitude toward the Temple in Jerusalem is consistent with his stance toward other Jewish practices. Jesus' cursing of a fruitless fig tree and its subsequent withering (Mark 11:12-14, 20-25) brackets the scene in which Jesus overturns tables in the Temple (11:15-19). The next two chapters show Jesus in mounting contention with Temple authorities, including a pointed parable about the caretakers of a vineyard whose murderous failure to produce fruit will result in the vineyard being given to others (12:1-12). Finally, at the instant of Jesus' death, the curtain of the Temple is torn asunder (15:38). This suggests both the eventual fate of the sacrificial cult (cf. 13:2) and the opening of access to the Divine Presence to the Gentile nations. Notice that it is a Gentile centurion who expresses profound insight in the very next verse. (Again, Jesus' actual deeds concerning the Temple are not the issue here, but, rather, Mark's arrangement and interpretation of the traditions about Jesus which he has received.)

---

[20] For the preceding paragraphs I am indebted to the analyses of E. P. Sanders in *Jesus and Judaism* (Philadelphia: Fortress, 1985) 264–267; and in his *Jewish Law from Jesus to the Mishnah* (Philadelphia: Trinity, 1990) 6–41.

From all of these indications, it seems that Mark must be ranked as a "Type Four" Christian according to the schema on p. 45. He rejects Jewish food laws and he sees no abiding significance in Jewish feasts or the cult of the Temple. For Mark, all of these things are irrelevant in the community of Jesus. Perhaps his position is epitomized in the saying that "no one puts new wine into old wineskins" (2:22).

And so, although the Gospel of Mark is concerned with a crisis of faith which has arisen in a church experiencing suffering, upheaval, and possibly persecution, the writer's stance toward Judaism is perceptible. The Marcan Jesus' comments about foods, purity, and the sabbath all convey the evangelist's belief that such customs are obsolete in the final days before the return of the Son of Man and, therefore, are not binding on either Jews or Gentiles in the Church.

## V. The Gospel of Matthew

### A. General Background

It is generally believed that Matthew's Gospel was composed about fifteen years after Mark's (circa 85 C.E.) and that the author actually used some form of Mark as one of his sources. The writer displays an impressive knowledge of the Hebrew Scriptures which he uses extensively to illuminate his understanding of the significance of Jesus. Indeed, the uniquely Matthean reference to the "scribe who has been trained for the kingdom of heaven . . . who brings out of his treasure what is new and what is old" (Matt 13:52) may reflect the author's estimation of his own work. He is a scribe who discloses the treasures of the old (the Hebrew Scriptures) in the light of Jesus' new conclusive interpretation of it.

While Jesus' passion is very important to him, Matthew's depiction of Jesus does not emphasize his suffering to the extent that Mark's Gospel does. Instead, the Matthean Jesus is presented as the definitive expression of the Torah who authoritatively teaches what God expects believers to do. The evangelist artfully conveys this conception of Jesus in several ways. For example, events in the life of the Matthean Jesus are often reminiscent of the original law-giver, Moses. It is only in Matthew's Gospel that the newborn Jesus must be rescued from the homicidal designs of an evil king, recalling the events surrounding Moses' birth (Matt 2:13-18; cf. Exod 1:15–2:10). Similarly, the scene of Moses on Mount Sinai is echoed when the Matthean Jesus delivers his great sermon about Torah sitting on a mountain (Matt 5:1-2ff), an event which in Luke's Gospel occurs on a level place (Luke 6:17-19ff).

It could also be said that the Matthean Jesus embodies the entire history of Israel. The implication of the genealogy at the opening of the Gospel (Matt 1:1-17) is that the whole story of the Jewish people coalesces in the birth of Jesus. This idea is verified by: (1) allusions to God's occasional *modus operandi* of acting through women with unusual sexual histories (Matt 1:3, 5, 6, 16, 18-20; cf. Gen 38; Josh 2; Ruth 3-4; 2 Sam 11); (2) the portrayal of Joseph as the recipient of knowledge through dreams (Matt 1:20; 2:13, 19, 22; cf. Gen 37:5, 9, 20; 40:8-19; 41:14-36); (3) implicit references to the whole People Israel coming up out of Egypt and being tempted in the desert (Matt 2:14-15; 4:1-10; cf. Deut 8:2; Exod 16:1-3; 17:1-2, 7; Exod 32:1-4); and (4) explicit assertions that in the life of Jesus the Hebrew Scriptures have been fulfilled (Matt 1:22; 2:15, 17, 23; 4:14; 5:17; 8:17; 12:17; 13:14, 35; 21:4; 26:54, 56; 27:9).

On this last point, religious educators should be aware of how these Matthean "fulfillment" passages function. At first glance it might appear that Matthew has simply observed that predictions made in the Hebrew Scriptures about the Messiah have come to fruition in Jesus. Actually, Matthew has done something far more subtle. This could perhaps be most vividly illustrated by examining Matthew 2:15 in which the evangelist suggests that Joseph's flight to Egypt with the child and his mother "was to fulfill what had been spoken by the Lord through the prophet, 'Out of Egypt I have called my son.'" The evangelist is alluding here to Hosea 11:

> When Israel was a child, I loved him,
>    and *out of Egypt I called my son.*
> The more I called them,
>    the more they went from me;
> They kept sacrificing to the Baals,
>    and offering incense to idols (Hos 11:1-2).

Seen in its own context, it becomes clear that the prophet, speaking for God, is commenting upon the past history of God's relationship with Israel. The son of God, Israel, was brought up out of Egypt in the Exodus, and even though it thus owes its very existence to God, Israel still consorts with pagan idols. Far from being a prediction about the eventual arrival of someone out of Egypt in the *future*, the passage is a wistful recollection of the *past*.

Matthew, however, has detected a resonance between the stories of Israel, son of God, and Jesus, Son of God. Both have been called out of Egypt by God, both pass through waters (Matt 3:13-17; Exod 14), and both experience temptations in the desert (Matt 2:1-10; Exod 16ff). Looking backwards into the Hebrew Scriptures through the lens of his post-resurrectional experience of Jesus, the evangelist perceives implications not apparent in the text itself. The Matthean Jesus has not simply carried out predictions made about him, for in reality the texts do not contain such "predictions." Rather, by reading the Hebrew Scriptures in the light of the Raised Jesus, the evangelist has come to believe that the story of Jesus recapitulates the story of Israel.[21]

Matthew can conceive of Jesus in this way because he also understands Jesus as the personification of the Wisdom of God. In several passages, the Matthean Jesus is described in terms reminiscent of God's Wisdom (Matt 11:16-19, 28-30; cf. Sir 6:18-37; 24:19-24; 51:23-27) with the result that those near Jesus are in the presence of something greater than the Temple, than Jonah, and than Solomon (Matt 12:6, 41-42). The Jewish tradition understood God's Wisdom as residing in the Temple in Jerusalem (Sir 24:8, 10) and as expressed in the Torah (Sir 24:24). Therefore, the Matthean Jesus—as the supreme expression of that Wisdom—transcends the importance of the Temple and is able to authoritatively interpret the Torah (see the "but I say to you" verses from the Sermon on the Mount in Matt 5:21-45).

Because Jesus thus brings the ultimate interpretation of the Torah, Matthew's Jesus is the teacher par excellence and Matthew's Gospel is the most consciously catechetical of the Gospels. In addition, Matthew emphasizes that the teaching of Jesus is something which must be put into actual practice and not merely spoken about (e.g., Matt 5:17-19; 7:21, 24-26; 12:12; 21:28-31; 25:14-30; 25:31-46; 28:19-20).

One last feature of Matthew's Gospel will impact on our assessment of the evangelist's position on Judaism. This is his attitude toward Gentiles. While there is no doubt that Matthew, like the other Gospel writers, supports the Church's Gentile mission (e.g. Matt 28:19), it is also true that his Gospel betrays a certain ambivalence toward Gentiles. For instance, there are several passages where Matthew urges his readers not to be like Gentiles, and where, occasionally, "Gen-

---

[21] This point about how the fulfillment passages operate relates to the statement in the Vatican "Notes," that the Hebrew Bible "retains its own value as revelation that the New Testament often does no more than resume" (par. 7). Similarly, *Within Context* observes that "such post-Resurrection insights do not replace the original intentions of the prophets" (below, p. 144). See also the Bishops' Committee on the Liturgy, *God's Mercy Endures Forever* (Washington: U.S.C.C., 1988) 15.

tile" is an epithet on a par with being a "tax collector" (See Matt 5:46-47; 6:7, 32; 18:17. Note that in the Lucan parallels [Luke 6:32-33; 11:1-2; 12:30; 17:1-4] this anti-Gentile rhetoric is absent.) Similarly, it seems that it is Gentiles who are referred to as "dogs" (Matt 7:6; 15:24-27; references again absent in Luke). Furthermore, it is made very explicit in Matthew that Jesus' mission is only to the "lost sheep of the house of Israel" (Matt 15:24) and that likewise his disciples are to "go nowhere among the Gentiles" but are to "go rather to the lost sheep of the house of Israel" (10:5-6).

This orientation, combined with the other items mentioned above, leads to the conclusion that the evangelist is Jewish. He thinks of Jesus in very Jewish categories, exhibits an extensive knowledge of the Hebrew Scriptures, may picture himself as a Christian "scribe," and displays mixed feelings toward Gentiles.

Unlike the Marcan Jesus who "declared all foods clean" (Mark 7:19) and simply nullified Torah instructions, the Matthean Jesus states emphatically that he has not "come to abolish the law [Torah] and the prophets" and "whoever breaks [or annuls] one of the least of these commandments, and teaches others to do the same, will be called least in the kingdom of heaven" (Matt 5:17a, 19a). It would seem that while Matthew agrees with admitting Gentiles to the Church, he believes that they must observe at least some Torah behavioral norms. This would appear to be the point of Matthew's addition to the Parable of the Guests Invited to a Feast (Matt 22:11-14). Though an uninvited guest is admitted to the banquet, he must be properly attired or face expulsion.[22]

Matthew, then, should be classified as a "Type Two" Christian according to the typology on p. 45. He upholds the ongoing legitimacy of the Torah, albeit as authoritatively interpreted by Jesus, and sees it as binding, at least in some respects, on Gentile Christians as well.[23]

---

[22] The tradition that Matthew's Gospel was composed in the vicinity of Antioch in Syria bears on this passage. Galatians 2:11-14 indicates that Peter and Paul argued publicly in Antioch about whether Gentiles should be required to observe certain dietary regulations (see also Acts 14:25–15:2; 15:19-21, 28-29). Since Peter seems to have prevailed, it is likely that in Antioch it became the established norm for Gentiles to eat kosher foods, a tradition which Matthew's Gospel reflects.

[23] Although Anthony J. Saldarini has recently observed that while Matthew carefully articulates his community's modifications of such Jewish customs as alms-giving, sabbath observance, Temple worship, purity rules, tithing, and conformity to Torah, no mention whatsoever is made of circumcision. Since Matthew is uninhibited about expressing his other, numerous differences with contemporary Judaism, the absence of contention about circumcision strongly suggests that the Matthean church simply takes circumcision for granted. It is possible, therefore, that Matthew might be a "Type One"

## B. Matthew and Judaism

The inherent Jewishness of Matthew's Gospel needs to be kept in mind when considering the Matthean attitude toward Judaism. This is particularly true when one comes upon the extremely polemical passages in chapters 21–23. Once again, the modern reader must be cognizant of the Stage Three context of the evangelist.

Matthew's Church is evidently a predominantly Jewish community in the mid-80s which understands itself as being authentically Jewish because it lives according to Jesus' authoritative presentation of the Torah. It is a community which feels itself called to incorporate Gentiles into its ranks, although with certain prerequisites. As such, the Matthean community is a minority sub-group among the various competing Jewish movements which are seeking to fill the vacuum created by the destruction of the Temple in 70 C.E. Consequently, the scribes and Pharisees are especially criticized in Matthew's Gospel because they are emblematic of those with whom the evangelist is vying for the post-Temple leadership of the Jewish community.

Matthew's polemic against contemporary opponents is evident in his version of the Parable of the Vineyard. This parable is found in one of Matthew's sources, the Gospel of Mark (Mark 12:1-12), but Matthew has added as an explanatory verse: "Therefore, I tell you, the kingdom of God will be taken away from you and given to a people (*ethnē*) that produces the fruits of the kingdom" (Matt 21:43). Additionally, the Matthean parable is addressed to the "chief priests and Pharisees . . . [who] realized that he was speaking about them" (Matt 21:45), but the Pharisees are absent in the Marcan account (Mark 11:27).

Matthew often pairs the Pharisees either with the chief priests or with the members of the priestly governing class, the Sadducees (Matt 3:7; 16:1, 6, 11, 12; 22:34; 27:62). By affiliating them in this way, the two groups become associated in his readers' minds.

In Matthew's estimation, the ethical poverty of the chief priests' leadership had been the cause of the Temple's destruction in 70 C.E. Their corruption is apparent in Matthew's passion narrative. It is the "chief priests and elders" (Matt 27:20) who had orchestrated Jesus' death and who incited the people of Jerusalem to utter the uniquely

Christian according to Brown's typology, who requires full observance of the Torah by Gentiles seeking membership in the Church. See Anthony J. Saldarini, "The Gospel of Matthew and Jewish-Christian Conflict in Galilee" (paper to appear in the English and Hebrew proceedings of the First International Conference on Galilean Studies in Late Antiquity, Lee Levine, ed.) 9–10.

Matthean exclamation: "his blood be on us and on our children!" (27:25).[24] Under such leadership, Jerusalem "kills the prophets" and is "desolate" (23:37, 38). Matthew's ideas about the fate of such leaders is plainly visible in his insertion into the Parable of the Guests Invited to a Feast. The king "sent his troops, destroyed those murderers, and burned their city" (Matt 22:7; an idea notably absent in the Luke 14:21 parallel).

By associating the Pharisees with the Temple leadership, the implication is made that just as the leadership of the chief priests had been corrupt and had proven to be fruitless (Matt 21:19, 33-44), so too the emerging leaders of Matthew's day are inauthentic blind guides who are also failing to produce true Torah living. In seven "woes" against the "scribes and Pharisees, hypocrites!" (Matt 23:13, 15, 16, 23, 25, 27, 29), the evangelist goes on to castigate his competitors for the hearts and minds of both Jews and Gentiles (woes 1-2), to reject their understanding of oaths, tithes, and purity (woes 3-5), and to portray them as lawless killers (woes 6-7). Matthew seeks to undermine the developing power of contemporary Jewish leadership because for him only a Jesus-centered understanding of Torah is legitimate. The evangelist insists that true guidance is to be found in the Jesus-centered Matthean community, the "people that produces the fruits of the kingdom" (21:43). Rival claimants to authority in the Jewish world are hypocritical blind guides who seem to be learned Jews but really are not. The fact that his Gospel is thus shaped against the background of what might be called an internal family feud only adds to the volatility of Matthew's rhetoric.[25]

In later Church tradition, as witnessed by the textbook quotations at the beginning of this chapter, it was common to understand these Matthean passages as meaning that the divine Election of Israel as the Chosen People had been transferred to Gentiles and that non-Christian Jews were dispossessed and accursed. Within his own context, however, it is more likely that Matthew takes the ongoing Election of Israel for granted. The conflict is about who accurately

---

[24] There has been debate about whether Matthew intends in this verse to issue a blanket condemnation of "the people as a whole" (27:25) or to impute guilt more precisely to "the chief priests and elders" (27:20). Such verses as 21:45-46 in which the "chief priests and Pharisees" fear the crowds who regard Jesus as a prophet favor the latter option.

[25] Some have suggested, incidentally, that during his ministry in the early 30s, Jesus may have become involved in disputes between the Pharisaic schools of Hillel and Shammai [e.g., *Within Context*, p. 143]. Whether traditions about such debates lie behind Matthew's presentation in chapter 23 is difficult to say. But the rancorous tone of the final form of Matthew's Gospel seems to stem more from the evangelist's own contentious situation in the 80s.

interprets Torah and, therefore, who should lead in the post-Temple epoch: the emerging authorities at Yavneh or the Matthean community of Jews and Gentiles living according to the Torah taught by Jesus.[26]

## VI. The Gospel of Luke and the Acts of the Apostles

### A. General Background

The third synoptic Gospel is the first part of a two-volume work which tells not only the story of Jesus' ministry but also recounts the growth of the early Church. Therefore, our discussion of the Gospel of Luke needs to reckon with the second volume, the Acts of the Apostles, as well. The twin works seem to date from approximately the same time as the Gospel of Matthew (circa 85 C.E.), but the author appears not to have been aware of his fellow evangelist's activity. Like Matthew, Luke also had access to some form of the Gospel of Mark.[27]

One of Luke's central convictions is that the time has come for salvation to be extended to all people. Besides explicit statements to that effect (e.g., Luke 2:32; 3:6; Acts 1:8), Luke-Acts also displays a certain understanding of the structure of human history. For Luke the time of Jesus' ministry is the pivotal moment of human history when salvation dawns upon the world. The time of "the law and the prophets," the Epoch of Israel, preceded Jesus' activities (Luke 16:16), but after Jesus comes the Epoch of the Church (Acts 1:6-8) when news of salvation must be brought to all of humanity.

Luke-Acts also features a complementary geographical structure. The Gospel begins and ends in Jerusalem. Acts begins in Jerusalem, but Jesus commands the disciples to witness to him "in Jerusalem, in Judea and Samaria, and to the end of the earth" (Acts 1:8). The end of the earth refers to the end of the book where the great apostle, Paul, is found preaching about Jesus "quite openly and unhindered" in the imperial capital of the known world—Rome (28:31). Thus, the goal of the Gospel is Jerusalem, while the goal of Acts is Rome. This structure dramatizes the principle that Jews must receive the Good

[26] On the importance of a Jewish or a Gentile context for the reading of Matthew see Benno Przybylski, "The Setting of Matthean Anti-Judaism," in *Anti-Judaism in Early Christianity*, Vol. 1, *Paul and the Gospels*, ed. by Peter Richardson (Waterloo, Ontario: Wilfrid Laurier University Press, 1986) 181–200.

[27] For an introduction to Lucan theology see Joseph A. Fitzmyer, *Luke the Theologian: Aspects of His Teaching* (New York/Mahwah: Paulist, 1989).

News before Gentiles (Acts 13:46), but it also establishes that mission of the Church is no less than the salvation of the whole world.

A related Lucan purpose is the desire to convince Roman readers that the Church poses no threat to imperial peace and ought to be granted legal status as a legitimate religion. The evangelist imparts this idea in several ways. The family of Jesus is portrayed as law-abiding Galilean peasants who dutifully comply with a Roman census (2:1-5). The adult Jesus responds to news about Pontius Pilate's latest atrocity, not by calling for revenge as Romans might expect of a native of troublesome Galilee,[28] but by calling instead for repentance on the part of his fellow Jews (13:1-3). A centurion who has built a local synagogue asks through Jewish intermediaries that Jesus heal a sick slave—a request that Jesus honors (7:2-5). Pilate himself finds Jesus innocent of any crime (23:4, 14, 22). The centurion at the foot of the cross in Luke's Gospel declares "Surely this man was innocent!" (23:47), unlike his cry in Mark and Matthew that Jesus was God's Son (Mark 15:39; Matt 27:54).

In Acts, the Roman centurion Cornelius is the first Gentile to be baptized (Acts 10:1-48), the Roman proconsul Gallio refuses to judge a religious dispute involving Paul (18:12-16), Roman soldiers save Paul from an irate Jewish mob in the Temple (21:30-32), they rescue him again from a contentious Jewish council (23:10), and a Roman tribune writes to the governor saying that Paul has done "nothing deserving death or imprisonment" (23:29), a verdict echoed by the Roman client-king Herod Agrippa and the Roman governor Festus (26:31).

These episodes tend to minimize the awkward fact that the founder of the Christian movement had been executed at the command of a Roman prefect as "King of the Jews" (Luke 23:38). This embarrassment is countered by picturing all the Romans who come into contact with Jesus or his followers as reacting favorably to them. It was the doing of the "chief priest, the leaders, and the people" (Luke 23:13) that a man declared to be guiltless by Roman authorities was crucified. Therefore, Rome should not hesitate to grant legal status to the movement begun by Jesus.

This positive portrayal of Romans has, what is for Luke, the welcome side-effect of distancing the Church from those Jews who had rebelled against Rome in 66 C.E. This detachment is intensified by the frequent depiction in Acts of Jews as hostile to the Church (e.g.,

---

[28] For a treatment of popular Jewish response to Roman rule see Richard A. Horsley with John S. Hanson, *Bandits, Prophets, and Messiahs* (San Francisco: Harper & Row, 1985). For an exploration of Jesus' ministry within this imperial sociological context see Horsley's *Jesus and the Spiral of Violence* (San Francisco: Harper & Row, 1987).

Acts 9:23; 13:45, 50; 14:4, 19; 17:5-9; 18:12; 20:2, 19; 22:30; 23:12; 24:27; 25:9, 24). Thus, as part of his apologetic aimed at Rome, Luke takes pain to distinguish Church members, whether Jew or Gentile, from non-Christian Jews, a distinction not always obvious to Roman eyes.

Luke's depiction of Jesus is consonant with his aims regarding Rome. The Lucan Jesus is the healing savior who brings reconciliation, forgiveness, wholeness, and peace. This is evident in several uniquely Lucan passages. It is foretold that John the Baptist will prepare for Jesus by being a guide "into the way of peace" (Luke 1:79). Angels proclaim Jesus' birth as the dawning of peace (2:10-11, 14). Old Simeon is gifted with peace by encountering the newborn infant 2:29-30). Jesus begins his ministry by referring to himself as the one anointed by the Spirit of God to announce Good News and to liberate the poor, the captive, the blind, and the oppressed (4:16-21). At the end of his ministry Jesus mourns for Jerusalem which has not recognized "the things that make for peace" (19:42). Although all the Gospels report the severing of someone's ear in the garden where Jesus is arrested (Mark 1:47-50; Matt 26:51-52; John 18:10-11), only the Lucan Jesus heals the injury (Luke 22:50-51). The mere presence of Jesus sparks a rapprochement between Pilate and Herod (23:12). Only the Lucan Jesus prays for forgiveness for his executioners (23:34), and only in Luke's Gospel does one of the men crucified with Jesus repent (23:39-43).

Another important aspect of the Lucan portrait of Jesus and the early Church is his emphasis on their Jewish origins. In the Infancy Narrative all of those close to Jesus are pious, faithful Jews (Luke 1:6, 59; 2:21-22, 25, 27, 36-37, 39, 41). Jesus himself is devout and prayerful (Luke 3:21; 4:16; 5:16; 6:12-13; 9:18; 9:28; 11:1; 19:47; 22:32, 41-42; 23:34, 46-47). Similarly, the early Church is composed of holy Jews who regularly pray at the Temple (Luke 24:53; Acts 1:14; 2:5, 46; 7:59-60; 21:26). Acts further indicates that great numbers of Jews responded to the apostles' preaching (e.g., Acts 2:41; 4:4; 5:14; 6:7; 9:42; 14:1).

The Jewishness of Jesus and of the early Church underscores another Lucan theme. Jesus has actualized the promises God made to Israel in the Hebrew Scriptures (e.g., Luke 1:54-55, 70-75; 4:21; 7:22; 18:31-33; 24:26-27, 44-46; Acts 3:18-26; 8:27-35; 10:43). Therefore, the death and raising of Jesus, the birth and spread of the Church, the inclusion of Gentiles in the Christian community—all of these things have happened in accordance with the plan of God.

Although it is debated whether Luke is a Jew or a Gentile, these features of Luke-Acts are consistent with the idea that Luke is a Gen-

tile "God-fearer." Godfearer is the name given to a Gentile who ad-
mired Judaism and had begun to observe certain dietary customs or
celebrate the sabbath and other Jewish feasts. There is archaeological evidence from the late second century C.E. that, by that time at
least, Godfearers actually held some sort of official membership in
diaspora[29] synagogues—their names appear in roughly equal numbers with the names of Jews who are memorialized as contributors
to synagogue building projects.[30] It has been suggested that it is
primarily such semi-Jewish Gentiles whom Luke depicts as becoming members of the Church, whereas pagan idolaters are avoided (see
10:2, 22, 35; 13:16, 26; 15:28-29).[31]

Understanding Luke as a Godfearer explains his familiarity with the
Hebrew Bible to which he frequently alludes, but it also accounts for
his occasional misconstruing of Jewish practices such as in Luke
2:22-24 where he confuses several different Jewish customs.[32] Given
the dietary norms for Gentile Christians which are established in Acts
15:28-29, Luke would appear to be a "Type Two" Christian according to the typology on p. 45. Circumcision is not demanded of Gentiles in the Lucan Church (Acts 10:44-48), but certain Torah practices are required.

### B. Luke—Acts and Judaism

An exploration of the complex presentation of Jews and Judaism
in Luke-Acts might begin by considering an important theme in Acts.
A recurrent feature of the speeches in Acts is that Jews are blamed
for the crucifixion of Jesus (Acts 2:22-23, 36; 3:15; 4:10; 4:27; 5:30;
7:53; 10:39; 13:27-29). Although in some of the passages Pilate or the
Romans are mentioned as bearing some responsibility for Jesus' death,
it is clear that the emphasis is primarily on the Jewish people's role.
Similarly, while chief priests and rulers are occasionally singled out,
the people at large are more often indicted. For some reason Luke
issues blanket accusations against "the Jews" (Acts 10:39) for the execution of Jesus, even though historically (and ethically) this is untenable.

---

[29] "Diaspora" refers to Jews who are scattered around the Mediterranean world in
contrast to Jews living in Judea or Galilee.

[30] Joyce Reynolds and Robert Tannenbaum, *Jews and Godfearers at Aphrodisias* (Cambridge, England: Cambridge Philological Society, 1987).

[31] Jacob Jervell, "The Church of Jews and Godfearers," in *Luke-Acts and the Jewish
People*, ed. by Joseph B. Tyson (Minneapolis: Augsburg, 1988) 11–20.

[32] Joseph A. Fitzmyer, *The Gospel According to Luke I–IX*, The Anchor Bible, Vol. 28
(Garden City: Doubleday, 1981) 424–426.

Two factors have already been mentioned: first, Luke's concern to portray Jesus as innocent of crimes against Rome causes him to tone down the fact that Roman authorities executed Jesus; second, a negative depiction of Jews harmonizes with negative Roman sentiments toward the Jews who had rebelled against imperial rule.

But the speeches also pertain to Luke's ideas about prophecy.[33] The Lucan Jesus is portrayed as the ideal model of a prophet who is rejected. From the programmatic scene in which Jesus is first accepted and then rejected by his townspeople because "no prophet is acceptable in his own country" (Luke 4:24), to his journey to the Holy City because "it cannot be that a prophet should perish away from Jerusalem" (13:33), to the last days in which "a prophet mighty in deed and word" (24:19) is not recognized in Jerusalem (19:44), Jesus is shown as the Ultimate Prophet who goes the way of all the prophets before him.

Seeing Jesus as the last and greatest of the slain prophets would obviously necessitate an emphasis on his own people's role in his death. It should be pointed out that the notion that Israel always abuses the prophetic messengers of God did not originate with Luke. The Chronicler, for example, believed that the rejection of the prophets caused the destruction of the first Temple (2 Chr 36:15-16). Likewise, Luke attributes the Second Temple's demise to the rejection of the Great Prophet, Jesus (Luke 23:27-31).

This prophetic theme underlies the demand for repentance which often accompanies the accusation of guilt for Jesus' death (Acts 2:38; 3:19; 5:31; 10:43; 13:38). The pattern of condemning transgressions and demanding a return to God is typical of Israelite prophetic utterances. Also typical is the harsh invective in which the cry for penitence may be couched. Indeed, in some prophecies there is no chance for repentance, but just a blunt decrying of the sins which have angered God (e.g., Ezek 23). The Lucan apostolic prophets of Acts demand repentance from Israel in similar harsh language.

The response to this call for repentance is notable. Acts often depicts Christian missionaries as successful in their preaching to Jews (2:41, 47; 4:4; 5:14; 6:1, 7; 9:42; 12:24; 13:43; 14:1; 17:11-12; 21:20).[34] This relates to Luke's emphasis on the Jewish origins of the Church, and

---

[33] It should be noted that the Bible understands prophecy as speaking on behalf of God, such speech usually exhorting the People to live in fidelity with the Covenant. Prophecy in the Bible does not primarily mean to predict the future as it does in colloquial English. The Lucan Jesus is God's ultimate spokesperson, not a mere soothsayer.

[34] Jacob Jervell, *Luke and the People of God* (Minneapolis: Augsburg, 1972) 44.

also to his conviction that "it was necessary that the word of God should be spoken first to [Jews]" (Acts 13:46).

Now there is no doubt that the author wishes to show how God's salvation has extended from Jerusalem to all Judea and Samaria and to the end of the earth (Acts 1:8). But the care taken to discuss the mission to Jews and its success among significant numbers of them makes it plain that for the author Gentiles have come to God *through* the witness of Jewish believers. For Luke, Gentiles have not come to salvation by replacing Jews as God's Chosen People, but by entering into association with those noble Jews who have heard the word of God and believed it. The author also feels that the extension of salvation to Gentiles through repentant or faithful Israel is the fulfillment of the promises which God had made to Israel long ago (see esp. Luke 2:30-32). The coming of Jesus marks the time of salvation for the Gentiles and the moment of greatest glory for Israel through whom that salvation comes.

The presence of Jews in the Church is thus of the utmost importance for Luke. In his eyes they are the faithful remnant who have heard the apostles' words and repented. Through them God not only fulfills the promises made to Israel but also extends salvation to the Gentiles. For Luke, the first believers in Jesus as Lord are the authentic Israel, sincerely repentant and ultimately faithful. They are the Jewish heart of the Lucan Church.[35]

This outlook suggests that the author of Luke-Acts wants to show that Christianity is the legitimate outcome of the preaching of faithful Jews. It is not some sort of falsification or aberration devised by Jewish apostates.[36] Although Jews are becoming more and more a minority in an increasingly Gentile Church, Luke shows that their growing isolation is not a sign of God's disapproval. He does this by presenting them as faithful Israel within the Church mediating salvation to the Gentiles.[37]

The author depicts the Jewish heart of the Church, perhaps epitomized by Paul, as Torah-observing Jews (e.g. Acts 2:46-47; 3:1; 16:3; 21:17-26). Despite Stephen's attack on the Temple (7:48-50), Christian Jews continue to be Temple-goers (21:17-26). It is they who define the criteria for Gentile membership in the Church (15:20; 21:25), and there is no evidence that Luke thinks this typically Jewish use of Leviticus 17–18 is outdated.[38] The reasonable conclusion

---

[35] Jervell, "The Mighty Minority," 41–43.
[36] Fitzmyer, *Luke I-IX*, 178, 58–59.
[37] Jervell, "Mighty Minority," 39–43.
[38] Ibid., 43.

is that Luke honors Christian Jews both in his account of the early Church and also in his own time period.

Since Luke conceives of Christian Jews as the faithful and authentic Israel of God, it is almost inevitable that those Jews who have not accepted the Christian message would be considered by him to be unfaithful and inauthentic. He holds that Jesus has caused a division between the faithful and unfaithful in Israel, an idea evident early in the Gospel (Luke 2:34, 35b). Israel's ultimate time of decision is triggered by the apostles' witnessing to the raising of Jesus. Since theirs is the promise (Acts 2:39), Israel is given the opportunity to hear, repent, be baptized, and receive the Holy Spirit (2:38). Jews are urged to save themselves "from this crooked generation" (2:40) because "every soul that does not listen . . . shall be destroyed from the people" (3:23). Jews who heed the apostles are truly faithful and will receive the Spirit, but the evangelist concludes that unresponsive Jews are losing their status as Chosen People.[39] For Luke, Israel is in the process of being reconstructed out of the faithful Jews who hearken to the apostles' preaching and out of believing, God-fearing Gentiles.

Luke portrays "the [non-Christian] Jews" as increasingly opposing the spread of the Church. A partial listing of such hostility includes Acts 9:23; 13:45, 50; 14:4, 19; 17:5-9; 18:12; 20:2, 19; 22:30; 23:12; 24:27; 25:9, 24. Associated with the theme of unrepentant Israel rejecting the prophets, these and other references convey the overwhelming impression that non-Christian Jews are the implacable foes of the Church. This undoubtedly relates to the situation in Luke's day. As we saw with Matthew, by the mid-80s some synagogues had marginalized the Christian Jews in their ranks. By depicting Jewish rejection of the Church as an opposition to God which deprives them of any claim to religious authority,[40] Luke seeks to counter any influence the synagogue might exert on his own church community.

In conclusion, the harsh language seen in Acts against "Jews" who are accused of killing Jesus and the portrayal of non-Christian Jews as the enemies of the Church must be understood within their Lucan context. The evangelist Luke attempts to convince Jews outside of the Church of the truth of the Christian message by patterning his apostolic speeches after the prophets of old. In the hope of spark-

---

[39] This conclusion is not reached without regret on the part of the evangelist. Lucan remorse about non-Christian Jews can be seen in the parable about an unfruitful fig tree which is to be fertilized for another year in the hopes of encouraging productivity (Luke 13:6-9), unlike Mark and Matthew who portray Jesus cursing and withering an unfruitful fig tree. It is also only Luke's Gospel which presents Jesus weeping over imperceptive Jerusalem (19:41-44).

[40] N.B. the episode in Acts 19:13-16.

ing repentance and belief, he seeks to prod Israel's conscience regarding Jesus in a typically prophetic manner. His bitter words must be understood as originally rooted in the long tradition of rigorous Jewish self-criticism.

Nevertheless, such Jewish self-criticism was seen as more of an attack on Judaism itself once it was read in a totally Gentile Church.[41] Luke-Acts readily lends itself to such an interpretation because the evangelist actually does believe that non-Christian Jews have "fallen," although it is not clear whether he feels that this fall is irrevocable. However, Luke's reverence for Christian Jews must be stressed. In Luke's context the edifying presence of Christian Jews was critical evidence of Christianity's continuity with Judaism. This continuity assured, Luke could prophetically condemn non-Christian Jews, though not without remorse. Thus, Luke's presentation is in some ways both the most pro-Jewish and anti-Jewish of the synoptic Gospels.

## VII. Conclusion: Teaching the Gospels "Within Context"

This chapter began with the observation that contentious language in the synoptic Gospels has been used over the centuries to promote hostility toward Jews and Judaism. Reading the Gospels within their own contexts of dispute, exhortation, rivalry, and the need to fix clear boundaries in a new community explains the origins of such rhetoric. A contextual awareness discloses that this polemic is the product of human conflict and does not represent timeless truths about God.

While earlier generations read the Gospels in ways which absolutized and universalized polemical assertions, thereby fostering anti-Jewish behaviors among Christians, a sensitivity to the historical contexts of the evangelists averts a similar reading today. This leads to several suggestions for religious educators about ways to teach the synoptic Gospels which minimize their anti-Jewish potentialities:

1) Promote a critical awareness of the Gospel texts. This can readily be done by noting their unique portrayals of Jesus and their individual concerns and emphases. This would help students come to appreciate the Gospels as theological reflections on the significance of Jesus which were designed to address local needs.

2) Foster an understanding of the principles contained in the Pontifical Biblical Commission's "Instruction on the Historical Truth of the Gospels." By becoming familiar with the three stages of Gospel development, people would be enabled to understand the evangelists'

---

[41] See Lloyd Gaston, "Anti-Judaism and the Passion Narrative in Luke and Acts," in Richardson, Anti-Judaism, 150–152.

individual contexts. They would also be less likely to regard the Gospels simply as transcripts of Jesus' ministry.

3) Highlight the real-life situation of each evangelist in order to show how their attitudes about Jews and Judaism were molded by their contexts. This situates and de-absolutizes their polemical rhetoric.

4) Compare Gospel remarks about Jews and Judaism with modern understandings. Ecclesial statements that Jews cannot be held liable for the crucifixion[42] should be recalled when reading Luke's accusations against Jews or Matthew's attacks on the Pharisees. Similarly, John Paul II's words that Jews remain "the people of God of the Old Covenant, never revoked by God,"[43] ought to be cited when the Gospels imply that Judaism is obsolete or rejected by God. A comparison of the Church's twentieth-century context with those of the Gospel would also be worthwhile.

These strategies, adapted for different ages and backgrounds, would help to provide that "objective and rigorously accurate teaching on Judaism . . . [which leads] to an exact knowledge of the wholly unique 'bond' which joins us a Church to the Jews and to Judaism."[44]

## Questions for Reflection and Discussion

1. Describe the attitudes toward Jews and Judaism displayed by Mark, Matthew, and Luke. What are their differences and similarities? What factors account for their unique presentations?

2. What aspects of this survey of the Synoptic Gospels were the most surprising or unsettling for you? Why might this have occurred? How might these areas be explored more fully? How might religious educators assist people in integrating new insights about the Gospels?

3. Matthew's reverent insistence on the permanence of the Torah and Luke's veneration of Christian Jews were not prominent sen-

---

[42] *Nostra Aetate,* 4. For recent ecclesial documents about Jews and Judaism see the two collections edited by Helga Croner, *Stepping Stones to Further Jewish-Christian Relations* (New York: Stimulus, 1977) and *More Stepping Stones to Jewish-Christians Relations* (New York: Paulist [Stimulus Series] 1985). Also see the World Council of Churches, *The Theology of the Churches and the Jewish People* (Geneva: WCC Publications, 1988).

[43] "Address to the Jewish Community," Mainz, West Germany, November 17, 1980. Fisher and Klenicki, 35.

[44] Vatican "Notes," 8. I would like to thank the following friends and parish religious educators for their helpful comment in the preparation of this chapter: Leon E. Abbott, Gail Capriole, Michael J. Corso, Harold Hartwell, Ann Kater, Denise LoConte, and William Mealey.

timents in the later Gentile Church. Are there ways in which these positive attitudes could be instructive in our present context?

4. What are the results of either reading or not reading the Synoptic Gospels "within context," particularly in terms of the presentation of Jews and Judaism?

# The Gospel of John and
# The Presentation of Jews and Judaism

*Urban C. von Wahlde*

## Introduction

The Gospel of John, the fourth of the canonical Gospels, is widely known as the "spiritual" Gospel. This is due to the fact that it presents such a lofty understanding of the role and identity of Jesus. It speaks of Jesus in a way that reveals a level of understanding of his role and identity that is generally recognized to be among the most profound in the New Testament.

Yet at the same time it cannot be denied that repeatedly throughout history this Gospel has been said to have encouraged anti-Semitic attitudes. That a book which Christians consider to be God's Word would be used, by Christians themselves, in such a profoundly non-Christian and non-religious way is deeply disturbing. It must be admitted that the Gospel of John is not always easy to understand and our purpose is to try to put forth the best available understanding of the Gospel in its historical context so that we may properly understand it and interpret it correctly.

## 1. The Gospel of John

Scholars have long recognized that the Gospel of John is a result of a complex editorial history. Although there is considerable disagreement about the specific contours of this editorial history, or indeed whether it can ever be adequately recovered, there is general agreement that the present Gospel is a result of three successive editings, each of which had its own structure and theological orientation.

Among those scholars who have dedicated their considerable efforts to recovering the contours of the Gospel's editing process, it is generally recognized that the first edition of the Gospel consisted of a relatively simple, straightforward document which focused on the miraculous activity of Jesus and the effects (both positive and negative) of that activity. This document probably included both a passion account and a narrative of the resurrection.

The second edition of the Gospel developed and amplified this first document by, among other elements, a number of discourses and dialogues between Jesus and various other persons. This edition was responsible for a much more profound reflection on the mystery of Jesus and provides what is known as the high Christology of the Gospel.

However many scholars suggest that the community felt that the document at the end of its second edition did not represent in a fully nuanced way the community's tradition and so further modifications and additions were made. This final edition complemented and nuanced a number of elements of the previous edition.

While this is not the place to review that editorial history in detail, it must be pointed out that our understanding of the Gospel is considerably complicated by the fact of this literary history. But at the same time, the complexity of this tradition may also hold the key to the solution of some of the Gospel's theological and literary problems.

## 2. The Jewishness of the Johannine Community and the Johannine Gospel

### a) The Community Represents One Strain of Jewish Christianity

In order to put the Gospel's attitudes toward the Jews in the proper context, we must remember first of all that the community itself, as were several other of the early Christian communities represented in the writings of the New Testament, was made up primarily of Jews who had converted to belief in Jesus rather than of Gentiles who had been pagans and non-Jews before becoming Christians.

Just as the first disciples were themselves Jewish, and just as Jesus himself was a Jew, the Johannine community was composed mostly of people who were Jewish by birth. They believed that Jesus represented the fulfillment of their religious hopes which they shared with their fellow Jews. These first followers of Jesus believed that they were recognizing the eschatalogical action of Yahweh which had been promised in their Scriptures.

### b) Jesus Is Presented as Standing Within the Jewish Tradition

Thus the Gospel of John reports that Jesus and his disciples took part in the Jewish feasts of Passover (2:13; 12:1, 12), Tabernacles (7:10), and Dedication (10:22-23) and went up to Jerusalem to celebrate them. In addition he acknowledged the Sabbath although he saw conditions under which the Sabbath laws did not apply (5:16-18, cf. 7:21-24). Jesus speaks of the one God of Judaism although he claims that that God is his Father (e.g., 5:17). Jesus believed in the Hebrew Scriptures and believed that they were fulfilled in him (6:31-32, 45; 7:37-39; 10:34-37) and frequently quotes the Scriptures in this regard. He saw himself as standing within the tradition of Jacob (4:12), Moses (6:30-31), and Abraham (8:58). Indeed Jesus himself affirms (4:22) that "salvation is from the Jews."

### c) Other Jewish Features

The Gospel of John also reflects an understanding of complicated principles of Jewish law such as the debate about whether God himself works on the Sabbath (5:17-18) and the Jewish laws of witness (5:31-40; 8:12-20). The Bread of Life Discourse (6:30-59) is structured in the typical form of a homiletic midrash used in the synagogue.

### d) The Use of the First Testament in the Gospel

Although there are fewer actual quotations from the First Testament, Jesus uses many of its most important and powerful symbols and applies them to himself: that of shepherd, of vine, of bread, of living water, of life. He is described by titles which are developed in the Jewish scriptures: prophet, prophet like Moses, son of David, Son of Man, son of God, Lord, and Messiah.

In short, not only does the Gospel of John clearly have a positive estimation for the Jewish tradition, but also the Jewish tradition is the very soul and life of the Johannine tradition. Without it, the Johannine understanding of Jesus would be impossible.

Whatever else we say about the Gospel's attitude toward the Jews and Judaism, this cannot be denied.

## 3. The Historical Situation of the Johannine Community

If the Gospel has gone through three separate editions, as the majority of present day scholars thinks, something needs to be said briefly about the circumstances of the community at each of the periods in order to situate each edition in its proper circumstances.

### 3a) Overview of the Community's History

Of the historical circumstances of the community, least is known about those of the first edition. This edition reflects a Jewish-Christian community with close ties to Judea and it enshrines some traditions about Jesus which are quite early and unique within the New Testa-

ment. It is only in this material that we find out that Jesus himself
conducted a baptizing ministry. It is this edition that contains the
remarkably specific and accurate geographical information (e.g., the
pool of Bethesda [5:2], the Stone pavement within the Praetorium
[19:13]). It also reflects a period during which, although there were
undoubtedly disagreements about the meaning of Jesus, the community continued to experience the fellowship of the synagogue.

The second edition reflects a somewhat later period (perhaps shortly
after the year 90 C.E.) a time when fellowship with the synagogue
was no longer possible. The community had recently experienced an
emotionally wrenching expulsion from the synagogue. Now the community had come to a clearer conviction that Jesus was fully divine.
There is a suggestion that some members were being put to death
for their belief in Jesus as the Messiah.

The third edition was composed at a time of a major division within
the Johannine community. This intra-Johannine struggle was concerned with the proper interpretation of certain elements of the tradition and did not reflect the community's relation with surrounding
Judaism at all. In fact, by the time of the third edition of the Gospel,
it is clear that the community was thought of as a separate entity totally independent of Judaism. This period also reflects a number of
concepts and the apocalyptic thought world similar to that of
Qumran.

### 3b) The Relationship with Judaism During the Second Period of the Community's History

As can be seen from this outline, the first and second periods are
the ones that most reflect the Jewishness of the Gospel and also the
community's tension with parent Judaism. It is particularly the second edition which affects the presentation of the Jews and Judaism
and which calls for greater attention.

*3b1) Alienation and Distancing.* This edition reflects a considerable
alienation and a distancing from parent Judaism. One of the clearest
means by which this alienation is evident is in the way the Jewish
religious authorities are identified. In the first edition they were referred to in their customary way as "Pharisees, chief priests, rulers."
However in the second edition these distinctions are blurred and now
the religious authorities are referred to as a group simply as "the Jews,"
a generalized and anachronistic term which indicates that now the
community sees itself as distinct from and as over against "the Jews."
As we shall see, it is the use of this term which accounts for much

of the serious misunderstanding and which has created numberless problems for understanding the gospel ever since.

Another way this distancing from its contemporary Judaism is reflected is the way the debates with "the Jews" do not reflect a more historically plausible growth in opposition to Jesus but rather present right from the start a heightened level of opposition such as must have existed at the time the community was being excluded from the synagogue.

Finally this distancing is evident in the way the disputes no longer seem to present specific historical encounters between Jesus and "the Jews" but rather represent summaries of representative debates between the Johannine community and the Judaism of its day.

*3b2) The Issue in the Debate: The Claims Made for Jesus.* At the time of the second edition, the issue was not just that Jesus was the Messiah but that he claimed to be equal with God and indeed his son. The debate at this stage was almost entirely christological, i.e., about the claims made for Jesus, rather than about Jesus' interpretation of the Law or about his ethical standards.

It is the debate over these claims that forms the problematic passages in the Gospel. We will look at these in more detail in section 4 below.

*3b3) Expulsion from the Synagogue and Persecution by Fellow Jews.* The final stage in the "distancing" of the Johannine Christians from their parent Judaism is clearly echoed in three passages which refer to the formal exclusion from the synagogue of those who believed in Jesus. These incidents which are anachronistically projected upon the ministry of Jesus reflect the circumstances of the community toward the end of the first century.

In 9:18-22, it is said that "the Jews" had determined that anyone who confessed Jesus as the Christ would be put out of the synagogue. A similar statement is made in 12:42, where it is stated that "many of the Pharisees" believed in Jesus but did not confess it openly lest they be put out of the synagogue. Finally during his last discourse with his disciples, Jesus predicts (16:2) that his followers will be put out of the synagogue and will be put to death and that those who do so will think that such persecution is a way of praising God.

This situation clearly reflects the historical circumstances near the end of the first century C.E. It is evident from the Acts of the Apostles that for some time after his death, Jesus' followers continued to worship in the Temple and in the synagogues. Although they were at times disciplined, there is no indication that they were formally excluded.

Many scholars consider the Johannine references to formal excommunication to be related to the curse on heretics found in the Eighteen Benedictions as formulated by the rabbinic council at Jamnia. Although the dating of the Eighteen Benedictions is not able to be done with precision, they stem from the period 85 C.E. to 115 C.E. In any event it is clear that these texts refer to events and decisions at the end of the first century rather than during the historical ministry of Jesus.

Not only did such excommunication mean a severing from one's parent religious tradition, but by separating the Christians from the protective status Jews enjoyed within the Roman Empire, it exposed the Christians to the possibility of persecution for failing to partake in the state worship of the Roman emperor.

The Gospel shows that there were a number of persons who believed in Jesus secretly. Nicodemus would seem to be an example of this faith since he comes by night (3:1), speaks of some openness to Jesus (7:50-51), and comes to bury him (19:38). Joseph of Arimathea (19:38) is listed as a secret disciple "for fear of the Jews." In the face of possible synagogue exclusion, these persons faced a particularly difficult decision. Some, represented by the man born blind in chapter 9, confessed Jesus and were probably excluded (see 9:34). Others like the man's parents were afraid to confess their faith openly "for fear of the Jews" (9:22). "Many of the Pharisees" (12:42) were said to believe in Jesus but were afraid to confess Jesus openly and so remained part of the synagogue.

It is, of course, clear from the material of the final edition of the Gospel as well as from the First Epistle of John that the excommunication was effective and resulted in the community becoming a separate, independent group apart from Judaism.

## 4. Polemic Against Opposition in the Synagogue in the Second Edition of the Gospel: "The Jews."

The historical circumstances of the community provide the backdrop for the study of the Johannine polemic. This study will be arranged in two parts. The first will examine the term "the Jews" which is used so often in the Gospel and particularly in the second edition. The second part will be in the section which follows (#5) and will deal with the specific content and style of the polemic.

### "The Jews" in the Gospel of John.

As we have seen above in the introduction, in spite of its essential respect for the Jewish tradition, the Gospel of John has the reputation for being a source for and seemingly a justification for the hatred of Jews not only in the time of Jesus but in various periods throughout the history of the Christian world down to our own time. In order to understand how this came about we need to look first and foremost at the phrase "the Jews" as it is used by the author.

### 4a) A Variety of Meanings

In the Gospel of John, the term translated in English by the word "Jews" is *Ioudaios* and in the plural *Ioudaioi*. The term occurs seventy-one times in the Gospel, much more frequently than in any other Gospel.

However not all occurrences of *Ioudaioi* have the same meaning. This complicates our understanding of the Gospel and poses problems for interpretation. Nevertheless it is essential to grasp these differences if we are to try to understand the meaning of the Gospel as the author intended it and if we are to avoid superimposing a meaning that was not intended.

There are a number of instances in which the term is used to refer to Jews as members of a political/religious group. Sometimes this is done in contrast to other political or religious groups (e.g., Samaritans or Romans).[1] This is the use intended in the title given to Jesus on the cross: "King of the Jews."[2] It is used in this way to refer to the Jewish religious/national customs, their feasts, or their authorities (e.g., "ruler of the Jews").[3] In all of these instances the use of the term is that common in the ancient world as a designation of this religio-political group.

The term is also used to refer to persons we would call "Judeans" since the same word (*Ioudaioi*) is used to refer to both.[4] These Jews are associated with the city of Jerusalem, which is situated in Judea. From their function in the narratives, these Judeans are identified as members of the common people who report to the authorities. They are divided in their assessment of Jesus, and they do not exhibit the hostility characteristic of the third group of "Jews."

---

[1]4:9a, 9b, 22; 18:35.
[2]18:33, 39; 19:3, 19, 21b, 21c.
[3]2:6, 13; 3:1; 5:1; 6:4; 7:2; 11:55; 18:20; 19:21a, 40, 42.
[4]3:25; 10:19; 11:19, 31, 33, 36, 45, 54; 12:9, 11; 19:20, 21.

The third, uniquely and characteristically Johannine use of the term occurs in the remainder of the passages in the Gospel.[5] This use is represented for example in 2:18-22 where "the Jews" demand a sign for Jesus' actions in the Temple; or in 5:15-19 where "the Jews" begin to persecute Jesus for performing miracles on the Sabbath. When Jesus explains that he is continuing the work of the Father, "the Jews" are said to be "even more determined to kill him." In 9:22 the Jews are said to have "already agreed that if anyone acknowledged him as the Messiah, that person would be expelled from the synagogue."

### 4b) *The Chief Characteristic of the Johannine "Jews": The "Jews" Represent Religious Authorities Not the Nation as a Whole*

It is this third group of uses that needs to be studied because it is the usage most clearly associated with the charges of anti-Semitism. It also must be pointed out that this usage is uniquely Johannine; it appears in no other literature with exactly these same connotations and function.

The first, essential, observation is that this characteristically Johannine use of the term "Jews" is intended to refer not to the nation or the people as a whole but to a group of religious authorities. Whatever else can be said of the impropriety of usage, the term in this sense (which appears in the passages where the greatest mutual hostility is evident) does not refer to the nation as a whole in a way that can be called racially anti-Semitic. This can be substantiated in four ways.

A first indication that this use of "Jews" does not refer to the people as a whole is the fact that these "Jews" are distinguished from other people who are themselves Jews by nationality / religion / culture. For example, in 9:22 we read that the parents of the man born blind do not want to discuss their son's condition "for fear of the Jews." Both the man born blind and his parents are certainly Jews by nationality, religion and culture. Yet they are said to fear "the Jews." Clearly the term must refer to a sub-group within the people as a whole.

The same phrase occurs in 7:13 where people who are Jewish by nationality are said not to talk openly about Jesus "for fear of the Jews." Finally on the Sabbath after the death of Jesus, the disciples who themselves are Jewish are said to be secluded in a room "for fear of the Jews." In each case the term refers to a sub-group within the nation.

[5] 1:19; 2:18, 20; 5:10, 15, 18; 6:41, 52; 7:1, 11, 13, 15, 35; 8:22, 31, 48, 52, 57; 9:18, 22; 10:24, 31, 33; 11:8; 13:33; 18:12, 14, 31, 36, 38; 19:7, 12, 14, 31, 38; 20:19.

Second, this sub-group of Jews functions in ways that are typical of the religious authorities. For example, in 9:22, it is said that "the Jews" have passed a formal edict of excommunication against anyone who would confess Jesus as the Christ.

Third, the term occurs in contexts where it alternates with other terms for religious authorities. For example, the religious authorities are called "chief priests" and "Pharisees" in 7:32 but the same group is referred to as "Jews" in verse 35. In chapter 9, the authorities are called "Pharisees" in verses 13 and 16 but "Jews" in verses 18 and 22.

Finally, there are passages where the authorities are identified as "Pharisees" but when the passages are referred to later the term "Jews" is substituted (cf. 11:45-52 and 18:3 which are later referred to in 18:12-14 with "Jews" substituted). As we have seen, this strange alternation in terms is due to re-editing of the gospel and reminds us that we must not be too confident we are able to fully understand this Gospel without careful study.

*4c) Other Characteristics of the Johannine "Jews"*

Beyond this important restriction of the term to a group of religious authorities, other important characteristics distinguish this use of the term.

These Johannine "Jews" express considerable hostility towards Jesus. They desire to kill him, to excommunicate him, to stone him, they accuse him of being possessed, of being a Samaritan, of blaspheming. At times the texts show a hostility which is less intense but is still representative of unbelief.

A second characteristic of these texts is that they represent a single undifferentiated reaction. There is no sign of an increase of hostility throughout the ministry. Rather their reaction is unified and monolithic. This is in contrast to the Jews in the 'neutral' sense, some of whom believe while some do not (cf. 10:19, 11:45). It is also in contrast to the authorities described as "Pharisees, chief priests, and rulers" who are also described at times as divided in their assessment of Jesus (cf. 7:45-52; 9:16). The "Jews" (in the characteristic Johannine sense) never give the slightest hint of anything but unanimity in their assessment of Jesus.

Thus there can be no doubt that the passages which are couched in these terms reflect a period of intense debate and hostility between Judaism and the Johannine community. Just as the edict of excommunication reflects the experience of the Johannine community more than the ministry of Jesus, so too much of the hostility and fierceness of the Jews toward Jesus is undoubtedly a partial reflection of the hostility between synagogue and community. In short, these Johannine "Jews" fit well the historical circumstances of the community during the second stage of the community's history.

## 5. The Content of the Polemic: Part Two: The Major Debates With "the Jews"

### 5a) Not About the Law But About Christology

In the earlier gospels (Matthew, Mark, Luke) the disputes between Jesus and the Jewish religious authorities show a clear pattern of disagreement regarding interpretation of the Law. For example, Jesus is accused of violating the Sabbath; he takes issue with the rules for cleansing eating utensils and food; he discusses the Great Commandments, the question of the resurrection, etc. However in the gospel of John this focus on interpretation of the Law is almost entirely absent. The "real" issue immediately becomes one of christology. Indeed it is the issue of "high" christology (the identification of Jesus as being a true son of God, as being I AM [the Septuagint designation of "Yahweh"], as being pre-existent) that occupies the central position in the theology of the second edition. It was in order to explain their position and justify their beliefs that the various arguments of the second edition of the gospel were composed.

An additional feature of the christology of the gospel is the theme of Jesus as a replacement of various elements of Judaism. While Jesus is seen as the spiritual fulfillment of the Law (1:17; 5:39), he nevertheless believes that it has a validity as a testimony to himself. While he seems to distance himself from the Law by referring to it as "your" law (7:19; 8:17; 10:34; 15:25), at least some (if not all) of these are rhetorical expressions designed to force the listeners to take the Law seriously. These must be taken in the context of the remainder of the Gospel where the witness value of Scripture is constantly attested (see e.g., 5:39-40, 45-47).

### 5b) The Major Debates With "The Jews"

In the debate about the meaning and identity of Jesus both the author and his opponents registered heated accusations about the other. A brief rereading of the chief debates brings us to the heart of the Johannine polemic. Almost all of the passages looked at in the following section come from the second edition although for the sake of simplicity all polemic is treated together.

In chapter 5, after the healing of the man paralyzed for thirty-eight years, Jesus justifies his actions by claiming that God is his Father and that he acts on the Sabbath just as his Father does. In response, the Jews claim not only that he violates the Sabbath but that he "makes himself equal to God." We are told that it is because of this claim that "the Jews" persecute him and seek to kill him. Jesus responds by affirming the Father's bestowal of the power of judgment and of giving life upon Jesus. In the ensuing debate, Jesus accuses "the Jews" of not having the word (5:38) or love (5:42) of God in their hearts. They do not seek the glory that comes from the one God (5:44). They do not believe Moses (5:46-47).

In chapter 6, after the feeding of the five thousand and after the miraculous crossing of the sea, "the Jews" ask him for a sign. Jesus responds by speaking of Moses giving the Israelites bread in the wilderness. He then asserts that not Moses gives them bread but his Father and that the Father gives them the true bread which is Jesus. The Jews cannot believe this claim that Jesus is the true bread come down from heaven since they know his parents (6:41-42). Jesus in response accuses them of "not being given" by the Father. He also says that they do not hear or learn from the Father (6:45). He then affirms the need to eat of the true bread in order to have life. The Jews cannot understand this (6:51-59); the result again is lack of belief.

In chapter 7, Jesus goes to the feast of Tabernacles and begins to teach. This occasions a series of controversies about his teaching, about where he comes from and where he will go, about his signs, and about his qualifications as Messiah. "The Jews" in turn seek to kill him (7:1, 19, 25). The issue of healing on the Sabbath comes up again and Jesus accuses them of not keeping the Law of Moses in this regard (7:19). When they challenge where he comes from he asserts that they "do not know either him or the Father" (7:28).

But it is in chapter 8 that the polemic of the Gospel becomes most bitter. The debate centers around the value of Jesus' witness (esp 8:12-20 but also 8:21-30), particularly the witness value of his word (8:31-59). Jesus accuses "the Jews" (8:22, 31, 48, 52, 57) of not knowing the Father (8:19, 55). They are from below; he is from above (8:23). Unless they believe that he is I AM, they will die in their sins (8:24). There follows a series of comparisons using the person of Abraham. First Jesus says that if "the Jews" continue in his word, they will know the truth and the truth will free them. They respond that they are children of Abraham and that they have never been slaves to anyone. Jesus affirms that they are "seed of Abraham" but says that they do the work of their Father. They respond that Abraham is their father but Jesus retorts that they do not do what Abraham would do. He then says that they are children of their father the devil and that they do his wishes (8:41,44), and that he is a liar from eternity. They are not "of God" (8:47).

In the final exchange of the chapter (8:48-59), "the Jews" accuse Jesus of being a Samaritan and being possessed. Jesus responds that, if they keep his word, they will not die forever. "The Jews" respond that Abraham and the prophets died and that his statement is final proof that he is possessed. They ask him rhetorically if he is greater than Abraham. Jesus responds that he does not seek his own glory but that Abraham saw Jesus. "The Jews" cannot believe that Jesus has seen Abraham since Jesus is less than fifty years old. Jesus in turn claims to have been I AM before Abraham came to be. "The Jews" then try to stone Jesus (8:59) but Jesus eludes them.

In chapter 9 Jesus heals a man born blind. In the ensuing debate, the major exchange is between the man and the religious authorities. However at the end Jesus describes his mission to the man as one in which Jesus has come into the world for judgment that the blind might see and that those who see might be blind. He ends by accusing the religious authorities of being guilty of sin because they claim to see whereas in fact they do not (9:39-41).

In chapter 10, Jesus delivers a parable about a shepherd and about the gate of the sheepfold (10:1-6). He then explains the parable by applying it to himself, to believers, and to the religious authorities (10:7-21). Once again the polemic is intense on both sides. The religious authorities are called "thieves and marauders" (10:8); they are said not to be "of his sheep." The hirelings leave the sheep and flee when danger comes. In turn his listeners accuse Jesus of being possessed (10:20). In a closely connected debate (10:22-39) "the Jews" attempt to stone Jesus (10:31) because he blasphemes by making himself equal to God. Again they try to seize him (10:39) but he escapes.

In chapter 12, a final judgment is placed on unbelievers (including the religious authorities). It is said that they were blind and did not believe and Isaiah 6:10 is applied to them and that they seek honor before humans rather than before God.

When we turn to the passion account, we find that again sets of terms for the religious authorities are mixed. Although the term Pharisees drops out after 18:3, the religious authorities are described sometimes as "chief priests" and other times as "the Jews." It is "the Jews" who introduce the religious charge against Jesus, saying that according to their law he must die because he made himself God's son (19:7). The chief priests then reply in 19:15 (in a way that was undoubtedly intended to show them degrading themselves) "We have no king but Caesar."

It must be remembered that although the Jews play a major role in the second edition of the gospel, it is not correct to say that the only passages which belong to the second edition are those where the term "Jews" occur. But this sampling of debate polemic shows the intensity of the exchange and the kind of polemical language used.

## 6. The Johannine Polemic in Historical Context and Perspective

However in order to properly understand this polemic, we must ask how a reader contemporary with the gospel would read and react to that polemic. Polemical language was widespread in the ancient world and so it is possible for us to gain some understanding of its nature and purpose.

Jewish writers such as Josephus and Philo used such polemic against Gentiles. They also directed it against fellow Jews. Polemic was also directed by Jews against Samaritans and would include the quite harsh reference in Sirach to the Samaritans as "the stupid people living at Shechem" (50:28). John's gospel reports what would appear to be a standard estimation of Samaritans in the accusation by "the Jews" that Jesus is "a Samaritan and (therefore) possessed" (8:48).

There is evidence from contemporary literature that three of the major accusations leveled at opponents in the New Testament (being a "hypocrite," being "blind" and being "possessed") all have parallels in contemporary Jewish polemic; and so give evidence of being "standard" types of rebuttal against one's opponents. Seeing polemic in this way suggests that it was not considered to be as harsh as we might think today.

When we turn to the Gospel of John to attempt to understand its polemic, we find the parallels equally if not more illuminating than those adduced for the remainder of the New Testament.

Some prominent features of Johannine polemic, such as the accusation that unbelievers do not "know God," that they are "liars," that they are "unable to repent" find close parallels in the prophetic critique of Israel in the First Testament and need to be interpreted within this context rather than as a unique phenomenon expressing a unique hatred. For example, Jeremiah says of the nation of Israel: "They ready their tongues like a drawn bow; with lying and not with truth, they hold forth in the land. They go from evil to evil, but me they know not, says the Lord. . . . They have accustomed their tongues to lying, and are perverse, and cannot repent" (9:2, 4 NAB). Clearly Jeremiah's words were a standard prophetic critique of the nation.

The Dead Sea Scrolls and the apocrypha, particularly the *Testaments of the Twelve Patriarchs* provide numerous examples of polemic directed by Jewish groups against fellow Jews. These parallels are particularly illuminating because they are so similar in phraseology to the rhetoric of chapter 8 of the Gospel, the polemic generally considered to be among the harshest of the Gospel.

For example, the Dead Sea Scrolls put forward a view in which some persons are presented as influenced by the Spirit of Truth and others as dominated by the Spirit of Falsehood and so as under the dominion of either God or of Satan. Members of the community are said to be "sons of light" (1 QS 3:13) or "sons of darkness" (1 QS 1:10; 1 QM 1:7). The opponents are also described as "sons of the pit" (1 QS 9:16; CD 6:15; 13:14). They are said to "do the works of" God or of Belial (Satan). In the Community Document from Qumran (1 QS) the Levites are told to curse all the men of the lot of Satan (i.e., Gentiles and Jews who are not part of the community) (1 QS 2:4-5).

This is quite similar to the language of John 8. "The Jews" are said to do the works of their father (8:41). Their father is said to be the devil (8:44). The devil is a murderer (8:44), a liar (8:44). The listeners are not able to hear the word of Jesus (8:43).

In the apocryphal Testament of Levi, the text exhorts the listeners to choose "either light or darkness, either the law of the Lord or the works of Belial" (19:1).

Equally illuminating is the example of 1 John. In 1 John we again find a rhetoric similar to that of John chapter 8 and to the Dead Sea Scrolls. What is instructive about this example is that here the rhetoric is not leveled at "the Jews" but at members of the Johannine community: at those former members who have defected from the community. Such people are liars (1:6; 2:4, 22 etc); they are in darkness (2:9); the darkness has blinded their eyes (2:11); they do not belong to God (3:10); they have not known him (3:6; 4:8); they belong to the devil (3:8); they are the devil's children (3:10); they are murderers (3:15); they are governed by the spirit of deception (4:6); the world has never recognized the son (3:1).

In the Book of Revelation similar rhetoric is directed against Jews (cf. the synagogue of Satan [Rev 2:9; 3:9]) but also against Romans who are described with the image of a beast and a harlot (17:1-18).

Thus we see that in dualistic, apocalyptic writing, this harsh rhetoric is found to be quite common. It is, in various places, found to be directed: (1) against Jews by Christians (Gospel of John); (2) against Jews by other sectarian Jews (Dead Sea Scrolls); (3) against Christians by other Christians (1 John); (4) against Romans by Christians (Revelation).

More detailed study of polemic in these and other works from the world contemporary with the New Testament (e.g., Josephus, Philo, Wisdom of Solomon, as well as pagan writers) suggests that such polemic was relatively widespread and that the polemic found in the New Testament is relatively mild. It also suggests that such rhetoric was intended to have an effect more on those within the community than on those outside. In a time of persecution, such contrasts as were expressed by the polemical language helped set firm and clear boundaries for what was and was not acceptable belief for the community. With the danger that fear of excommunication or even death might result from confessing one's belief, such clear boundaries would be necessary in order to prevent apostasy.

Thus putting this polemic into a clearer historical context can be said to relativize such polemic and to call into question interpretations of it which read its intensity in a way such polemic would have in a modern context. Rather, by reading it "with first century eyes" we are able to see it as a stylized form of debate designed to separate the opponents, to identify them, and to dissociate them from the goods represented by the author and his community. However, on the basis of the widespread use of such polemic, it is probably inaccurate to say that the polemic is anti-Semitic.

## 7. Reading the "Jews" Passages of the Gospel Today

We have seen that the concern that the Gospel of John is anti-Semitic (or alternatively anti-Jewish) is based primarily on three features of the Gospel: (1) the frequent use of the term "the Jews" to refer to the opponents of Jesus; (2) the portrayal of the Jews in the passion accounts; (3) the intensity of the polemical language and the images used in that polemic.

Our review of the Gospel has led us to propose a nuanced understanding of each of those issues. While the term Jews is used more frequently than in any other Gospel, the term has a variety of meanings and those need to be distinguished from one another. Even the instances with the most hostile connotations are used in a way that is intended to refer to religious authorities rather than the entire nation.

The portrayal of the Jews in the passion account is also subject to the same nuancing that was called for in the other texts. There is no indication that it was the author's intention to assign responsibility for the death of Jesus to the entire nation.

Finally, the polemic used in the debate with fellow Jews is indeed harsh to our ears, but when it is seen in the general context of religious polemic in the first century C.E., there is less reason to think that it is any different than that which Jews directed to other Jews and which Christians directed to other Christians. In short we must learn to listen to it with first-century ears and not with twentieth-century ones.

Our approach to the topic of the Gospel's presentation of the Jews and Judaism has been from the point of view of the biblical scholar, attempting to point out the original meaning of the Gospel's language and attitudes within their historical context. This has been done in the hope that the more precision is introduced into the understanding of the Gospel the more likely we are to be able to use the Gospel intelligently and with sensitivity in the Church today. Nevertheless the topic cannot be said to be finished without some reflection on how we today should treat the topic of "the Jews" and the overall presentation of Judaism within the Gospel. It is for this purpose that the following observations are offered.

We have sought to understand Johannine rhetoric by placing it within its historical context. However once we have listened to this rhetoric, we must be indeed careful not to repeat it ourselves, today. What may have been an understandable form of rhetoric in the first century has no place in the twentieth. The situation of persecution and separation from the synagogue with all the perils that that could entail and the very likelihood that many of the Johannine community would not find the strength to confess their convictions in these circumstances called for efforts to identify clearly the issues and the opponents.

However to repeat that polemic today would only lead to the very hostility and rejection that the New Testament in its larger dimensions seeks to avoid. Whatever the Gospel of John may have achieved in terms of other elements of its theology, its attitude toward unbelievers and toward outsiders clearly needs to be balanced by the perspectives found within the remainder of the canon.

It remains true that the presence of "the Jews" passages in the Gospel will be dangerously misleading to the average reader. We have seen in our study that a carefully nuanced reading of the gospel demonstrates that there are no legitimate grounds for a charge that the Gospel is anti-Semitic. But the fact remains that the complexity of the editing process as well as of the historical process which gave birth to the Gospel and the conventions of polemical language make a misreading of the passages easy, perhaps even likely. How are we to deal with this?

Suggestions have been made that texts used in public reading should be modified in such a way as to make the meaning of the terms clear. This has arisen particularly regarding the passion account in the Gospel which is read during the Holy Week services.

This proposal has the important benefit of recognizing that a simple literal translation of the text will be, almost inevitably, misleading. However the production of translations for public liturgical use is properly a matter for the appropriate Church bodies. Unless such retranslations or paraphrases of the text are approved, the solemnity of the service is marred, and in some cases poor scholarship and mistaken information can lead to even greater errors in the presentation of the text. But a second concern is even more fundamental. Modification of the text itself runs the risk of distorting the integrity of the text as an historical document.

This then leads to an alternate suggestion: if clarification is needed, then this should be done through explanation rather than by means of modification of the text. This is the proposal of R. Brown who says,

> In my opinion a truer response is to continue to read the whole passion, not subjecting it to excisions that seem wise to us; but once having read it, then to preach forcefully that such hostility between Christians and Jews cannot be continued today and is against our fundamental understanding of Christianity. ("The Passion According to John: Chapters 18 and 19," *Worship* 49, 3, 131.)

To follow the full text with an explanation accomplishes several worthwhile goals. First, it respects the integrity of the text. Second, such explanation can go a long way toward impressing on persons the complexity of the process by which God's word comes to us. It provides an opportunity to speak of the manner of God's revelation in Scripture. Third, by explicitly addressing the issue of the presentation of the Jews in these texts, presumably such explanation would involve some of the elements we have discussed in this study: the complexity of the term "Jews," the complexity of the history of the community and of the Gospel, and finally the need for understanding the Johannine polemic with the conventions of rhetoric contemporary with the Gospel.

This explanation process provides not only an opportunity to set the text straight but also to add further positive words about the necessity of a genuinely "Christian" understanding of the Jews. Thus our preaching and teaching today can help correct the unfortunate history of misinterpretation of this Gospel and the regrettable attitudes toward Jews that such misinterpretation has inspired.

## Bibliography

R. E. Brown, *The Gospel According to John* (AB 29, 29a; New York: Doubleday, 1966, 1970).

_____, "The Passion According to John: Chapters 18 and 19," *Worship* 49, 3 126–134.

J. L. Martyn, *History and Theology in the Fourth Gospel* (2nd ed.; Nashville: Abingdon, 1979).

L. T. Johnson, "The New Testament's Anti-Jewish Slander and the Conventions of Ancient Polemic," *Journal of Biblical Literature* 108, 3 (Fall, 1989) 419–441.

J. T. Townsend, "The Gospel of John and the Jews: The Story of a Religious Divorce," in *Anti-Semitism and the Foundations of Christianity* (New York: Paulist, 1979) 72–97.

U. C. von Wahlde, "The 'Johannine' Jews: A Critical Survey," *New Testament Studies* January 1982, 33–60.

_____, *The Earliest Version of John's Gospel* (Wilmington: Glazier, 1989).

## Questions for Reflection and Discussion

1. Outline the three editions of the Gospel of John described in this essay, together with the circumstances occurring at the time of these editions. Why is it important to be aware of this history, especially the events which unfolded during the writing of the second edition?
2. What are some features of John's Gospel that bear on the relationship of the Johannine community to the Jewish synagogue?
3. Describe the different meanings apparent in the Gospel's use of the term "the Jews" (*hoi Ioudaioi*).
4. What can religious educators do to enable their students to hear the polemic of the Gospel of John "within context"?

# Jesus: Opposition and Opponents

*David P. Efroymson*

"Has God rejected his people? By no means!" (Rom 11:1). Such is the emphatic position of Paul in the Letter to the Romans and the clear teaching of the Catholic Church at Vatican II (*Nostra Aetate* 4). Mary Boys has shown in another essay of this collection not only the importance of this affirmation, but also the tragic fact that the opposite claim long held sway in the Christian tradition: the allegation that God *had* rejected his people and replaced them with a new, Christian people. The Christian "story," as long generally understood, included that "rejection" and "replacement" as key elements.

Why in the world would a just and loving God have rejected his people? Because, it was alleged, "the Jews" and "Judaism" rejected Jesus, crucified him, and thus left God no choice but to reject and replace them. This, of course, was the way the story was popularly understood prior to the biblical and theological developments to which Boys refers: an understanding based in part, but going beyond, a naive and distorted reading of the Gospels.

The Gospels are dealt with elsewhere in the essays by Cunningham and von Wahlde, and the narratives on the trial and death of Jesus by Fisher. There are, however, specific passages in which Jesus appears in conflict with certain of his fellow Jews. Misconstrued versions of that conflict can lead to a distorted understanding and presentation of Judaism, thus preserving the "teaching of contempt."[1] This essay will examine that conflict or opposition with an eye to such questions as: What was it really about? How serious was it? How extensive? Did Jesus have identifiable "opponents"? If so, who are they likely to have been?

Before beginning the examination, however, an important preliminary point must be made: the stakes here are high. When it is

---

[1] *The Teaching of Contempt* is the title of an important book by Jules Isaac (New York: Holt, Rinehart and Winston, 1964), which pointed to some of the Christian roots of anti-semitism.

(wrongly) claimed that the opposition concerned "a conflict of Jesus with the Torah,"[2] or that what was really revolutionary about Jesus was that he "revolted against the Torah of his fathers,"[3] what is involved is not only a distortion of *Judaism* and its Torah. It also entails a serious misunderstanding of *Jesus* and what he was up to, and of the *God* of Israel in whose behalf Jesus worked and whom we claim to serve.

In order to make the point, allow me to cite a few examples of what can be shown to be exaggerated and seriously distorted claims, made by theologians and scholars whom we all respect, in books we all read; these claims, however, are wrong and dangerously misleading. Joachim Jeremias, for example, claims that Jesus' "criticism of the Torah," among other things "shook the foundations of the ancient people of God."[4] Wolfhart Pannenberg emphasizes that

> . . . the conflict with the law in the background of Jesus' collision with the authorities must remain apparent in all its sharpness: either Jesus had been a blasphemer or the law of the Jews—and with it Judaism itself as a religion—is done away with. That the latter is the case became clear from the perspective of Jesus' resurrection.[5]

So Jesus' "conflict with the law" "shook the foundations" of Israel and "did away with" the law and with it "Judaism itself as a religion."

With Hans Küng, *God* enters the picture. For Küng, it was "conflict with the law and its understanding of God which had brought death to Jesus."[6] He admits: "It is not a new God that he proclaims: now as always it is the God of the Covenant. But it is this old God of the Covenant in a decidedly new light . . . He is not a God of law, but a God of grace."[7]

[2]Helmut Merkel, "The Opposition between Jesus and Judaism" in *Jesus and the Politics of His Day,* ed. by Ernest Bammel and C.F.D. Moule (Cambridge: Cambridge University Press, 1984) 138.

[3]Ernst Bammel, "The Revolutionary Theory from Reimarus to Brandon," ibid., 56.

[4]Joachim Jeremias, *New Testament Theology. The Proclamation of Jesus.* (New York: Charles Scribner's Sons, 1971) 211.

[5]Wolfhart Pannenberg, *Jesus—God and Man* (Philadelphia: Westminster, 1968) 255. It should be pointed out that in an "Afterward" to the second edition of this work, Pannenberg wrote: "Today I regret this conclusion, which seemed to me inescapable at the time. It involved . . . a view widespread in German Protestantism, that the religion of the Law and the Jewish religion are identical." He apparently still holds that Jesus' conflict was with the Law.

[6]Hans Küng, *On Being a Christian* (Garden City: Doubleday, 1976) 406.

[7]Ibid., 314. Elsewhere (pp. 273–74) he contrasts the "God of Judaism" with Jesus' conception, especially as it bears on forgiveness.

John Riches moves along the same lines and is at least as emphatic that God is involved:

> Jesus' teaching . . . thus shows clearly the way in which he understands the will of God as the will of a loving and forgiving father rather than of a God who will have dealings only with the pure and righteous . . . .[8]

He speaks of "the deep break" which Jesus had made "with their basic apprehension of God," and claims that "Jesus in his preaching and call to discipleship attacked the basis of current Jewish strategies by challenging the beliefs about God on which they rested."[9]

For Norman Perrin, "Palestinian Judaism was confronted by a crisis when Jesus proclaimed the eschatological forgiveness of sins, and 'tax collectors and other Jews who had made themselves as Gentiles' responded in glad acceptance." Jesus came, claiming that the Jews "were wrong in their understanding of God and his attitude to these outcasts, and so striking a blow at the fundamental convictions which upheld the Jewish people."[10]

As a final bad example, Jon Sobrino, s.j., will suffice. In a book in which he rightly attempts to re-focus Christological reflection on Jesus' humanity, his human situation and his message of human liberation, he feels compelled to set Jesus and his message in complete opposition to a Judaism which is seriously and consistently misrepresented. A series of Sobrino's assertions should make the point fairly clearly:

> Even more important than the fact of his conflict with the Pharisees is his frontal assault on the mechanisms they use to manipulate God to their own end . . . .
>
> These arguments about the true essence of religion take on a concrete and graphic tinge in his dealings with the Pharisees as official representatives of Jewish religion. Here Jesus appears in a prophetic role, as someone from the outside who fights them in God's name.[11]
>
> At bottom he sought to unmask a way of manipulating the "mystery of God" that served to oppress human beings and to justify such oppression . . . .
>
> In the last analysis Jesus is hostile to the religious leaders of his day and is eventually condemned because of his conception of God.[12]

---

[8]John Riches, *Jesus and the Transformation of Judaism* (New York: Seabury, 1982) 135.
[9]Ibid., 163, 168.
[10]Norman Perrin, *Rediscovering the Teaching of Jesus* (London: SCM, 1967) 97, 103.
[11]Jon Sobrino, s.j., *Christology at the Crossroads* (Maryknoll: Orbis, 1978) 205.
[12]Ibid., 206.

Jesus' polemics with the religious authorities were not just a didactic exercise; . . . Jesus presented people with a God who stands in complete contradiction to the existing religious situation. His God is distinct from, and greater than, the God of the Pharisees.[13]

They would have to choose between the God of their religion and the God of Jesus . . . .[14]

Jesus was condemned for blasphemy, not for heresy.

Thus his conception of God was not only different from, but radically opposed to, that held by the established religion of the standing order.[15]

It isn't enough for Sobrino that Jesus attacked their "oppressive" religion and its conception of God. "Is it possible," he asks rhetorically, that *God* "accepted Jesus' death on the cross so that he might overcome the old religious schema once and for all . . . ?"[16] The "old religious schema" which was to be "overcome" by God and Jesus is, of course, Judaism, or at least the Judaism of the time of Jesus.

To repeat: the assertions paraded above are not meant as a general indictment of the work of Jeremias, Perrin, Pannenberg, Küng, or Sobrino. We have, most of us, learned from them and, in varying degrees, are in their debt. But in their collective treatment of Jesus' "conflict" with "the Pharisees" or with "Judaism," they are wrong, and convey a picture of Judaism, of Jesus and his aims, and of God, which cannot withstand scrutiny. They all seem to share a picture of Judaism of the time of Jesus which had degenerated, having become legalistic, oppressive, and corrupt. That picture was never accurate, and has been demonstrated to be and to have been indefensible.[17] The aforementioned claims about Jesus' "conflict"

---

[13]Ibid., 207.

[14]Ibid., 208–209.

[15]Ibid., 367.

[16]Ibid., 209. It may be worth adding here that, for all the creativity and sense of justice which liberation theology has given us, some of its practitioners share many of the distortions found in Sobrino. See, for example, John Pawlikowski's critical assessment in his *Christ in the Light of the Jewish-Christian Dialogue* (New York: Paulist, 1982) 59–75.

[17]See the essay by Saldarini and the remarks by Boys in this collection. Charlotte Klein presents a good survey of how pervasive among Christians the older, inaccurate picture was, in *Anti-Judaism in Christian Theology* (Philadelphia: Fortress, 1978) 15–91. There were earlier refutations of it by George Foot Moore, Solomon Schechter, and others, but no one seemed to have listened. What may now finally have gotten some attention is the magisterial work of E. P. Sanders, *Paul and Palestinian Judaism* (Philadelphia: Fortress, 1977). After a scathing attack on the intolerable "persistence" of the distorted view (33–59), he spends nearly 400 pages (59–428) examining all the extra-biblical Jewish literature that has survived from about 200 years before the time of Jesus until about 200 years after. None of it offers any evidence of the alleged "degenerate" state. Two other works on the Judaism of the period are: Anthony Saldarini,

with some of his contemporaries, however, do serve to highlight the importance of trying to "get it right." Was there "conflict" or "opposition"? How serious was it? What was it about? From what quarters is it likely to have arisen?

### "Revolt Against the Law"?

The most common claim is probably that historically there was conflict, that it was serious, and that it concerned Israel's Torah: God's "instructions" for Israel on how the people were to respond to God's gracious act of having liberated them and having fashioned them as a people. The claim is that Jesus "attacked" or "revolted against" this Torah. As evidence, what is frequently adduced is a series of "conflict stories" in Mark (2:1-3:6; 7:1-23 and parallels) and two further sabbath healings in Luke (13:10-17; 14:1-6). Space does not allow a full treatment of such passages here, but certain observations may help to provide a necessary historical perspective.

> 1. Some of the settings seem so artificial and unrealistic as to suggest that several of the stories were created by the Church to provide an occasion for a "pronouncement" by Jesus on an issue which may have been faced by the early Church rather than by the historical Jesus. Examples of such apparent artificiality would be: Pharisees "organizing themselves into groups to spend their Sabbaths in Galilean cornfields in the hope of catching someone transgressing (Mark 2:23f.)" or making "a special trip to Galilee from Jerusalem to inspect Jesus' disciples' hands (Mark 7:1f.)"[18]
>
> 2. In three cases, the alleged "perpetrators" are the disciples and not Jesus: not fasting (Mark 2:18-22); plucking grain on the sabbath (Mark 2:23-28); eating with unwashed hands (Mark 7:1f.; Jesus is reported not to have washed before dining with a Pharisee in Luke 11:37-38). Thus in these cases Jesus does not *do* anything in violation of any law.
>
> 3. In two cases, Jesus heals on the sabbath but is not described as doing anything (except healing): a man with a withered hand (Mark 3:1-5) and a man with dropsy (Luke 14:1-6). There is a similar case in John (5:2-10), although the healed former cripple does then carry his pallet.

*Pharisees, Scribes and Sadducees in Palestinian Society* (Wilmington: Michael Glazier, 1988), and Shaye J. D. Cohen, *From the Maccabees to the Mishnah* (Philadelphia: Westminster, 1987).

[18]E. P. Sanders, *Jesus and Judaism* (Philadelphia: Fortress, 1985) 265. Much of the argument which follows is indebted to this book (hereinafter: *J&J*) and to the same author's more recent *Jewish Law from Jesus to the Mishnah* (Philadelphia: Trinity Press International, 1990) especially 1–96.

4. In only one case[19] (Luke 13:10-17), Jesus does "lay his hands" on a crippled woman on the sabbath. According to the evidence provided by Sanders, this would be "extremely minor in the context of the period," so that Jesus as depicted in the synoptic Gospels (as well as John) "behaved on the sabbath in a way which fell inside the range of current debate about it, and well inside the range of permitted behaviour."[20]

5. Thus there is no *action* of Jesus which would constitute a clear transgression of the Law.

6. Did Jesus *teach* or *say* anything against the Law? Again, not in these passages. The issues of the authority Jesus claimed for himself, and his "eating with tax collectors and sinners" will be treated below.

7. Fasting (except on the Day of Atonement) and handwashing (except for priests) are not biblical precepts. Thus Jesus' defense of his disciples is not against the Law.

8. According to Mark 7:15, Jesus is reported to have said: "Nothing that enters one from outside can defile that person; but the things that come out from within are what defile." Mark follows this with his own parenthetical, editorial remark (7:19): "Thus he declared all foods clean." If this were what Jesus had actually said, and if Mark were right about what it meant, Jesus would here have abolished Jewish food laws. Here we would have a case of Jesus teaching against the Law. However, if this were the case, the disputes about the Law, and especially about food, in the early Church (in Gal 2:11-14; Rom 14:1-6; Acts 10:9-17; 11:1-10; 15)[21] would make no sense. That is, if Jesus had actually said something this clear and this definitive, how did it happen that Peter and others were unaware of it, that there were disputes about it later, and that no party to the dispute refers to any teaching of Jesus to settle the matter? In light of considerations such as these, some have argued that Jesus must not have actually said anything like this, and the saying was created, probably by a post-Pauline church, to justify their nonobservance of certain (or most) Jewish food prohibitions.[22]

9. Others would claim that Matthew's version of the saying (15:10) may well be closer to something Jesus actually said, and that it was meant as a *comparative* assertion, the intent of which would have been something like: "It is not only what enters someone which defiles; what

---

[19]It is reported in one other passage, John 9:6, that Jesus makes clay to heal a blind man, but we are not informed until 9:14 that it was on the sabbath, thus suggesting the artificiality of this story, created to set up the conflict which occupies the whole of John 9.

[20]*Jewish Law*, 22–23; the evidence for how the sabbath was observed and debated at the time is presented on 6–23.

[21]The issue of whether Jewish followers of Jesus may eat with Gentile followers is an issue about whether they may eat non-kosher food.

[22]Heikki Räisänen, "Jesus and the Food Laws: Reflections on Mark 7:15," in *Journal for the Study of the New Testament* 16 (1982) 79–100; Sanders, *J&J*, 264, 266.

defiles *even more* (or: what defiles in a more radical sense) is what comes out of someone's mouth."[23]

10. Jesus may well have said that human need, or the coming of the Reign of God, or even that following him was more important than certain sabbath prohibitions, and warranted the performance or the omission of certain actions (e.g., Mark 2:25-28; 3:4; etc.).[24] While not all would have agreed with him, it would be difficult to place any such instance outside the range of debate of the time. Were Jesus to have said something like, "No more sabbath observance!" or "From now on we will observe the first day of the week (Sunday) and *not* the seventh (sabbath)," then we would have anti-sabbath and anti-Law teaching. This is not, of course, what we have, and not what Jesus said.

11. One might also add the many passages in which Jesus is depicted as observant of the Law (e.g., Mark 1:44), or as teaching observance of the Law (esp. Matt 5:17-20 and 5:21-48)[25]—as finally and definitively interpreted by Jesus himself. This again raises the question of the *authority* which Jesus claimed for himself, to be treated below.

12. Thus no *action* of Jesus is against the Law, nor can any *teaching* be described as against the Law. He probably did claim that *some* things (the Reign of God? following him?) were, at *this* time (the end of this age; the time of God's definitive appeal to his people), more important. This may have led to opposition, but in this context the focus of the opposition would have been on the *authority* by which he made such a claim. Opposition strictly on issues of the Law and its interpretation would have been no more serious than other debates of the time, and are not likely to have led to his death.

[23]This is the position of James D.G. Dunn, "Jesus and Ritual Purity: A Study of the Tradition-History of Mark 7:15," in *Jesus, Paul, and the Law* (Louisville: Westminster/John Knox, 1990) 37–60. He argues persuasively that Mt's version (and the similar version in Gospel of Thomas 14) lacks the "radicalizing" features of Mark and is earlier (and not dependent on Mark). The basic position is also defended by: Barnabas Lindars, "All Foods Clean: Thoughts on Jesus and the Law" in *Law and Religion. Essays on the Place of the Law in Israel and Early Christianity*. ed. by Barnabas Lindars (Cambridge: James Clarke, 1988), 61–71; Roger P. Booth, *Jesus and the Laws of Purity* (Sheffield: JSOT Press, 1986); Ben F. Meyer, *The Aims of Jesus* (London: SCM, 1979) 149; Sanders, *Jewish Law* (see n. 18, above) 28.

[24]The passage (Matt 8:21f; Luke 9:59f) in which Jesus may have placed following him ahead of the biblical obligation to bury (and thus honor) one's parents should probably be understood in the same way.

[25]While it has been asserted that Jesus "abrogated" two or three biblical commands in the "antitheses" of Matthew's Sermon on the Mount (5:21-48), the position enunciated by Sanders (*J&J*, 260) better catches their spirit; there is no "abrogation": "it is not against the law to be stricter than the law requires"; the antitheses "affirm the law, but press beyond it." For an elaboration of this position, see: Neil J. McEleney, "The Principles of the Sermon on the Mount," *Catholic Biblical Quarterly* 41 (1979) 552–70; Meyer, *The Aims of Jesus*, 137–53 ("Torah for a graced and restored Israel," p. 141); Benedict T. Viviano, O.P., "Matthew," *New Jerome Biblical Commentary* 641–44; Ulrich Luz, *Matthew 1–7: A Commentary* (Minneapolis: Augsburg, 1989) 255–351; David Hill, *The Gospel of Matthew* (Grand Rapids: Eerdmans, 1972), 117–31, especially 120.

### Associating/Eating with Tax Collectors and Sinners

Probably more serious, and apparently a source of real conflict, was Jesus' seeking out and eating with "tax collectors and sinners." Since this is frequently misunderstood or distorted, certain preliminary observations are called for.

First, what Jesus was up to: his "aim."[26] The heart of what he proclaimed was that the Reign of God was breaking in, that God's final saving act was now, already, operative in Israel. This proclamation was at the same time, for Jesus, an appeal or a summons to Israel to become the Israel that God wanted her finally to be: "eschatological" Israel, a "restored Israel coming into being in response to his call."[27] Jesus' symbolic actions gave expression to and supported that proclamation and appeal: the calling and sending of disciples, and especially of "The Twelve" (*all* Israel: the twelve tribes); the healings and exorcisms, probably to be construed as signs of the breaking-in of salvation (healing = the wholeness of Israel) and the overcoming of the resistant evil one. It is in this context that Jesus' seeking out and eating with "tax collectors and sinners" is to be understood. If *all* of Israel is to be summoned and restored, then not to be neglected were those who in some sense had "lost" their place in the Israel ready for judgment: Jews who had sinned seriously, and Jewish collaborators who were collecting taxes for the Roman occupying force. Thus Jesus sought out these "tax collectors and sinners" because of his sense of mission, because of the Reign of God, because God is forgiving, and because the "restored" Israel would not be whole without them; it was not because Jesus found them particularly "attractive" or "interesting" people.

A critical reading of the Gospels makes the historicity of the issue certain: Jesus is *reported* as associating and eating with such people; he is *accused* of it, as an offense of some kind; and he *defends* the legitimacy of what he was doing. Thus we can be certain that Jesus sought out and ate with "the wicked," and nearly as certain as to *why* he did so. We can also be certain that some found it *offensive,* and that it led to *conflict.* What is controverted is what the conflict was about, what was offensive about Jesus' behavior in this case.

We can be sure that the conflict was not about Jesus defending *"the oppressed,"* or *the common people.*[28] Jesus' concern for the poor and the oppressed need not be called into question. The point here is that,

---

[26]What immediately follows is based on Ben F. Meyer, *The Aims of Jesus* (cf. n. 23, above) 129–168.

[27]Ibid, 142

[28]Sanders, *J & J* (cf. n. 18, above) 174–200.

in this case ("eating with tax collectors and sinners"), this is not what Jesus is accused of, nor what he defends himself against. The parable of the prodigal son (Luke 15:11-32), a part of Jesus' "case" for his actions, in no way defends the younger (errant and "prodigal") son as oppressed by the father or anyone else. In the parable of the laborers in the vineyard (Matt 20:1-16), it is not the need of those who worked only one hour which defends the action of the landowner. It is the generosity of the landowner, as it was the generosity of the father, which Jesus emphasizes.

Was the issue, then, *forgiveness?* Was Jesus offering something "new" in Israel: the claim that sinners could be forgiven? It is mind-boggling that anyone might suggest that Israel had never before heard of forgiveness, or that Israel's allegiance was to a God conceived as unforgiving. No one who had ever read Jeremiah 30 and 31, or Ezekiel 18:23 and 33:11, or Hosea 11, or Micah 7:18-20, or Jonah, could seriously defend such a claim. It is held, of course,[29] but such a claim cannot be defended and should be abandoned in Christian teaching and preaching.

If the issue, the offense, was not the poor and not forgiveness, what was it? Some have argued[30] that the issue was *ritual purity* and the *group boundaries* which it helps to maintain. According to this view, the *haberim* (those who belonged to a *haburah*, a "fellowship"), a reformist group in Israel contemporaneous with Jesus, and probably identifiable with some among the Pharisees, had a reform program which they observed themselves and which they urged upon others in Israel. A significant part of the program was the observance of elements of ritual purity—especially of not sharing table fellowship with those who might not be ritually pure (handwashing before meals *could* have been a relevant issue at this time) or whose food might not be pure, or might not be tithed. According to this same view, Jesus' practice of eating with tax collectors and sinners endangered these group boundaries and challenged the reformists' (the Pharisees?) program for Israel. Such a view cannot be dismissed out of hand. Anthony

[29]Sanders, *J & J*, 200–204, is forced to spend a few pages refuting Perrin, Riches, Kasemann, and Fuchs, all of whom make roughly the same claim. Were anyone to argue that God's forgiveness had been "forgotten" in Israel around the time of Jesus, that person might quickly be corrected by consulting the index entries under "forgiveness," "repentance" "grace," "God as merciful" and similar headings in Sanders, *Paul and Palestinian Judaism* (cf. n. 17 , above), the book in which he reviews most of the Jewish literature which has survived from that time. God's forgiveness had *not* been forgotten.

[30]Most recently by James D. G. Dunn, "Pharisees, Sinners, and Jesus," in *The Social World of Formative Christianity and Judaism*, ed. by Jacob Neusner et al. (Philadelphia: Fortress, 1988) 264–89, reprinted in *Jesus Paul, and the Law* (cf. n. 23, above) 61–88.

Saldarini has shown[31] that what we can know of the Pharisees suggests that they had a program for Israel, and that, to the extent that Jesus can also be described as having a "program," the programs differed, and competition and conflict of some kind were likely. The issue of ritual purity and group boundaries may have been a point where conflict occurred.

If that were the case here, however, it would mean that the "sinners" were not really "sinners," but only the potentially ritually impure. It would mean, further, that the conflict would have been between two Jewish strategies for how Israel was to be restored. And, if the Pharisees were the actual opponents, it would mean that *this* dispute did *not* lead to Jesus' arrest and death, since the Pharisees at this time had no power to impose such a penalty, nor do they appear in any of the trial narratives.[32]

Sanders has serious objections to the view outlined above (of what was "offensive" about Jesus' association with sinners).[33] His own tentative proposal is more provocative: "that the novelty and offense of Jesus' message was that the wicked who heeded him would be included in the kingdom even though they did not repent as it was universally understood,"[34] that is, without restitution, sacrifice, and a formal "turning" to the law. This clearly would have been offensive, and not only or even especially to the Pharisees. Except for those who followed Jesus, and were convinced that he spoke and acted with God's authority, most of the observant and pious in Israel would likely have been offended. This accounts for the offense and the conflict, but much of the gospel material on repentance and the moral demands of Jesus' teaching would have to be dismissed as non-historical.

Ben Meyer's slightly less radical suggestion seems more persuasive: Jesus reversed the "classical biblical structure of repentance" (conversion first, communion/fellowship second). The *emergency* (the inbreaking Reign of God)—and Jesus' sense of both mission and authority—led Jesus to associate and share table fellowship with sinners, in the *hope* of their conversion or repentance; contact was to

---

[31]Briefly in the essay in this collection, and more fully in *Pharisees, Scribes and Sadducees in Palestinian Society* (cf. n. 17, above) *passim*, but especially 283, 290–91, 293. Both Saldarini and Dunn acknowledge the indebtedness of all of us to the work of Jacob Neusner.

[32]On what power and influence the Pharisees may have had during Jesus' time, see Saldarini's *Pharisees. . . . passim;* for the trial narratives, see the essay by Eugene Fisher in this collection.

[33]His objections are to be found in *J & J*, 176–99 and, more fully on ritual purity and the Pharisees, in *Jewish Law* 29–42 and 131–250.

[34]*J & J*, 207. The argument runs through 206–210.

trigger repentance.[35] There were risks involved: the sinners might not repent, and Jesus could easily appear to be playing irresponsibly with the seriousness with which human beings are accountable to God for their actions. He could appear to be offering, solely on *his own authority,* and on *his* claim that this was an *emergency* situation, God's forgiveness, and offering it too cheaply.

This last position seems most adequately to account for all the likely historical data. Here, too, offense could be taken and conflict could result. It is important, however, to be clear on what the real root of the conflict would then have been in this case. It is *not* that Jesus spoke and acted for a "forgiving" God as opposed to a "God of law" or a "God who will have dealings only with the pure and righteous."[36] The God of Jesus is, of course, forgiving, but no more so than the God of Hosea, or Ezekiel, or Micah, or the author of the book of Jonah, and no more so than the God of the Pharisees or of most other Jews known to us at the time of Jesus.[37] The real issue, as it would most probably have been perceived by his contemporaries, would have been whether *Jesus* had the *authority,* or the *right,* to "offer" what he was offering, to *these* people, at *this* time, and with *this* risk. *Was* the Reign of God breaking in? Now? Who said so? *Was* the crisis such as to warrant *these* measures? Who said so?

It is, to be sure, possible for the generosity-beyond-calculation of the God of Israel to be forgotten. It was forgotten at times, in Israel; otherwise there would have been no need for the prophetic "reminding" alluded to above. It has been forgotten by Christians. It *may* have been forgotten by some in Israel at the time of Jesus, and Jesus may well have engaged in some prophetic "reminding" of his own. But Jesus *did* what he did (the initiative toward "sinners") on his sense of *mission* and his sense of *emergency,* each based on his own *authority.* When his opponents, whoever they may have been, objected, he *defended* what he did by appealing directly to them about what he believed he and his opponents *shared:* a conviction about the readiness-to-forgive of the God of Israel. As Ben Meyer[38] puts it, in connection with Jesus' defense of this initiative in parables:

> It should be emphasized that this was not the defense of an embattled man concerned with his own honour, nor was it a polemical put-down of his critics. It was above all an appeal, one repeatedly renewed and

[35]*The Aims of Jesus* (n. 23), 160–62.
[36]These are the claims of Küng and Riches cited earlier in this essay; Perrin says roughly the same thing.
[37]Cf. n. 29, above.
[38]*The Aims of Jesus,* 162.

recast, designed not to humiliate the opposition but to win it over. Such was the intended thrust of the parables of the Two Sons, of the Two Debtors, of the Lost Sheep, of the Lost Drachma, and, above all, of the Prodigal Son, where the appeal to the *dikaioi* is particularly evident and poignant.

The opposition, then, and the conflict, would have been, at least at root, about the authority which Jesus apparently claimed for himself.

### The Authority Claimed by Jesus

Thus both the conflict over the inclusion of sinners, and whatever opposition there may have been about the Law—about Jesus' alleged transgressions, the controversial interpretations, and the claim that following him, or the Reign of God, was more important than certain legal stipulations or prohibitions—lead back to the *authority* which Jesus appears to have arrogated to himself. Whether explicit or implied, Jesus' claim about himself was significant and seems clearly to have provoked opposition.

A few of the dimensions of that claim to authority are worth noting. He claimed to know what God was doing—what he was up to— in the history of Israel: God has now, Jesus said, initiated his Reign and his claim upon Israel. He claimed to know the will of God: that God now demanded *more* of Israel (Matt 5:17-48, at least parts of which seem authentic);[39] that God wanted healing done, even on the Sabbath (e.g., Luke 13:10-16; 14:1-6); that God wanted following Jesus to take precedence even over the obligation to bury a parent (Matt 8:21-22). He claimed to know whom God wanted in the Kingdom, and under what conditions, at least now in a situation which Jesus construed as an emergency. He thus claimed to *speak* for God, and, at least in his summons to Israel and his initiative toward sinners, to *act* for God.[40]

This is a massive claim. Christians today are accustomed to it, accept it, and sometimes wonder at the seeming blindness of those Jews of Jesus' time who did not accept it. But historically, it is important to keep in mind that the Jesus who made this enormous claim, had not been raised from the dead and vindicated by the One whom he called his Father (at least to the satisfaction of those to whom the

---

[39]On this, see Meyer, *Aims*, 137–53.

[40]Sanders would add a further element: an implied claim to be the messianic "king" in the in-breaking Kingdom: *J & J*, 232–35 with 144–48, and especially 306–308. His argument seems to me not quite conclusive, but it would explain Jesus' execution by the Romans as "King of the Jews." If Sanders is correct, it would add one more element to those already mentioned.

risen Jesus had appeared). Perhaps historically, the surprising thing was rather that some accepted the claim, and not that some were not persuaded.

But beyond simple non-acceptance, what about *oppostion?* What kind of opposition would have been provoked by the claim? From what quarters would it have arisen? How serious would it have been? Persons who make exorbitant claims can easily be dismissed, at least when no one is "taken in" by the claims, when the claimant has no following. But when Jesus drew a certain "critical mass" of followers, then those who did not or could not see things the way he did could perceive him as a "seducer," "leading Israel astray." So there could well have been resistance from among those who did not share the vision of Jesus and his followers. How much? Perhaps enough to have provoked from Jesus some of the frustration expressed in the criticisms of "this generation": e.g., Matthew 11:16-19//Luke 7:31-35, where Jesus complains that people criticized the Baptist's asceticism and then accused Jesus of being "a glutton and a drunkard, a friend of tax collectors and sinners."

More serious would have been the opposition from among the priestly leadership, especially if they were to come to believe that his claim to authority, now taken seriously by the aforementioned "critical mass" of followers, was a direct challenge to theirs, that his claim was that he, *rather than they,* spoke for God. The occasion for such a challenge, if there was one, would have to have been that event usually described as Jesus' "cleansing" of the Temple.

### Jesus and the Temple

It seems virtually certain that Jesus engaged in some kind of symbolic "demonstration" in the Temple area, and said something about its destruction.[41] This seems to have triggered the series of events in Jerusalem which culminated in his arrest, trial, and death at the hands of the Romans. It is at this point where, whatever the conflict was about, it became deadly.

The matter, however, is not simple, and some brief observations may help prevent misunderstanding and oversimplification. The synoptics report Jesus predicting the Temple's destruction (Mark 13:2; Matt 24:1-3; Luke 21:5-7; in John 2:19 it is conditional). Mark 14:58 (followed with modifications by Matt 26:59-61) refers to an accusation against Jesus at his trial that *he* would destroy the Temple *and*

---

[41]Sanders' analysis of the relevant texts seems to demonstrate the historicity of both the event and at least approximately what Jesus said: *J & J*, 61-76. His interpretation of what Jesus *meant* is subject to some dispute.

rebuild it, but it is reported as a false accusation, by false witnesses. The accusation is repeated by passers-by as Jesus is on the cross (Mark 15:29). It is difficult to avoid the impression that Jesus must at least have said something about the Temple's destruction. Who would destroy it, and whether "rebuilding" was part of what he said, are far more problematic.

As to the demonstration itself, it seems that there was a disturbance of some kind, including the overturning of some tables (of the money-changers). But what Jesus *says* during the demonstration is different in John[42] (2:16: "you shall not make my Father's house a market-place") from what he says in the synoptics (roughly: "It is written: 'My house shall be called a place of prayer,' but you have made it into a 'den of thieves' "). Since the synoptic saying is a composite scriptural citation (Isa 56:7 in the first half, and Jer 7:11 in the second), it may come from the evangelist or a source, and may not throw light on what *Jesus* meant by what he did.

There was an older, "conventional" view according to which Jesus was attacking external religion, or the buying and selling in the Temple area, or even sacrifice itself. But it is not at all probable that Jesus struck out at sacrifice itself; he seems to have accepted it (the "altar" in Matt 5:23-24 is the Jewish altar of sacrifice, not the altar in a Catholic church). If there is to be sacrifice, suitable animals must be available for sale, especially for pilgrims coming to the Temple from a distance. If Roman coins are unacceptable, provision must be made for changing them.

In light of this, Sanders[43] argues that Jesus overturned the tables as a sign of the Temple's impending destruction, as part of the demise of the old order, and probably at least implying that it would be replaced by a new Temple appropriate to the new order now breaking in. What Jesus *said* must have been a word about destruction, interpreting what he had done. Sanders offers evidence that such a symbolic gesture would have been generally intelligible.[44] He further argues that the demonstration was not directly against the priests, since otherwise one would expect to find more of the same in the gospels, where charges of priestly corruption, immorality and dishonesty are conspicuously absent.[45] Nevertheless, such an affront to the Temple (as part of an old order that was to be destroyed to make

---

[42]Who of course places the whole scene at the *beginning* of Jesus' ministry, to set the stage for the conflict he wants to emphasize throughout the gospel.

[43]*loc. cit.* in n. 41.

[44]*J & J*, 77–90.

[45]Ibid., 65–66.

way for something "new") would have been offensive to most Jews and especially to the priesthood, who would then have collaborated with the Romans to seek Jesus' death.[46]

Others,[47] in specific reaction to Sanders, have argued that the demonstration was indeed directed at the priesthood. They offer evidence from *Jewish* sources critical of the high priesthood around Jesus' time[48] and of hints in the Gospels of more animosity between Jesus and at least some of the priests[49] than Sanders allows. Further, if there were an expectation or a hope abroad that the "old" (second) Temple was to give way to a new, eschatological Temple, as Sanders holds,[50] one can question why Jesus' claim that this expectation was about to be realized would be offensive enough to account for his arrest and death. For this, Jesus' demonstration would have to be construed as a direct challenge to, or critique of, the priesthood.[51]

The evidence is such that we may not be able to settle the difference between these two positions, or to obtain certitude. Inference is necessary, and will have to suffice. Jesus had come to Jerusalem not in order to die,[52] and probably, not in order to pick a fight. He had come, apparently, in order to confront the Jerusalem leadership with his proclamation and summons. The Temple demonstration would seem to have been purposeful, "calculated to . . . bring the imminence of God's reign abruptly, forcefully, to the attention of all,"[53] especially to the highpriestly leadership. He had come to lay a claim, and the claim was refused or opposed by many, perhaps most, of the priestly leadership.[54] This may have led to some sharp criticism from Jesus, perhaps along the lines of the parable of the tenants/vineyard keepers (Mark 12:1-9 and parallels). Before long,

[46]Ibid., 301–305.

[47]Most recently, Craig Evans, "Jesus' Action in the Temple: Cleansing or Portent of Destruction?" in *Catholic Biblical Quarterly* 51/2 (1989) 237–70; Richard Bauckham, "Jesus' Demonstration in the Temple," in Lindars, ed., *Law and Religion* (as in n. 23, above) 72–89 (+ notes, 171–76).

[48]Evans, 256–64, offers evidence of accusations of corruption, but then concludes that there "must have been" corruption; Bauckham, 78–81: "commercialism rather than corruption" (79).

[49]Evans, 243–48.

[50]In *J & J*, 77–90.

[51]So Bauckham, 87–89.

[52]See the helpful survey by John Galvin, "Jesus' Approach to Death: An Examination of Some Recent Studies," *Theological Studies* 41/4 (1980) 713–44.

[53]Meyer, *Aims*, 197.

[54]References in the tradition to some support for Jesus among the leadership (e.g., John 12:42), as well as to Nicodemus in John and to Joseph of Arimathea, should give us some pause about referring to the opposition of "the" priests or "the" Sanhedrin as an undifferentiated bloc.

Jesus is arrested, tried, and executed, probably by some coalition of Romans and Jerusalem priests who collaborated with the Romans.

Why? Jesus' claim to authority, especially as expressed dramatically in the Temple demonstration, was almost certainly taken by elements of the Jerusalem leadership as a threat to their authority and, as they saw it, to Israel. The disturbance by Jesus and his followers would have been enough to involve the Romans. This man had to be stopped.[55]

## Opponents?

So much for the opposition. Is it possible now to identify "opponents," based on the preceding analysis?[56]

To the extent that there were Jews involved in Jesus' death at the hands of the Romans, these opponents would have to have come from among the *Jerusalem priestly leadership,* since collaboration with the Romans would have been necessary. The issue was not the Law, but Jesus laying a claim and proclaiming a summons, in a way that underlined his authority and apparently threatened theirs. The issue would have been Jesus' authority, and his "leading Israel astray." The incident in the Temple might have offended others, perhaps many others, from among the ordinary people, if it appeared that Jesus were attacking the Temple.

There could well have been opposition, or at least resistance, from many among the *pious* and *observant,* especially concerning the initiative toward sinners and the authority by which Jesus claimed the right to speak and act for God in this matter. Some of the same people might have been offended by his interpretation of the Law, or his claim about the priority of the Reign of God. It does not seem that this opposition from these people would have been serious enough to have contributed to his death.

There may have been opposition of sorts from some *Pharisees,* on matters of interpretation of the Law, or on ritual purity, table fellowship, and group boundaries.[57] If there were such opposition, it would

---

[55]The fuller account of all this in Sanders, *J & J,* 294–318, is as plausible as any we are likely to get for awhile.

[56]For much of what follows, see Sanders, *J & J,* 270–93.

[57]This is to accept Saldarini's case for at least the historical probability of a clash or competition of "programs" here (as in n. 31, above); it is also to accept, with reservations, the thrust of Dunn's "Pharisees, Sinners, and Jesus" (n. 30, above), including his argument that at least some few of the gospel traditions which include the Pharisees date from a time *before* the Pharisees became the dominant group (70–85 C.E.) and the principal opponent of the early church in the land of Israel. The evidence collected by Sanders, *Jewish Law,* 131–250, especially 236–50, is not such as to exclude Saldarini's point, but it is enough to demand caution.

have been both less extensive than the impression created by the gospels,[58] and less serious. At the time of Jesus, the Pharisees were only one of many reformist groups competing for influence in Israel. They did not become dominant until the years after the war with Rome in 66–70. Since they then seem to have become the principal opponents of the Jesus movement in Israel, many of the gospel passages actually reflect their disputes with the early Church, rather than actual conflicts between them and Jesus.

It may well be that the whole business of "opponents" has been overdone. The word tends to imply a Jesus who set out to establish a set of controversial legal or theological positions, and then to debate those who held contrary positions. But this is not the Jesus of history.[59] Or it suggests a Jesus who had come to attack certain positions or to pick fights with certain people. This, too, is a distortion. Jesus proclaimed, in word and in deed, the breaking in of God's reign and a summons to Israel. What he said and what he did, and the authoritative way in which he said and did it, met some resistance and some opposition, as well as some acceptance.[60] There may have been disputes or debates along the way, with various people, on the implications of what he said and did. The final trip to Jerusalem and perhaps especially the incident in the Temple, as expressive of a last-ditch, climactic and emphatic appeal to and claim on Israel, did not succeed. To the extent that some leaders in Jerusalem perceived his vision of what God wanted for Israel, and the authority with which he expressed and advanced that vision, as a threat to their vision and their authority, the opposition became serious. In collaboration with the Roman occupying forces, who must have seen Jesus as dangerous, the combined opposition became deadly and the matter was settled.

## Conclusion

There is not much merit in repeating what has already been said. Two further points, however, demand brief attention, especially for

---

[58]Saldarini points out the many passages in Matt and even more in Luke in which the Pharisees have been *added* as opponents: *Pharisees, Scribes, and Saducees,* 157–73 for Matthew, and 174–87 for Luke. Dunn, in the article cited immediately above, acknowledges this, even though he argues for *some* conflict between Jesus and some Pharisees: see pp. 272–74 of the original article, and 69–71 in *Jesus, Paul, and the Law.*

[59]See Sanders, *Jewish Law,* 94–95.

[60]The basic reconstruction offered by Ben F. Meyer, *The Aims of Jesus,* 122–73, is the most persuasive and coherent known to me. In only one or two minor instances (lumping together clean/unclean and righteous/sinners, 159, and on "Torah piety," 162–63) Sanders serves as a useful corrective: *J & J,* 174–211 and 245–69.

those who deal with Jesus in teaching or preaching. Whatever opposition there was to Jesus, it is a distortion and a serious oversimplification to call it "Judaism." As one scholar[61] has recently put it:

> Jesus' views may have annoyed powerful people, and so may have led to his prosecution and death, but we should refrain from making the views of those people normative, or of turning them into Judaism.

There was far too much diversity, and too many competing positions, in Israel at this time for any one of them to be identified as Judaism.[62] For at least two hundred years before Jesus, and for some time after, "the people of Israel had a number of strategies for preserving their identity and adapting their traditions in changing and often hostile circumstances."[63] These strategies were usually based on different visions of what God wanted Israel to be. Their proponents took them seriously, and frequently opposed those with competing visions. Jesus had such a vision, but he neither opposed nor was opposed by "Judaism." His God was the God of Israel; his vision, his strategy, and his proclamation were Jewish.

This leads to the second point. Christians need more fully to appreciate that we have all we need in Jesus and his vision of God and what God is doing, and what God wants in response. We do not need to "highlight" this, to make it seem somehow brighter by contrast with whatever alternate visions may have opposed, or not been persuaded by, his. Those alternate visions deserve to be studied and understood, but for their own sake, not for what is allegedly "lacking" in them. We do not need "opponents" to make Jesus more believable, or more acceptable. If we understand the opposition, we are richer for it. If we make Jesus and his vision dependent on "superiority" to the opposition, Jesus is trivialized and we are poorer for it.

---

[61]Philip S. Alexander, "Jewish Law in the Time of Jesus: Toward a Clarification of the Problem," in *Law and Religion* (n. 23, above) 58.

[62]This point is increasingly emphasized in contemporary scholarship. Saldarini's essay in this collection points to it clearly. See also, in addition to Saldarini and Cohen (n. 17, above), Gary Porton, "Diversity in Postbiblical Judaism" in *Early Judaism and Its Modern Interpreters,* ed. by Robert A. Kraft and George W.E. Nickelsburg (Atlanta: Scholars, 1986), 57–80; Robert Murray, S.J. " 'Disaffected Judaism' and Early Christianity: Some Predisposing Factors," in *To See Ourselves As Others See Us,* ed. by Jacob Neusner and Ernest S. Frerichs (Chico, Calif.: Scholars, 1985), 263–82; *Jewish and Christian Self-Definition, Vol. 2: Aspects of Judaism in the Greco-Roman Period,* ed. E. P. Sanders (Philadelphia: Fortress, 1981).

[63]The sentence is from Saldarini's essay in this collection.

## Questions for Reflection and Discussion

1. This essay makes several points about claims that Jesus was opposed to the Judaism of his day. Discuss this idea in terms of the Torah, Jewish ideas about God, and the Temple. Did Jesus reject any or all of these elements of first-century Jewish life? Why or why not?
2. Why might different segments of first-century Judaism have had adverse reactions to Jesus? Were any of these negative responses serious enough to threaten Jesus' life?
3. Discuss the "demonstration" conducted by Jesus in the Temple and issues of authority. Why might Jesus have caused this incident? What response was he seeking? What response did he provoke?
4. How do you feel most Christians conceive of the relationship between Jesus and his Jewish contemporaries? Does this have any implications for religious education?

# The Passion and Death of Jesus of Nazareth: Catechetical Approaches

*Eugene J. Fisher*

## I. Historical Context: The Councils of Trent and Vatican II

"Within Context" devotes a major section of its presentation on "Catechetical Principles" to the classroom presentation of Jesus' death because of the centrality of the issue within the ancient Christian teaching of contempt against Jews and Judaism. The collective guilt charge against the Jewish people for Jesus' death formed the linchpin of the negative view of the Jewish people and their religious tradition that prevailed in so much of Christian teaching until the Second Vatican Council.

"The" Jews, it was uncritically opined, rejected Jesus' religious teachings, which they regarded as blasphemous, and in their rejection moved to have his voice stilled. God, in turn, rejected the Jewish people, causing the Temple of Jerusalem to be destroyed in the year 70 A.D. (or C.E., i.e., "Common Era") and the people to be dispersed to wander the earth, visibly suffering as a sign of divine punishment until they repented of their rejection, accepted Christ as their Savior and converted to Christianity. This conversion of the Jews, many of the pious thought, would open the way for Christ's return, just as "the" Jews' continuing rejection of Jesus continued to block that return. The Jewish people, so conceived not only as the murderers of Christ ("deicides," as if God could be killed by human hands) but also as the primary block against the final coming of God's Kingdom on earth, gradually became fair game within "Christian" Europe for repressive legislation, forced conversion, exile, and ultimately massacres and pogroms.

The history of Christian persecution of the Jews in the name of the New Testament God of mercy and love (as opposed, of course, to the "Old" Testament God of justice and vengeance) is a long and often (though not unrelievedly) tragic one. It has been well told by

104

Rev. Edward H. Flannery, one of the great pioneers of Catholic-Jewish dialogue, in his volume, *The Anguish of the Jews: Twenty-Three Centuries of Antisemitism* (Paulist, 2nd ed., 1985). It does not need a complete retelling here. Suffice it to say that at the heart of Christian mistreatment of Jews over the centuries lay a simplistic and false syllogism: "The Jews rejected and killed Jesus. Therefore, God must want to punish them, to make them suffer for this crime. Therefore, we Christians should help God by increasing the sufferings of the Jews."

Today, we have been called by the Second Vatican Council to rethink the questionable historical and theological categories that lead Christians to the notion of collective Jewish guilt for Jesus' death. Interestingly, this was not the first attempt of an ecumenical Council of the Church to clarify the doctrinal muddle that was the deicide charge. In the 16th Century, the Roman Catechism commissioned by the Council of Trent stated very clearly that:

> In this guilt are involved all those who fall frequently into sin; for, as our sins consigned Christ the Lord to the death of the cross, most certainly those who wallow in sin and iniquity crucify to themselves again the Son of God, as far as in them lies, and make a mockery of him. This guilt seems more enormous in us than in the Jews, since according to the testimony of the apostle: If they had known it, they would never have crucified the Lord of glory; while we on the contrary, professing to know him yet denying him by our actions, seem in some sort to lay violent hands on him (Heb 6:6; 1 Cor 2:8) (*Catechismus Romanus,* Article IV).

The Roman Catechism in fact represented the authentic Christian faith over the ages concerning the death of Christ. That Christ died freely "because of the sins of all, so that all might attain salvation" (*Nostra Aetate,* no. 4) merely reiterated a core teaching of the Church. The official Creed of the Church, for example, never ascribed guilt to Jews but simply stated that Jesus' death took place "under Pontius Pilate." The deicide charge against Jews was thus rightly perceived by the authors of the *Roman Catechism* to be a digression from what should be central to Christian teaching on the matter: that Christians shoulder their own responsibility, in faith, for the crucifixion. For to the extent that we Christians, by contemplation of the Cross, are lead to repent our sins, so we may die to sin and rise again in Christ to new life. Blaming the Jews, however, as Trent knew, not only allows Christians to dodge this responsibility but also in effect cuts the Christian off from the source of grace.

## II. *Nostra Aetate* and Biblical Interpretation

But, some will argue, even if one grants the Creed and the Tridentine Roman Catechism the doctrinal point they are making, is there not still a biblical and historical issue? The New Testament speaks of Jews as being involved in plotting Jesus' death, even if it was actually carried out by Roman soldiers under the orders of Pontius Pilate. Surely, this should be taken into account in our teaching?

Yes, it should. But the burden of history, of Christian sins against Jews rationalized by false appeals to a collective deicide charge, equally make it incumbent on contemporary teachers to exercise scrupulous caution in approaching the topic. The 1974 Vatican "Guidelines for Implementing *Nostra Aetate*" call for "an overriding preoccupation" to deal with this problem "especially when it is a question of passages which seem to show the Jewish people in an unfavourable light" (no. 2). *Nostra Aetate* itself took into account this objection in its condemnation of the deicide charge: "True, authorities of the Jews and those who followed their lead pressed for the death of Christ (cf., John 19:6); still, what happened in His Passion cannot be blamed upon all the Jews then living, without distinction, nor upon the Jews of today. Although the Church is the new people of God, the Jews should not be presented as repudiated or cursed by God as if such views followed from the holy Scriptures."

In other words, all of the negative statements, controversy narratives, even polemics within the New Testament notwithstanding, one cannot conclude either that "the Jews" killed Jesus (or as some would have it, manipulated Pilate to do so) nor that they were or are rejected by God or being punished by God as a people. A remarkable but too little noted passage of the 1985 Vatican "Notes on the Correct Way to Present Jews and Judaism in Preaching and Catechesis," upon which *Within Context* is based, carries forward the Conciliar discussion by quite consciously turning the ancient teaching of contempt on its head. Whereas the old teaching interpreted the Jewish Diaspora and Jewish suffering over the centuries as a sort of inverted "proof" of the divinity of Christ (See how they suffer! God must be angry at them for rejecting Jesus!), the Vatican *Notes* place a positive valuation upon the Diaspora as part of God's plan of salvation even after the coming of Christ. And they understand Jewish suffering—often at the hands of misguided Christians—as an authentic act of martyrdom ("heroic witness"): "The history of Israel did not end in 70 A.D. It continued, especially in a numerous Diaspora which allowed Israel to carry to the whole world a witness—often heroic—of its fidelity to the one God and to 'exalt Him in the presence of all the living' (Tobit 13:4), while preserving the memory of their forefathers at the heart of their hope (Passover Seder)" (*Notes,* VI, 25).

How then can the teacher reconstruct for her or his students a presentation of the death of Jesus in a way that does justice to the historical and spiritual message of the four Gospels while at the same time avoiding a false or negative approach to Jews and Judaism? This is the catechetical task outlined in *Within Context* which will be filled in a bit more here.

### III. Four Gospels, Not One

One of the main dangers facing Christian teachers approaching the presentation of the Passion and Death of Jesus lies in the natural human tendency to try to "neaten up" the four Gospel accounts by reducing them to one, harmonized version. From the theological perspective, the problem with this is that God did not inspire one, harmonized Passion narrative, but rather four separate accounts. These accounts agree in the essence of the narrative structure of the historical events, as we shall outline below. But they differ also in certain significant details.

The four accounts are:

|              |              |
|--------------|--------------|
| Matthew 26–28 | Luke 22–23  |
| Mark 14–15   | John 18–19   |

It would be helpful to have these at hand when going through this section.

### IV. The Problem of Harmonization: The Example of the Passion Plays

One can see the potential for serious difficulties in the history of the medieval development of Passion plays. These plays, which were educational in intent, as were the earlier mystery and morality plays, attempted to bring together elements from the four Gospels into one dramatic unity. But when the point of selection of the various elements from the four Gospels is (as it was) the vibrancy of the drama rather than the authenticity of the theological message of the gospels (as articulated by the Council of Trent) or historical accuracy (as stressed in biblical studies in our own time), the danger of stereotyping Jews and Judaism becomes very strong. After all, what is more "dramatic" than a simple "good guy/bad guy" narrative?

Passion plays developed in the Middle Ages in the period which Father Edward Flannery has called the "period of woe" for Jews in Christendom. After 1096 tens of thousands of Jews were massacred by rampaging Crusaders, despite the remonstrations of the popes and such great figures as Bernard of Clairvaux. In the thirteenth and fourteenth centuries Jews were accused of poisoning wells to cause great plagues and of murdering innocent Christian children for the ritual use of their blood. Again the popes condemned these accusations for the false canards against Jews that they were, but again the papal condemnations fell on largely deaf ears among Catholic clergy and laity alike.

In the thirteenth century the IV Lateran Council institutionalized the ghettos, some historians would say as a means of providing protection for Jews as well as separating them from the general population. By the end of the fifteenth century, Jews had been forcibly expelled from England, Spain, most of Germany, much of France, and their numbers limited even in Italy, countries in which the Jewish presence often predated the Christian presence by centuries.

The earliest extant texts of Passion plays come from Germany, the thirteenth-century Benediktbeuren manuscripts. Already these manuscripts illustrate problems of conflation that were to recur over the centuries in Passion plays and catechetical texts down to our own times.

Each Gospel has distinct features. The Gospel of John, for example, having been written very late in the first century, has, unlike the Synoptics, a very simple view of the people among whom Jesus passed his life. Whereas the earlier Gospels speak of numerous groups among Jews of Jesus' time (Sadducees, Pharisees, Herodians, etc.), the Gospel of John often speaks simply of "the Jews" as if all thought and acted with a single mind and voice, something like speaking of "the Americans" when dealing with the civil rights struggles of the 1960s!

Recent scholarship has shown that the author of John's Gospel uses the term *"hoi Ioudaioi"* (usually translated as "the Jews") in more than one sense. When used historically, the author normally means "Judeans" as opposed, for example, to Galilean Jews (as in the Gospel of Luke). But often John's use is not historical but theological and contemporary to his own time. In this sense he means not "the Jews" as a people as we would understand the term today, but rather "the opponents of Jesus" or, more precisely, the opponents in John's own time, whether Christian or Jewish, of John's own high Christology. Only with such explanation, for example, can one understand such otherwise inexplicable usages of the term as that found in John 20:19, where the author has the disciples—Jews themselves one and all—hiding behind closed doors "for fear of the Jews."

Pejoratives that historically were meant more precisely to refer to this Jew or that, especially among certain Jewish leaders, are lent a collective nuance in John's Passion narrative that in itself has been very problematic over the centuries in misleading Christians to think of "the Jews" killing Jesus. In Jesus' time, in fact, far more Jews lived outside Judea and the Galilee than inside. Most could not have heard of him, much less have had a chance to accept or reject him. And even of the Jerusalem Jews, only a very tiny percentage could have fit into Pilate's courtyard. Many would probably not even have been aware of Jesus' arrest and crucifixion.

Yet the Passion plays and much of Christian catechesis has often simply spoken of "the Jews" in a devastatingly collective sense. The Passion plays added something even worse. In Matthew's text, and only in Matthew's text, there is a phrase attested nowhere else in the gospels and ascribed to the small crowd gathered in Pilate's court-yard: "His blood be on us and on our children." This is a phrase which appears to exculpate Pilate and blame the Jews, though many scholars would question this as Matthew's original intent.

If one conflates this unique phrase from Matthew's text with the collective *"hoi Ioudaioi"* of John's Gospel, one can go very quickly to an invidious portrait of all Jews not only of Jesus' time but of all times and generations as guilty of the death of Jesus. Demonizing the Jews as enemies of God and a potential source of all sorts of conspiratorial evils is, of course, only a short step away from such a portrait.

Indeed, one can see this line being crossed in the earliest Passion Plays. The thirteenth-century German Benediktbeuren manuscripts put into the mouth of the Blessed Mother herself the following "planctus" (lament) about her own people:

> Oh the zeal, Oh the crime of this hateful race!
>   Oh the animal-like hands of those crucifying you!
> What crime, what shameful thing this barbarous people commits.
>   He is made to suffer chains, beatings, wounds. . .
> Oh blind deplorable race, repent!

And in an alternate lament in the Carmina Burana manuscript 265/4b:

> He who is innocent is condemned by a damnable people. . .
> Men of blood rage against the Lord of salvation with iniquitous zeal
>   and all the while feign virtue.

In 1988, the Bishops' Committee for Ecumenical and Interreligious Affairs of the National Conference of Catholic Bishops issued a detailed set of "Criteria for the Evaluation of Dramatizations of the Passion" for parish and classroom use. In English and Spanish, it can be recommended as a highly practical tool for teachers.

## V. What The Texts Have In Common

*Within Context* lists briefly the elements of Christ's Passion that the Gospels share in common. As the text notes these common elements represent a high degree of historical probability, handed down as they were by the different traditions, liturgical and oral, which the various New Testament authors had at hand in constructing their Gospel narratives. These are:

**A.** A growing hostility to Jesus on the part of the Jerusalem Temple authorities. It should be noted that the Gospels, while in greater or lesser degree positing a conflict between Jesus and "the Pharisees" (another unfortunate collective term) do not mention Pharisees as being involved in the events leading to Jesus' death. When Jesus predicts his death, he does not even mention the Pharisees, but only the chief priests of the temple, scribes and elders (Mark 10:32-34; Matt 20:17-19; Luke 9:22). The Gospels are also clear that the desire on the part of the Temple authorities to do something about Jesus had to be carried out covertly because of Jesus' popularity with the people of Jerusalem. Thus, Mark states: "The chief priests and the scribes heard about this and began to look for a way to destroy him. They were at the same time afraid of him because the whole crowd was under the spell of his teaching" (Mark 11:18). Luke's Gospel shows Pharisees coming to Jesus before his journey to Jerusalem for the Passover to warn him that there was a plot against his life. Far from wishing Jesus' death or fearing him in any way, then, one can say that the Pharisees, though eager to debate the nuances of Torah observance with Jesus as they did among themselves, would have seen Jesus as a natural ally in their own major conflicts with the Temple priesthood, a priesthood that they, like Jesus, saw as corrupt. The context of Mark 11:18, of course, is precisely the scene in which Jesus overturns the tables of the temple moneychangers.

**B.** A Last Supper with the apostles, whether or not this was in fact a passover seder. The Synoptics interpret it, theologically, as such, which is what is of major importance to catechesis. On this see Anthony Saldarini, *Jesus and Passover* (Paulist, 1984).

**C.** Betrayal by Judas to the Temple authorities. Here, the catechist needs to exercise some caution because the name "Judas," related to "Judea" and the modern term, "Jew" (German, Jude), has in the past lead some Christian commentators to see in Judas a symbol of the Jewish people in his betrayal. He is not. He is an individual representing, historically, only himself, and, theologically, ourselves as Christian sinners.

**D.** Arrest at night outside the city. In the Synoptics (Matt 26:3; Mark 14:1; Luke 22:2) it is very clearly the chief priests of the Temple and not the Pharisees who have Jesus arrested to deliver him to Pilate as an insurrectionist. When Jesus predicts his Passion, he does not mention the Pharisees, only the chief priests and scribes (Matt 20:17-19; Mark 10:32-34; Luke 9:22). In John's Gospel, the arresting force is a Roman cohort accompanied by Temple guards (John 18:3, 12). Unlike the Temple, the Pharisees, as a popular religious reform movement, did not have troops, but only the authority of their piety and scholarship with which to convince the people. The fact that the arrest had to be outside the city and at night because of Jesus' popularity with the people of Jerusalem is, again, a telling detail shared by all the Gospels. It shows that the conflict lay not with the Jewish people or with Judaism as such, but rather with certain of the "powers that be." In the case of Jesus the "power" was Rome's. The chief priests of the Temple were directly appointed and controlled by the Roman procurator (governor) and answered to Rome. What threatened the Temple, therefore, would be perceived as a political threat to Rome, and vice-versa.

**E.** Interrogation before a high priest. Again, what is shared by the Gospels is only an appearance before the high priest prior to Jesus being sent to Pilate for the disposition of his case, which was not in any event in the hands of Jewish authorities but only Pilate. Many scholars question whether there was a full Sanhedrin trial, since what is depicted in the New Testament violates the known laws of capital trials as these can be reconstructed from biblical and subsequent Jewish tradition. Likewise, a formal trial under the law is not necessary to the essence of the historical event as shared by the Gospels. John's Gospel, for example, has no Sanhedrin trial scene at all, but only a questioning before the two chief priests at dawn (19:18). It is not, in any event, Jewish law that is applied in the case, but Roman law and Roman punishment—crucifixion, a punishment unknown in biblical or later Jewish penal law.

**F.** Condemnation by Pilate as the legally responsible authority (cf., the Creeds, which mention only Pilate).

**G.** Crucifixion by Roman soldiers while the Jews of Jerusalem mourn, with the cause of execution clearly stated as a political crime against Rome: "King of the Jews." It is not accidental, perhaps, that Jesus was crucified along with two "insurrectionists."

H. Death, Burial, Resurrection: the key faith elements of the Passion narratives.

## VI. Ambiguities of Presentation

Contemporary Catholic religious education materials can at times present an ambiguous portrait of Jews and Judaism. While general statements about Judaism are most often quite positive and even corrective in tone, specific statements about events in Jesus' life, such as the "controversies" with Pharisees or the Passion narratives, can undercut the more general, positive assertions of respect for Judaism. In the teachers' manual for Grade 2 of one textbook series, for example, there is the statement that Advent

> . . . is a fitting time to tell the children about the Jews, to teach them to love and esteem this people as God does. Anti-Jewish prejudice should be presented by calling attention to God's love for the Jews. Explain to the students that Jesus is a Jew.

But the manual for Grade 3, dealing with the Passion, summarizes the four narratives this way:

> Now Pilate knew the real reason why the people wanted Jesus to die— because Jesus claimed to be the Son of God. They want no King but Caesar. This is their final apostasy, their final rejection of God.

This latter statement is misleading in almost all its particulars, from the generic use of the term "the people" where the Gospel texts show only a small "crowd" to the odd notion that some kind of collective "rejection of God" was involved in the affair. As evidenced by two major Jewish revolts against Rome in the period following Jesus' death, "the people" most definitely did *not* want Caesar as their king in any sense.

Unfortunately but perhaps inevitably, such misleading statements are usually found in the curricula in very close conjunction with vivid depictions of Jesus' agonies. This, of course, can leave in the minds of students lasting and very negative, if latent, attitudes toward Jews and Judaism.

It should be made clear in the presentation that crucifixion was a Roman form of punishment, one meted out particularly for "political" offenses, not religious ones. In Jewish law, the punishment for blasphemy was death by stoning at the hands of "all Israel." That is, the people themselves must participate in the execution of the blasphemer because blasphemy involves a violation of the Covenant itself, and thus threatens the covenantal relationship between God and the people Israel (Lev 24:10-16).

If Jesus had been convicted of blasphemy by a formal Jewish court under biblical law, crucifixion by a third party would not have satisfied the requirements of the law. If some Jews were concerned about possible blasphemy in Jesus' teaching, they would not have been satisfied that death by crucifixion rather than the required stoning actually responded to the threat to the Covenant. The sentence was the wrong one and carried out by the wrong people. Thus it is unlikely that Jesus was formally charged or convicted by Jews of blasphemy under the law.

Nor is there anything in Jesus' teaching that would constitute "blasphemy" in a legal sense under Jewish law. The claim of his followers that he was the Messiah, while having distinct political overtones, as Pilate would have recognized, was from a Jewish point of view simply something true or false. In the second Jewish revolt against Rome, for example, the great Rabbi Akiba openly proclaimed Bar Kochba, the leader of the revolt, to be the Messiah. When Bar Kochba was defeated by Rome this claim came in for some clever satire by the rabbis, but there is no indication that the claim itself was seen as in any way blasphemous, only, in retrospect, foolish.

As seen above, Jesus did appear to represent a threat to the religious authority of the temple priesthood and, by his popularity with the people, to Roman rule itself, though he seemed to have argued otherwise by acknowledging that one ought to give to Caesar what was due the secular power. The Gospels are quite clear that Jesus was condemned to death for political reasons (Luke 23:2-5). The official charge posted on the cross was insurrection: "King of the Jews" (John 19:19).

Because of the potential for misunderstanding, the teacher needs to be very clear on these basic points.

## VII. The Role of Pilate

Pilate is often viewed as a symphathetic figure in religious education materials. The Gospel of Matthew is taken to be a source for this portrait of a kindly ruler who believes in Jesus' innocence but is pushed by Jews into killing Jesus. Since the Gospels were written at a time when the survival of the Church depended upon Roman toleration, one can understand today that the Gospel writers would not have wanted to point too obvious a finger of blame against Pilate as the villain of the narrative. Charges were already being levelled against Christians that they were insufficiently loyal to the Roman empire.

Ancient accounts of Pilate contemporary with his own time, however, reveal another side to the man than the one often presented of him in Christian teaching, a sincere but weak individual easily swayed by the machinations of "the Jews." It is known that Pilate was ultimately called back to Rome because his excessive brutality toward the native population was leading to ever greater resentment of Roman rule. At one point, he lined the road between two towns with crucified Jews in retaliation for an attack on a Roman patrol in the vicinity. Under his reign, the slightest hint of "revolutionary" potential seems to have been sufficient cause for a Jew to be crucified. Jesus was likely one of these.

A letter of the period reveals what many of Pilate's contemporaries felt about him. It accuses him of "corruptibility, violence, robberies, ill-treatment of the people, grievances, continuous executions without trial, endless and intolerable cruelties."

New Testament scholar Gerard Sloyan concluded in his study *Jesus on Trial* (Fortress, 1973) that:

> Jesus' historical opponents, therefore, were certain of the chief priests and their associates. It is probable that they became the whole Sanhedrin in a (later) dramatization of the story in Christian circles (131).

As I concluded in my own treatment of the topic in my book *Faith Without Prejudice* (Paulist, 1977):

> The Gospels as a whole present us with sufficient evidence, when viewed objectively, to reconstruct a true picture of Jesus' death. That picture does not include "the Jews" or even "the Jewish leaders." It is an event in which the Roman governor is the primary actor, along with certain key figures of the temple party which he controlled. (83)

### VIII. Precision in Presentation

One must, in the words of the 1974 Vatican Guidelines, learn to treat the issue of the presentation of the Jewish figures involved in Jesus' death with an "overriding preoccupation" for precision and accuracy. Linked conceptually with the death of Jesus, for example, is the death of the first martyr, St. Stephen, who was, perhaps not coincidentally, in fact stoned to death. We tend in our minds to think of Stephen's martyrdom as something done by "the Jews" in their alleged "rejection" of Christianity. But read more closely, the text of the New Testament is here much more precise. The harsh words of Peter and Stephen in Acts, in the first instance, are not addressed to the Jewish people as such nor even to the inhabitants of Jerusalem, but to the leaders of the city. The trial of Stephen was never completed, the text says (Acts 7), but taken over by a mob.

Acts 5:17 is very clear that it was the high priest and his supporters among the Sadducees who arrested the apostles and brought them before the Sanhedrin. In this case, unlike that of Jesus or Stephen, a full trial seems to have been concluded under Jewish law. Interestingly, it was "a Pharisee named Gamaliel, a teacher of the Law, honored by all the people," who risked the wrath of the Temple authorities to defend the apostles and their right to preach the Gospel even in the Temple precincts. His argument was simplicity itself. If the Christian claims about Jesus have been fabricated ("made by men"), they will sooner or later fall of their own weight. But if, Gamaliel argues, they are in some way inspired by God, nothing can silence them and you (Sadducees) may find yourselves vainly trying to oppose the will of God. To their credit, the Sadducees saw the wisdom of this argument. The lives of the apostles were saved by a classical example of Pharisaical reasoning, which is to say reasoning permeated with piety, wit and compassion. Even more interestingly, it must be remembered that here we have the lives of all of the apostles at stake, which is to say the very existence of the early Church, saved by a Pharisee.

Perhaps Catholic teachers could set aside one day during Holy Week, say Monday or Tuesday, to remember the Pharisee Gamaliel, the Preserver of the Church, in our classrooms.


## IX. Case Study: "Blasphemy" in the Gospel of Mark

In Section VI, above, we discussed briefly some of the reasons to doubt the historical accuracy of the notion that Jesus was formally charged and convicted of blasphemy by a Jewish court. While the issue is not a major one in terms of literary-critical scholarship in New Testament studies, it is of more than passing importance catechetically. First, because of its implications for Christian theology and secondly, because of its implications for Christian understandings of Judaism.

The theological implications of the blasphemy charge are straightforward, since it is linked in the Gospels with the sacramental understanding of the forgiveness of sins, especially in Mark as we shall see, and also, in post-Resurrection understanding with our Christian awareness of the divinity of Christ. It is not an issue, therefore, that the catechist should approach lightly.

The implications of the blasphemy charge for Christian-Jewish relations over the centuries, however, have been devastating. If one presumes a formal Sanhedrin trial, then one can see in the evangelists' accounts a neat reversal whereby, in effect, it is Judaism as such that is on trial and found wanting. Briefly put, if Jesus' teachings and claims about himself were, historically, such that a formal trial according to Jewish law would have to result in his conviction as a blasphemer for those teachings, then the Christian would of necessity see Judaism as essentially opposed to Christianity and the Jewish people as inevitable and eternal enemies of Christians by reason of their very faithfulness to Jewish beliefs and practice. Indeed, as we have seen, this is just how many Christians in subsequent centuries saw the relationship between Judaism and Christianity, not only as different interpretations of God's Word in the Scriptures, but as necessarily opposing interpretations, such that the affirmation of the one automatically implied implacable hostility toward the other.

Such a situation of theological hostility, of course, is not what the New Testament authors had in mind, as one can see most clearly in St. Paul, Romans 9–11. Rather, the New Testament authors were interested in putting forward a positive theology about Jesus. The use of the blasphemy charge in the Gospel of Mark is a case in point, and will also provide the teacher an example of how this doubly sensitive issue (for Christian theology and for Christian appreciation of Judaism) may be handled.

In the Hebrew Torah (Lev 24:10-23), cited above, a person is to be condemned to stoning if he or she "curses (*qillel*) the Name" of God. Subsequent Jewish legal tradition (e.g., Babylonian Talmud, Sanhedrin 7, 5) defined blasphemy very narrowly requiring that the person actually have pronounced the sacred tetragrammaton (YHWH) for the punishment of stoning to be invoked, even though the Greek translation of the Bible, the Septuagint, uses the term, *blasphemein*, in related contexts outside the Pentateuch in a wider sense.

In Mark's Gospel, which is the earliest according to scholars, the blasphemy charge appears in Jesus' first controveresy with some of his fellow Jews at the beginning of the Gospel (Mark 2:1-12) and his last, in the trial narrative (Mark 14:61-64, cf., Matt 26:65, omitted in Luke). In the first, the confrontation is with the scribes, who react to Jesus' affirmation to the paralytic, "Your sins are forgiven" by saying "in their hearts" that Jesus was blaspheming, since only God can forgive sins. Some verses later, this interior questioning leads the scribes, now Jesus' enemies, to begin plotting against his life (Mark 3:6). This plot, first seen in the narrator's uncanny ability to read minds, finds its denouement in Jesus' last confrontation with fellow Jews, in this case the high priest (Mark 14), where the denouement of the drama unfolds in the rending of garments and the pronouncement of blasphemy despite the fact that the required two witnesses have not been found: "What further need have we of witnesses? You have heard the blasphemy" (Mark 14:64), though here it is related to certain titles ascribed to Jesus by the early Church (Messiah, Son of the Blessed One, Son of Man).

Numerous scholars, Jewish and Christian, have shown that none of these titles, as such, could possibly have triggered an actual charge of blasphemy, unless understood with the later, post-Resurrection faith of the Church in the divinity of Christ. It is in the light of this faith, then, that this aspect of the Markan scene before the high priest and the charge of blasphemy are best undersood. As E. P. Sanders, whose recent study of the issue is closely followed here, concludes:

> The combination "messiah, son of God" is no more blasphemous than each term separately—except, of course in Christianity. The two favorite Christian titles came to be "Messiah" (in Greek "christos") and "Son of God," and Jesus was thought to be the Messiah and the Son of God in some very special way. Thus Christians might be accused by Jews of blasphemy. These facts stand behind the (scholarly) skepticism which many feel about the exchange between the high priest and Jesus: the combination of "messiah" and "Son of God" is Christian, and the accusation "blasphemy" is a reasonable Jewish response to Christian thought about Jesus. I fully share the view that we have here a (later) Christian composition. (*Jewish Law from Jesus to the Mishnah*, SCM and Trinity Press, London and Philadephia, 1990, 64)

In other words, the blasphemy charge in the trial scene of Mark's Gospel has everything to do with the development of Christian theology in the early Church, but little to do with the likely response of the Jews of Jesus' time. Sanders, and increasingly more and more scholars, posit the overturning of the tables in the Temple as the actual event which triggered the animosity of the Temple priesthood and led them to turn Jesus over to Pilate as a potential troublemaker for the Empire and its clients (themselves). That is, the conflict lay not in abstract doctrine but in very real action and natural reaction in a particularly volatile period of Jerusalem's often troubled history.

It is important to recall that Mark effectively brackets his description of Jesus' public ministry with the blasphemy charge. What begins with his first confrontation ends with his death. This is a very telling and theologically significant narrative device of importance for understanding Mark's theology. But it can be devastating, as we have seen, if presented to students in a literalist and fundamentalist sense, ignoring the context and purpose of Mark's Gospel as a coherent unit.

With regard to the notion that Jesus' affirmation that the paralytic's sins were forgiven would have led to a charge of blasphemy "in their hearts," Sanders notes that it is evident that this is a narrative device, and that it is in the passive voice: "Your sins are forgiven." Jesus does not in fact here put himself in the place of God, forgiving sins, but rather as one who knows the will of God to forgive sins. This might strike some Jews as a bit arrogant, but not blasphemous. Nor was the claim to be able to interpret the will of God without plenty of precedent in Jewish tradition!

It may be of interest, though Sanders dismisses it, that the claim to announce God's forgiveness, like the altercation in the Temple, might have been seen as challenging the prerogative of the priests to declare the validity of the sin-offering in the Temple. In any event, this possiblity does conform to the neatness of Mark's theological "bracket" linking Jesus' public ministry to his arrest by the Temple authorities.

## X. Case Study Two: Matthew's Passion Narrative

Jesus' final journey to Jerusalem for the Passover initiates the climactic events of his public ministry, his death and resurrection. The additions inserted by Matthew into the earlier material that he shares with Mark's Gospel reveal quite a bit about the context in which the evangelist wrote his gospel and also something of the way in which the notion of collective Jewish guilt may have gotten its start.

From the earlier to the later Gospels there is, as we have seen, an increasing tendency to exculpate Pilate and place increasing blame upon the Jewish participants in the events. Whereas Mark and Luke, for example, speak of a "crowd" before Pilate, Matthew, writing in the late 80s or early 90s of the first century, speaks of "the whole people" and John, writing even later, of "the Jews." As shall be seen, such usage has a sociological setting in the desire by leaders of the early Church in the wake of the first Jewish revolt (which led to the destruction of the Jerusalem Temple in the year 70) to disassociate themselves from the rebellion and to reassure the Roman authorities that Christianity, though Jewish in origin, was not inimical to the secular power of the Empire. Such details can also have a theological point bearing on the interreligious polemics of the period between early Christianity and the other great Jewish movement that survived the destruction of the Temple with a claim to possessing "the definitive" interpretation of the Hebrew Bible for the times, i.e., early rabbinic Judaism. Hence, for example, Matthew's insertion of "the Pharisees" into the earlier accounts of the giving of the law of love. In Mark 12 and Luke 10, the scene is a simple exchange between two Jews interpreting the Commandments by citing from the Torah. Matthew 22:34-40, however, changes this scene of Jewish amity into a confrontation between Jesus and Jewish religious leaders, ironically making use of the law of love itself as a polemic against the rabbis of his own time!

Some of Matthew's insertions into the earlier materials reflect his own rather literal sense of biblical fulfillment. All four Gospels show Jesus entering Jerusalem riding, in "fulfillment" of the words of the prophet Zechariah (9:9), "on an ass, on a colt, the foal of an ass." Matthew, however, seemingly relying on a Greek translation of the original Hebrew, cites Zechariah 9:9 with an extra word not found in Hebrew: "mounted on an ass *and* on a colt, the foal of an ass." The extra "and" leads Matthew, following his principle of literal fulfillment, to develop a somewhat humorous scene: "The disciples . . . brought the ass and the colt, and put their garments on them, and he (Jesus) sat thereon" (Matt 21:6-7). So while the other Gospels show Jesus' entry into Jerusalem to the cheering crowd sitting on a single animal, Matthew's image is that of Jesus uneasily astride two animals of two different sizes.

In this instance the actual historical event can be relatively easily separated from Matthew's overly literal interpretation. The discrepancy is harmless, though illustrative, again, of the care the modern reader needs to take in realizing that there are four, not just one, Gospel accounts which cannot, in all their details, be harmonized into one. More devastating, however, are some of the other Matthean additions to the narrative.

Matthew's additions, reflecting the pressures of his own times, are often small but provocative. The confrontation over authority subsequent to the overturning of the tables of the moneylenders in the Temple, for example, is clearly with the Temple priests, as Matthew himself acknowledges (Matt 21:23). But Matthew's additions to the parable of the tenants, which is depicted as a part of this same confrontation within the Temple precincts, illustrates how far the break between rabbinic Judaism and Christianity had gone by Matthew's time. As told in Mark 12 and Luke 20, the vineyard is Israel and the wicked workers, appropriate to a Temple confrontation, are Sadducees and priests, whom Jesus in very Pharisaic fashion charges with corrupting the worship of the people. Matthew records the same parable in Matt 21:33-46. But instead of a condemnation of the Temple priesthood's abuse of their authority as in the earlier Gospels, Matthew widens the scope to include "the chief priests and the Pharisees" (v. 45) and includes a much harsher and more final judgment than anything in Mark or Luke: "Therefore, I say to you, the kingdom of God will be taken away from you and given to a people that will produce its fruit." These words, with their supersessionist implications, are found in neither Mark nor Luke and, if taken literally by the catechist, would constitute a contradiction of St. Paul's view of God's enduring love for the Jewish people in Romans 9–11, e.g., the statement that "the gifts and the call of God (to the Jews) are irrevocable" (Rom 11:29).

Similarly, the parable of the marriage feast, which follows immediately (Matt 22:1-14) escalates the language and scope of the same parable as found in Luke 14. In Luke, the invited guests merely fail to show up. In Matthew they brutally seize and murder the king's messengers. In Luke, the king reacts simply by inviting other guests. In Matthew, "the king was enraged and sent his troops, destroyed those murderers, and burned their city" (Matt 22:7). This last image, of course, clearly refers to the destruction of Jerusalem in the year 70 by the Romans. In Matthew 23, likewise, Matthew collects together and aims at "the Pharisees" several sayings concerning religious hypocrisy, sayings which in Luke 20 and Mark 12 are directed not against Pharisees but scribes.

Matthew adds two key sentences to earlier versions of Jesus' appearance before Pilate which not only reflect his own times but which have been used for centuries by later Christians to rationalize mistreatment of Jews. These are:

> When Pilate saw that he was not succeeding at all, but that a riot was breaking out instead, he took water and washed his hands in the sight of the crowd, saying "I am innocent of the blood of this man. Look to it yourselves." And the whole people said in reply, "His blood be upon us and upon our children" (Matt 27:24-25).

These two verses are unique to Matthew. They would seem to reflect a "fulfillment" of Deuteronomy 21:1-8, the ritual handwashing prescribed when a corpse is found between two or more cities but the murderer is unknown. The leaders of the nearest city, according to Deuteronomy, are to wash their hands while declaring in the name of their communities, "Our hands did not shed this blood." Given the escalation of language from "crowd" to "the whole people" and from the present generation to the next, one can easily discern the lines of Matthew's polemic against the Jewish community of his time, over a generation after the time of Jesus' death. Likewise, the whitewashing of Pilate's unsavory character is here complete. Whereas Mark, in an attempt to appease Roman sensitivities, had portrayed Pilate as somewhat hesitant about whether or not to condemn Jesus to death, Matthew's Pilate is convinced of his innocence and actively seeks to free him.

The elements of this scene are clearly not historical but inventions of the evangelist. The notion that Pilate, with the power of life and death over all Jews under his domination, would not have been able to free Jesus had he so wished, is not historically credible. The phrase, "see to it yourselves," is also unlikely, since Romans alone could carry out a death sentence at the time (John 18:31), and in fact that is how Matthew himself describes what happened next: "Then the soldiers of the governor took Jesus. . . ." (Matt 27:27). "The whole people" could not have been present, nor does Matthew give any rationale for why those present should be in any sense representative of "the whole people." Likewise, the ritual washing of hands in this context was a purely Jewish custom, reflecting biblical law not Roman law. It is unlikely that a Roman governor known for his contempt for the Jewish people would even have known about the prescriptions of Deuteronomy, much less been willing to follow them. Finally, it is odd and perhaps telling that Matthew does not cite the conclusion of the hand-washing ritual from Deuteronomy: "Absolve, O Lord, your people Israel, whom you have redeemed, and let not the guilt of shedding innocent blood remain in the midst of your people Israel. Thus they shall be absolved from the guilt of bloodshed, and you shall purge from your midst the guilt of innocent blood" (Deut 22:8-9).

Whereas in Matthew, "the whole people" are implicated by the evangelist's editorial insertions, in Mark and Luke a sharp line is drawn between the will of the people and the specific acts of individuals, i.e., of the high priests and the Roman governor and his troops. In Luke, "the people" are struck with sorrow over the Roman sentence meted out to the innocent Christ: "Now there was following him (Jesus) a great crowd of the people, and of women, who were bewailing and lamenting him" (Luke 23:27).

The scene in which the priests and "the Pharisees" (two groups that agreed, historically, on almost nothing) assemble together to convince Pilate to place guards at the tomb (Matt 27:62-66) is another scene found only in Matthew. So too is the dream of Pilate's wife (27:19), which serves to bolster the idea that Pilate thought Jesus to be innocent. Further, Matthew alone adds the detail that the priests bribed the guards at Jesus' tomb to spread the rumor that Jesus' body was stolen by his followers (Matt 28:11-15). This may well reflect a response by the evangelist to a contemporary Jewish retort to Christian claims concerning the resurrection, rather than an event from Jesus' time.

## Conclusion

The above reflections illustrate the care with which the catechist should present the events of the last days of Jesus' life. Collective language such as "the Jews" or "the Pharisees" should be avoided entirely. Precision and not a little reflective reconstruction based upon the discrepancies between the Gospel accounts should be involved in the lessons. Jews as such should not be presented as "rejecting" Jesus or his teaching. The role of Pilate (which of course does not reflect upon all Romans of Pilate's time nor upon the Italians of today) should be shown in all its historical negativity. The theological truths of the sacrifice and divinity of Christ will not, properly done, in any way be watered down by developing a more mature catechesis. Rather, these truths will be clarified by removing from their presentation distracting features which from history we know will foster animosity toward and even hatred of Jews and Judaism. The story of Christ's Passion is not a story of scapegoating and blame-calling. It is a story, we believe the ultimate story, of God's infinite love and mercy.

## Questions for Reflection and Discussion

1. Why is the natural tendency to harmonize the four Gospels especially dangerous in regard to the passion narratives?
2. How was blasphemy understood in the time of Jesus? Why do some scholars doubt whether Jesus was ever charged with blasphemy, let alone whether he was guilty of the charge. Be alert to the post-resurrectional nature of the Gospel texts.
3. What is known about the character and history of Pontius Pilate? What factors influenced the Gospels' portrayal of him?
4. What historical and theological points about Jesus' death should be stressed in religious education settings?

# Paul, the Law, and the Jewish People

*Terrance Callan*

The letters of Paul frequently refer to the Law and the Jewish people, but it is not easy to understand what he is saying about them. This difficulty arises largely because Paul wrote letters. Each letter is half of a conversation which can be understood only by reconstructing the other half, mainly on the basis of the letter itself. There is always more than one way to do this. And taken together, Paul's letters do not constitute a systematic presentation of his thought; rather, they are halves of a series of conversations with different groups at different times. These must be synthesized by the interpreter, and again there is more than one way to do this.

Despite, or perhaps partly because of, this difficulty, understanding what Paul says about the Law and the Jewish people has always fascinated readers of his letters. And this has become a principal focus of Pauline scholarship in recent years. Thus far (as we will see) various interpretations have been proposed, and none has been universally acknowledged as satisfactory However, there is widespread agreement among scholars on certain points.

One point which now seems clear to most scholars is that Paul rarely speaks directly about non-Christian Jewish people in his letters. Paul's letters were written to Christian communities that were largely made up of Gentile converts to Christianity, though they also included Jewish converts to Christianity (at least in some cases). And when Paul speaks about the Law and the Jewish people in his letters, he generally does so in an attempt to persuade his Gentile converts to Christianity not to take up Jewish practices. The suggestion that they should adopt Jewish practices has come from other Christians, either Jewish converts to Christianity or Gentile converts who themselves have adopted Jewish practices. Thus, what Paul says about the Law and the Jewish people is a contribution to a discussion which is occurring within the Christian Church. This Church is composed of both Jewish and Gentile converts to Christianity, and it is split over

123

the question of how far it is appropriate for Gentile Christians to keep the Jewish Law. Paul is aligned with those who say that Gentile Christians should not keep the Jewish Law, and against those who argue the contrary. This position may have implications for non-Christian Jews, but is not directly concerned with them.

Another way of putting this is that Paul's letters derive from a very different context than the one in which we read them today. Today the Christian Church is almost exclusively Gentile, and the question of whether or not Gentile Christians should keep the Jewish Law is hardly a live one. We spontaneously read Paul's letters as though they speak directly to our situation in which the Gentile Christian Church and the Jewish people face one another as separate entities with a long and troubled history of mutual interaction. The single most important thing for us to realize in trying to understand what Paul says about the Law and the Jewish people is that his situation was very different from ours. He himself is a Jewish Christian; the Church of his day was made up of Jews and Gentiles; and he tries to resolve a question which we have laid to rest (partly because of Paul's efforts).

## Paul on the Jewish People

Although it is true that in general Paul does not speak directly about non-Christian Jewish people, there are at least two passages in his letters where he does speak directly about them.

### 1. Romans 9–11

The most important of these passages is Romans 9–11. In his Letter to the Romans, Paul concludes a lengthy argument that Gentile Christians should not keep the Jewish Law by speaking about non-Christian Jews. One reason for this may be that the Christian community in Rome seems to have included a sizeable number of Jewish Christians.

Paul begins this section with an expression of his anguish at the fact that many of his fellow Jews have not believed in Christ. (Some understand this anguish as caused by something other than not believing in Christ, as we will see below). He says, "For I could wish that I myself were accursed and cut off from Christ for the sake of my brethren, my kinsmen by race" (9:3). But as he continues his discussion, it becomes clear that the biggest problem which their unbelief raises for him is the possibility that "the word of God [has] failed" (9:6), i.e., that God has not succeeded in saving the people of Israel by sending Jesus as Messiah. Paul then goes on to argue that the unbelief of some Jews need not mean that the saving plan of God has failed. The history of Israel shows that God has always chosen some and rejected others (9:6-29); God could now have chosen those Jews who believed in Jesus and rejected those who did not. This leads Paul into a discussion of why some Jews have not believed in Jesus (9:30–10:21). He attributes their unbelief to a failure to understand God's purposes. He says, "I bear them witness that they have a zeal for God, but it is not enlightened" (10:2).

Paul now returns to the possibility he himself had earlier suggested, i.e., that God has rejected those Jews who did not believe in Jesus. At this point Paul emphatically rejects this suggestion. "I ask, then, has God rejected his people? By no means!" (11:1). This makes it clear that the earlier argument was incomplete. It would be possible to show that the unbelief of some Jews did not mean the failure of God's plan of salvation by supposing that God had rejected them. However, this is not Paul's actual solution to the problem. His actual solution is that the unbelief of some Jews was part of God's plan. Mysteriously, God intended this in order to extend salvation to the Gentiles; and after the salvation of the Gentiles has been accomplished, all Jews will also be saved. Because of this, Gentile Christians should not consider themselves better than non-Christian Jews. (This concern also surfaces in Eph 2:11-22). As Paul says, "Lest you be wise in your own conceits, I want you to understand this mystery, brethren: a hardening has come upon part of Israel, until the full number of the Gentiles come in, and so all Israel will be saved" (Rom 11:25-26). This is Paul's definitive statement about non-Christian Jews. Because "the gifts and the call of God are irrevocable," (11: 29) God will surely save all Jews, those who have believed in Jesus and those who have not.

### 2. 1 Thessalonians 2:14-16

The other passage in which Paul speaks directly about non-Christian Jewish people presents a somewhat different picture. In this passage Paul says that the Thessalonian Christians have become imitators of the Christian Churches in Judea. They have imitated them in accepting the Gospel which Paul preached as the word of God (cf. 2:13) and in remaining faithful to it despite opposition from their countrymen (v. 14). Paul then comments on the non-Christian Jews who opposed the Christians in Judea, saying that they "killed both the Lord Jesus and the prophets, and drove us out, and displease God and oppose all men by hindering us from speaking to the Gentiles that they may be saved—so as always to fill up the measure of their sins. But God's wrath has come upon them at last" (vv. 15-16).

This is a very different perspective on non-Christian Jews than the one we find in Romans 9–11. It even includes elements which later contributed to Christian anti-Judaism, notably the accusation that the Jews killed Jesus. Mainly because of the tension between this passage and Romans 9–11, many scholars propose that 1 Thessalonians 2:14-16 was not originally part of Paul's Letter to the Thessalonians, but was added later by someone else. Another possibility is that Paul changed his mind in the course of time. 1 Thessalonians is the earliest letter of Paul which has survived; Romans is one of the latest. Paul's view of non-Christian Jews might have changed between the composition of 1 Thessalonians and the composition of Romans.

However, it is important to realize that the tension between Romans 9–11 and 1 Thessalonians 2:14-16 is not as great as it might first seem to us. Although Paul ordinarily uses the word *Ioudaios* to mean members of the Jewish people wherever they live, in this context he uses the word more restrictively. He is comparing the treatment which the Thessalonian Christians have received from their countrymen with the treatment which the Churches of God in Judea have received from the *Ioudaioi*. It is clear that *Ioudaioi* here means primarily Judeans, not all Jews everywhere.

Further, the meaning of the sentence which the Revised Standard Version translates, "God's wrath has come upon them at last," would be more accurately reflected by the paraphrase, "The wrath (of the last day) has drawn near to them in the end." It is true that this sentence literally says that wrath has already come upon them. But Paul also refers to this wrath in 1 Thessalonians 1:10; 5:9; and in these passages it seems clear that this wrath still lies in the future. However, with the arrival of the Messiah, the last day has begun to dawn, and Paul can say that both the righteousness and the wrath of God have been revealed (Rom 1:17-18). What this means is that the coming of the Messiah has now made it clear that acceptance of the Messiah means righteousness before God, and that non-acceptance of the Messiah leaves one liable to wrath. In this sense wrath has drawn near to the Judeans who opposed the Gospel.

In his discussion of non-Christian Jews in Romans 9–11, Paul considers the possibility that God makes use of them to show forth wrath (9:22). As we have seen, he ultimately rejects this possibility in Romans 9–11. Perhaps a similar clarification is taken for granted in 1 Thessalonians 2:14-16, but is left unspoken because Paul is not mainly concerned here with the situation of non-Christian Jews. However we interpret 1 Thessalonians 2:14-16, we must remember that Romans 9–11 is Paul's final statement on this matter and should take precedence over 1 Thessalonians 2:14-16 in any reconstruction of what Paul says about the Jewish people.

## Paul on the Jewish Law

Although Paul rarely speaks directly about non-Christian Jewish people, he often discusses the Jewish Law. One of the main themes of his letters is that Gentile Christians should not keep the Jewish Law. This is the principal argument of Paul's Letters to the Galatians and Romans, and an important element of his Letter to the Philippians. We also find this theme in the Letter to the Colossians, which may not have been written by Paul.

It seems quite likely that Paul's argument that Gentile Christians should not keep the Jewish Law would reveal Paul's view of the Law, and perhaps indirectly of non-Christian Jewish people. However, we must keep two things clearly in mind. The first is that Paul discusses explicitly only the case of Gentile Christians and the Law. He never says clearly whether or not Jewish Christians should keep the Law, and certainly never addresses the issue of non-Christian Jews and the Law. This means that we do not have Paul's complete view of the Law, but can only infer it with some caution from his argument that Gentile Christians should not keep the Law.

The second thing we must keep in mind is that the reason why Paul believes that Gentile Christians should not keep the Jewish Law is not entirely clear. In fact it is currently among the topics most debated by scholars. One reason for this unclarity is that in addition to arguing that Gentile Christians should not keep the Law, Paul can also speak favorably about keeping the Law (e.g., Gal 5:14; Rom 13:8-10). Another reason for this unclarity is that Paul presents different arguments in support of his contention that Gentile Christians should not keep the Law. Unless Paul's view of the Law is inconsistent, only some of these arguments express the reason why Paul believes Gentile Christians should not keep the Law; the others are supporting arguments. The way we construe Paul's argument determines to a great extent what implications we will see in it for a view of the Law and of non-Christian Jewish people. Recent scholarly discussion has produced at least five different ways in which we may understand Paul's argument that Gentile Christians should not keep the Jewish Law.

### 1. The Qualitative Interpretation

Many have understood Paul's argument that Gentile Christians should not keep the Jewish Law as based on the inherent character of the Law. The very existence of a religious law seems to imply that human beings can achieve righteousness, and so qualify for salvation, by their efforts to keep the Law. Paul, however, thought that righteousness was possible only as a gift from God. Thus there was no place for any effort to achieve righteousness, or for the Law which would guide such efforts. Paul seems to express this sort of critique of the Law when he refers to himself as "not having a righteousness of my own, based on law, but that which is through faith in Christ, the righteousness from God that depends on faith" (Phil 3:9).

If this is Paul's basic reason for arguing that Gentile Christians should not keep the Jewish Law, then he obviously finds the Law itself deficient, at least in the sense that human beings inevitably misuse it. And it hardly seems that Paul could view positively those Jews who try to keep the Law, whether they are Christian or non-Christian. When the Law is regarded in this way, anyone who tries to keep it seems to have misunderstood God's will in a fundamental way.

Until recent times this has been the dominant understanding of Paul's argument that Gentile Christians should not keep the Jewish Law. It is still espoused by influential scholars such as E. Käsemann. In itself this understanding of Paul's argument makes sense, and there clearly are passages in Paul's letters which seem to support it. However, for two reasons many scholars today consider it unlikely that this interpretation goes to the heart of Paul's argument. First, as E. P. Sanders has argued at length, first-century Jews did not regard the Law as a means by which they could be righteous before God by their own unaided effort. In Jewish thinking keeping the Law was combined with reliance on God. Of course, there probably were individual Jews who tended toward self-reliance, but this was not characteristic of the Jewish people as such.

Even if this is so, it is possible that Paul came to see the Law as intrinsically connected with self-reliance. However, most of those who have interpreted Paul's objection to the law along these lines, have supposed that self-reliance was characteristic of Judaism in Paul's day. If it was not, we must explain in some way how Paul came to this understanding. This understanding itself is not the ultimate basis of Paul's argument.

Second, even if Paul does criticize the Law as an instrument of self-reliance, this does not seem to be his most prominent concern about the Law. As K. Stendahl has argued, Paul is more concerned about the way the Law affects Gentile participation in God's salvation of Israel. Other interpretations of Paul's argument that Gentile Christians should not keep the Jewish Law do greater justice to this concern.

## 2. The Quantitative Interpretation

Another common interpretation of Paul's argument that Gentile Christians should not keep the Jewish Law sees it as based on the view that it is impossible to keep the whole Law. Since one cannot keep the entire Law, an attempt to do so is certain to be unsuccessful and thus to result in one's being liable to punishment for failing to keep the Law. Paul seems to express this understanding of the Law when he says: "For all who rely on works of the law are under a curse; for it is written, 'Cursed be everyone who does not abide by all things written in the book of the law and do them'" (Gal 3:10).

Like the qualitative interpretation, the quantitative interpretation of Paul's argument that Gentile Christians should not keep the Jewish Law implies that the Law is inevitably deficient whenever human beings actually try to keep it. Because reliance on the Law can only lead to condemnation, it seems that Paul could only view negatively those Jews who try to keep it, whether Christian or non-Christian.

This interpretation of Paul's argument that Gentile Christians should not keep the Jewish Law is often combined with other interpretations. For example, H. Hübner understands Paul's argument in Galatians as quantitative, and his argument in Romans as qualitative. However, many scholars today doubt that this interpretation goes to the heart of Paul's argument, and for the same reasons that doubt has arisen about the qualitative interpretation. Neither does justice to Paul's concern for the participation of Gentiles in God's salvation of Israel, and neither reflects the understanding of the Law current in Paul's day. Moreover, not only is the view that it is impossible to keep the whole Law not a common view among first-century Jews, even Paul does not maintain it consistently. In Philippians 3:6 he describes himself in these words: "as to righteousness under the law blameless."

## 3. The Retrospective Interpretation

Because of the problems with the qualitative and quantitative interpretations, others have proposed a very different understanding of Paul's argument that Gentile Christians should not keep the Jewish Law. E. P. Sanders has proposed that Paul's argument is not based on a problem with the Law, but rather on the implications of faith in Jesus. In other words, before he became a follower of Jesus, Paul saw no problem with keeping the Law. But after he became a follower of Jesus, his faith in Jesus implied that it was not appropriate for Gentile Christians to keep the Law. Paul believed that Jesus had been sent by God to save all, Gentiles as well as Jews. But the very sending of Jesus implied that the Law could not lead to salvation; if the Law could provide salvation, the mission of Jesus was unnecessary. Thus there was no reason for Gentile Christians to keep the Law, and attempting to keep it would seem to imply doubt about the sufficiency of faith in Jesus. Paul expresses this view when he says, "if justification were through the law, then Christ died to no purpose" (Gal 2:21).

According to Sanders, then, becoming a follower of Jesus led Paul to conclude that the Law was not necessary for salvation. But this required him either to argue that the Law was not from God (something he could not do as a Jew) or to explain why God gave the Law. And Paul explains that God did not give the Law so that people might keep it and be righteous before God. God gave the Law, knowing that people could not keep it, in order to prepare them to accept salvation through the mission of Jesus (see Gal 3:19-25; Rom 5:20-21).

Thus Sanders argues that Paul does not reject the Law because of qualitative or quantitative problems. But having rejected the Law because of the implications of faith in Jesus, Paul supports this by retrospectively viewing the Law as deficient. Paul begins with the conclusion he wants to reach and develops a variety of arguments for that conclusion. The center of Paul's thought about the Law is the incompatibility of the Law and faith in Jesus. Everything else Paul says about the Law supports this. Scholars who interpret Paul along these lines differ concerning the degree to which Paul's view of the Law is consistent. Paul's explanations of the purpose of the Law do not seem fully consistent, nor do his positive and negative statements about the Law. Sanders considers Paul's position coherent, though unsystematic; H. Räisänen argues that Paul is simply inconsistent.

If we understand Paul's argument that Gentile Christians should not keep the Jewish Law as based on the implications of faith in Jesus, then it is possible that Paul finds nothing wrong with the Law at all. It could not bring salvation, but within its limits, it may be entirely good. And this would mean that Paul could regard positively the Jews who try to keep the Law. Because salvation comes from faith in Jesus and not from keeping the Law, Paul would regard non-Christian Jews as missing something essential. But he might have no problem with Jewish Christians who both keep the Law and believe in Jesus.

It is true that according to this view Paul sees the Law as having a negative purpose, and this in turn might have negative implications for his view of those who keep the Law. But if Paul's explanations of the purpose of the Law are supporting arguments, and not the center of Paul's thought about the Law, it is easy to suppose that they are limited, partial statements about the character of the Law, which would be supplemented by other perspectives if Paul were giving a full account of the Law and not trying to dissuade Gentile Christians from keeping it.

### 4. The Sociological Interpretation

J. D. G. Dunn has argued that the retrospective interpretation (and presumably others as well) finds Paul's treatment of the Law inconsistent because it does not take sufficient account of the social function of the Law. Dunn argues that keeping the Law, and especially circumcision and the food laws, served the social function of establishing the identity of the Jewish people and marking the boundary between them and other groups. But Paul believes that God is God of all, Jew and Gentile, and that Jesus was sent to save all. To require Gentile Christians to keep the Jewish Law is to require them to become Jews, implying that God is God of Jews only. To avoid this implication Gentile Christians must not keep the Jewish Law, thereby becoming Jews. Paul expresses this view when he says, "Or is God the God of Jews only? Is he not the God of Gentiles also? Yes, of Gentiles also, since God is one; and he will justify the circumcised on the ground of their faith and the uncircumcised through their faith" (Rom 3:29-30). But if Paul objects to the Law only as something which divides Jew and Gentile, he can still affirm the need to keep the Law. Both Jew and Gentile must keep the Law, but in such a way that it is not a barrier between them. In practice this means that circumcision and the food laws must be seen as matters of indifference. In this way Dunn reconciles Paul's positive and negative statements about the Law and argues that his treatment of the Law is consistent.

This understanding of Paul's argument that Gentile Christians should not keep the Jewish Law implies that Paul rejects only part of the Law, i.e., circumcision and the food laws, and is favorable toward the rest. If so, it seems that he would regard positively all who tried to keep the latter part of the Law, both Jew and Gentile. But he would regard negatively all who thought it was important to circumcise and keep the food laws. This would include most Jewish Christians and non-Christian Jews.

Although Sanders himself is aware that Paul finds the Law incompatible with faith in Jesus because of the inclusion of Gentiles in the Christian community, Dunn has emphasized this point and developed it in a helpful way. However, it seems unlikely to me that Paul is arguing only that Gentile Christians should not be circumcised and keep the food laws. It seems most likely that Paul, like other Jews, regards the Law as a unity which must be kept in its entirety. In arguing that Gentile Christians should not keep the Law, he argues that no part of it is binding on them. Of course, this means that there is at least some tension between Paul's positive and negative statements about the Law.

## 5. The Restrictive Interpretation

All of the previously discussed interpretations of Paul's argument that Gentile Christians should not keep the Jewish Law imply an understanding of the Law and a view of those who keep it which is negative in some degree. Recently however, L. Gaston, followed by J. Gager, has proposed that Paul's discussion of the Law is exclusively concerned with the relationship of the Law to Gentile Christians and says nothing about the Law in itself, or about those who keep it. No single passage expresses this view directly, but Gaston and Gager argue that it underlies everything that Paul says about the Law. When understood in this way, Paul's argument is compatible with the view that Jews are saved through the Law. This provides a simple explanation of Paul's positive statements about the Law. According to this view, Paul's only critique of non-Christian Jews is directed against their refusal to accept that God is saving Gentiles through Jesus apart from the Jewish Law. In Romans 9–11 Paul is concerned with this refusal and not with lack of faith in Jesus.

Obviously, this way of understanding Paul's argument that Gentile Christians should not keep the Jewish Law is the most attractive in its implications (or rather, lack of them) for Paul's view of the Law and the Jewish people. Understood in this way Paul says nothing negative about the Law in itself, and there would be no reason to suppose that he regards negatively the Jewish people who try to keep it. Paul is exclusively concerned with the way God has chosen to save Gentiles. All Jews need do is acknowledge that God is saving Gentiles in this way.

This proposal is revolutionary, and it is so new that scholars have only begun to evaluate it. It takes very seriously something which is beyond doubt—Paul is arguing that Gentile Christians should not keep the Jewish Law. But it maintains that this argument has no implications for a view of the Law or of the Jewish people. This is far from certain.

All five of these ways of understanding Paul's argument that Gentile Christians should not keep the Jewish Law have contemporary adherents. Scholarly discussion has not yet produced any consensus on this matter, and such consensus may never develop. The biggest unresolved question is whether or not the last interpretation will prove satisfactory. At present the retrospective interpretation is probably the most widely held. This is partly because of the influence of Sanders but also because Sanders articulated a view which had been emerging from the work of various other scholars, such as W. D. Davies, J. Munck, H. J. Schoeps, K. Stendahl and N. A. Dahl.

As may already be obvious, I also find the retrospective interpretation most satisfying. But I am inclined to combine the qualitative, quantitative, and sociological interpretations with it, seeing the retrospective interpretation as fundamental to the others. As I have pointed out above, the sociological interpretation, properly qualified, can be seen as an elaboration of the retrospective interpretation. Further, although Sanders does not do so, the qualitative and quantitative interpretations can be combined with the retrospective interpretation by seeing them as arguments to which Paul appeals in support of the retrospective interpretation, explaining how the Law leads to sin rather than to righteousness.

The only one of the interpretations for which I cannot find a place is the restrictive interpretation. Because of its important implications it must be scrutinized carefully by scholars. And perhaps it will finally be proved the best interpretation, or at least the equal of any other. However, at present it does not seem as satisfying as my modification of the retrospective interpretation, for the reasons which follow.

Although Paul makes the argument in order to convince Gentile Christians that they should not keep the Jewish Law, arguing that if the Law were the source of Justification, then Christ died in vain seems to imply the insufficiency of the Law not only for Gentile Christians but also for Jews. And when Paul supports this view by arguing that the Law could not lead to righteousness, this too seems to imply the insufficiency of the Law for Jews.

At least some of this can be read restrictively as Gaston and Gager propose. But if Paul intended this, we must ask why he did not say so explicitly. At least part of the reason that Gentile Christians were drawn to keeping the Jewish Law is that not keeping it seemed equivalent to disobeying God. To have explained clearly that the Law was God's will for Jews, but that God had established a different means of salvation for Gentiles would surely have been helpful.

The part of Paul's discussion of the Law which is hardest to interpret restrictively is his explanation of the purpose of the Law. While Paul uses this to support the argument that Gentile Christians should not keep the Law, its direct application would be to Jews. On any interpretation Paul does not think that Gentiles should ever keep the Law. Thus its purpose could only be accomplished in those who kept it, i.e., Jews. And this purpose, as Paul sees it, was to serve as a negative preparation for the coming of Christ.

Even though Paul never directly expresses such a view, it seems very likely to me that Paul regarded the Law itself as deficient and would have been critical of Jews who relied on it alone; in Paul's view the Law was intended to lead to faith in Jesus. If this is so, however, it must be qualified in three ways. First, it is clear that Paul did not think Gentile Christians should keep the Jewish Law, but it is not clear that Paul thought Jewish Christians should stop keeping the Law. If they adopted Paul's perspective, they could not suppose that righteousness came from keeping the Law. But if they regarded righteousness as deriving from faith, it is not clear that Paul would have objected to their keeping the Law. They might have done so as a way of preserving their identity as the people of Israel, which Paul would surely have seen as a good. Likewise, Paul would have made no argument that non-Christian Jews should cease keeping the Law, only that they should accept Jesus as the Messiah.

Second, Paul is critical of the Law and of non-Christian Jews because he himself is a follower of Jesus. His criticism of the Law does not arise from an analysis of the Law in itself, and his critique of non-Christian Jews has nothing to do with the way they keep the Law. Before Paul became a follower of Jesus he saw nothing wrong with the Law or Jews; on the contrary, he regarded the Law as God's will for the human race and Jews as uniquely privileged to possess it. What caused him to view this somewhat differently was becoming a follower of Jesus. This means that what Paul implies about the Law and the Jewish people will seem very strange to anyone who does not share his faith in Jesus or at least perceive that this is Paul's starting point. What Paul says about the Law and the Jewish people is not objective analysis, but an analysis from the perspective of faith in Jesus. Its truth depends entirely on the truth of that faith.

Third, although Paul may have been critical of non-Christian Jews, we must remember that this criticism was limited. As we can see from Romans 9–11, Paul thought that God' s faithfulness to Israel was unconditional. Even if part of Israel rejected God's plan by not accepting Jesus as the Messiah, God did not reject them in return. In the end God' s promise to save Israel will be kept.

## Conclusion

It is critically important not to read Paul as if he were a representative of what we today call Christianity and speaking about what we today call Judaism. Paul was a Jew who came to believe that Jesus was the fulfillment of God's promises to Israel and who thought that this fulfillment was open to Gentiles as Gentiles. This faith led Paul to a radical reinterpretation of what it meant to be a Jew. And this in turn made Paul critical of those who did not share his new view of what it meant to be a Jew. In my opinion both of these emerge indirectly, by implication, as Paul argues that Gentile Christians should not keep the Jewish Law.

Later history makes this implicit view of Paul's look like anti-Judaism. Now Christianity and Judaism regard one another as separate religions and Paul is understood as speaking for Christianity against Judaism. But in his own context Paul is involved, with other Jews, in a disagreement concerning the true nature of Judaism. Earlier I said that Paul's letters were a contribution to a conversation occurring within the Christian Church. But they were simultaneously a contribution to a discussion within Judaism because in the first century the two groups overlapped. Many first-century Christians, including Paul himself, were Jews. And it was initially Jewish Christians who differed as to whether or not Gentile Christians were obliged to keep the Law. Those who said Gentile Christians must keep the Law did so because they understood Judaism in the same way non-Christian Jews did. Those, like Paul, who argued that Gentile Christians should not keep the Law did so on the basis of a new understanding of Judaism.

Such differences over the nature of Judaism have arisen again and again in the history of the Jewish people (and in the history of most other groups). In the time of the prophet Jeremiah there was a division among the prophets as to whether God would give Judah into the hands of the Babylonians or would save Judah from them (Jer 27–28). In the time of the Maccabean revolution there were Jews who wished to embrace Hellenistic culture and others who saw this as incompatible with faithfulness to God (1 Macc 1; 2 Macc 4). At the present time Reformed and Orthodox Jews differ over the true nature of Judaism.

Seeing Paul as a Jew who came to a new understanding of Judaism probably does not make his views any more congenial to twentieth-century Jews than they were to those 1st century Jews who disagreed with him But it does give a more satisfactory sense of what is involved as Paul takes his position. And we must always remember that Paul continued to regard the Jews who disagreed with him as the people of God and held that God's promises to them were irrevocable.

## Bibliography

The foregoing is heavily indebted to the treatment of Paul by George Smiga in *Pain and Polemic: The Problem of Anti-Judaism in the New Testament,* soon to be published by Paulist Press.

For a brief description of the process by which Christianity became a religion separate from Judaism, showing the place of Paul in that development, see T. Callan, *Forgetting the Root: The Emergence of Christianity From Judaism* (New York: Paulist, 1986).

Books mentioned in the foregoing discussion:

Dahl, N. A., *Studies in Paul* (Minneapolis: Augsburg, 1977).

Davies, W. D., *Paul and Rabbinic Judaism* (Philadelphia: Fortress, 1948).

Dunn, J.D.G., *Jesus. Paul and the Law: Studies in Mark and Galatians* (Louisville: Westminster/John Knox, 1990).

Gager, J., *The Origins of Anti-Semitism* (New York: Oxford, 1983).

Gaston, L., *Paul and the Torah* (Vancouver: University of British Columbia Press, 1987).

Hübner, H., *Law in Paul's Thought* trans. by J.C.G. Greig (Edinburgh: T. & T. Clark, 1984).

Käsemann, E., *Commentary on Romans* trans. by G. W. Bromiley (Grand Rapids: Eerdmans, 1980).

Munck, J. *Paul and the Salvation of Mankind* trans. by F. Clarke (London: SCM, 1959).

Räisänen, H., *Paul and the Law* (Tübingen: J.C.B. Mohr [Paul Siebeck], 1987).

Sanders, E. P. *Paul and Palestinian Judaism* (Philadelphia: Fortress, 1977).

_____, *Paul, the Law and the Jewish People* (Philadelphia: Fortress, 1983).

Schoeps, H. J., *Paul: The Theology of the Apostle in the Light of Jewish Religious History* trans. by H. Knight (Philadelphia: Westminster, 1961).

Stendahl, K., *Paul Among Jews and Gentiles* (Philadelphia: Fortress, 1976).

## Questions for Reflection and Discussion

1. Why are Paul's exact thoughts about the Torah difficult to ascertain? Why did he rarely refer to non-Christian Jews? How is the social context of Paul's addressees different from our own?
2. What fundamental point about the Jewish people does Paul make in Romans 9–11? Why might his thoughts be important to the modern Church as it seeks to reform its supersessionist past?
3. What are five scholarly approaches to Paul's ideas about the Jewish Law, the Torah? Which of these seems to be the most reasonable to you? Why? What are the possible effects of these various approaches on one's attitude toward modern Jews and Judaism?
4. How has this essay impacted on your own understanding of the Apostle Paul?

## Final Reflections

1. What are your thoughts after completing this exploration of the New Testament and its presentation of Jews and Judaism? Are there ideas of which you have become more convinced? which you had to change?
2. It has been suggested that false or inaccurate knowledge of Judaism will cause Christians to have distorted ideas about their own faith. Discuss this proposal in terms of one's understanding of God, of Jesus, and of the Church.
3. What are the most important things that religious educators can do to promote an accurate knowledge of Jews and Judaism? What should be taught? What teaching strategies might be used?
4. Are you aware of local resources to which you can turn for assistance in teaching about Jews and Judaism in the New Testament? What are the diocesan or regional offices, local synagogues, Catholic or Jewish agencies, or colleges and universities which can provide additional information?
5. What are specific actions or policies which your school or parish can undertake to enhance its education about Jews and Judaism? What can be done during certain special seasons, such as Lent, both catechetically and liturgically?

# Appendix
# Within Context: Guidelines for the Catechetical Presentation of Jews and Judaism in the New Testament

## Introduction
## Why New Guidelines?

"Because of the unique relations that exist between Christianity and Judaism—'linked together at the very level of their identity' (John Paul II, March 6, 1982)—relations 'founded on the design of the God of the Covenant' (ibid.), the Jews and Judaism should not occupy an occasional or marginal place in catechesis: their presence there is essential and should be organically integrated."

This statement is taken from the recent *Notes on the Correct Way to Present the Jews and Judaism in Preaching and Catechesis of the Roman Catholic Church,* issued by the Holy See on June 24, 1985 (USCC Publication No. 970). The guidelines which follow aim to provide a practical and readable tool that can be used by the average teacher in an American context to implement the universal catechetical principles set forth by the Vatican *Notes.*

The discussion of the drafting committee, and consequently these guidelines, centered especially on sections III, IV and V of the *Notes.* These sections of the *Notes* deal with the New Testament portrayal of Jews and Judaism, and with the origins of Christian liturgy in Second Temple Judaism. The table of contents illustrates some of the major themes of the *Notes* which have been expanded in the present document.

No attempt has been made here either to resolve the theological questions raised in other sections of the *Notes* or to delineate for class-

Prepared in cooperation with the Secretariat for Catholic-Jewish Relations, National Conference of Catholic Bishops; Adult Education Section, the Education Department, U.S. Catholic Conference; and the Interfaith Affairs Department, Anti-Defamation League of B'nai B'rith.

room use the many complex historical issues of Christian-Jewish relations over the centuries (*Notes,* Section VI). The present attempt has been to stay well within the parameters of what is already clear and certain in the official teaching of the Church since the Second Vatican Council, leaving for a future effort issues still under consideration by the magisterium and in the ongoing dialogue between the Church and God's people, Israel.

It must be stated, however, that the consensus that emerged in the working sessions of the drafting committee, and which is reflected in these guidelines is remarkable. The unanimity of view is especially significant given the often tragic nature of the long history of relations between Christians and Jews that set the inevitable background of our discussions. Two decades of dialogue may appear a fragile screen to interpose between the present and two millenia of troubled past. Yet, in the words of the *Notes,* a "common hope in Him who is the master of history" and, if I may say, a common faith in the redeemability of history sustained us. At this level, we came to learn, whatever other differences we might have, that essential messages in both Testaments can find a deeper convergence, making possible a joint witness of shared hope and reconciliation.

May, 1986                                          Eugene J. Fisher

### The Background of *Within Context*
### Catechetical Renewal in the United States

It is important to situate the guidelines which follow in the context of efforts already taken in the United States to implement the Second Vatican Council's historic call for a renewal of Catholic teaching regarding Jews and Judaism.

With the promulgation in October, 1965 of *Nostra Aetate,* the Second Vatican Council's Declaration on the Relationship of the Church to Non-Christian Religions, a new page was turned in the ancient relationship of the Church to the Jewish people, and therefore in the Church's understanding of its own mission and nature. This was followed in 1975 by the promulgation by the Holy See of its "Guidelines and Suggestions for Implementing the Conciliar Document, *Nostra Aetate,* No. 4," and in 1985 by the issuance of the above mentioned catechetical *Notes* by the Holy See's Commission for Religious Relations with the Jews.

Meanwhile, work in the United States to implement *Nostra Aetate* was also progressing. In 1967, the Secretariat for Catholic-Jewish Relations of the National Conference of Catholic Bishops (NCCB) issued the first "Guidelines for Catholic Jewish Relations." These were updated in 1985 to reflect advances in understanding through dialogue in the intervening years (USCC Publication No. 966). In November of 1975 the NCCB issued its "Statement on Catholic-Jewish Relations," which carried further the theological task of interpreting the New Testament text, especially the Epistles of Saint Paul.

In 1978 the USCC Department of Education and the Anti-Defamation League of B'nai B'rith (ADL) cooperated in the publication of *Understanding the Jewish Experience,* which provided model teacher-training programs for Catholic educators.

In 1979, the ADL and the NCCB Secretariat for Catholic-Jewish Relations cooperated in publishing and distributing nationally *Abraham Our Father in Faith,* a religion teachers' curriculum guide produced by the office of the Superintendent of Schools of the Archdiocese of Philadelphia, which has since been translated into Spanish for distribution throughout Latin America by CELAM, the Latin American Bishops Conference.

Underlying and supporting such national efforts over the years have been countless academic exchanges and diocesan sponsored dialogues and studies in every region of the United States and Canada. Special recognition should be given here to textbook studies originally initiated by the American Jewish Committee. The first Catholic self-study of religion texts was done by Sister Rose Thering as a doctoral dissertation for St. Louis University in 1961. For a report on the Thering study, see Rev. John Pawlikowski, O.S.M., *Catechetics and Prejudice,* Paulist Press, 1973. This study was updated in 1976 to include post-Conciliar teaching materials (also in the form of a doctoral dissertation for New York University), by Eugene Fisher, *Faith Without Prejudice,* Paulist Press, 1977, and again by Philip Cunningham for Boston College in 1992.

Thus there existed a rich background, not only in official documentation but also in religious education programming and textbook analysis, which the group was able to bring to bear on the task of interpreting the Vatican *Notes* and rendering them into practical principles for use in classroom and adult education settings. *Within Context* can also be used as a helpful evaluative tool for the production of catechetical textbook series and audiovisuals on all educational levels.

### Guidelines for Teachers

What follows is meant to provide insight and direction for catechists, homilists and textbook publishers in their presentation of the subjects treated. It is hoped that they will help to correct misunderstandings, enlarge vision and, through proper interpretation of the New Testament text in its fuller context, point to deeper interfaith understanding between Christians and Jews today.

## Historical Perspectives

### The Jewishness of Jesus

Jesus was born, lived and died a Jew of his times. He, his family and all his original disciples followed the laws, traditions and customs of his people. The key concepts of Jesus' teaching, therefore, cannot be understood apart from the Jewish heritage. Even after the Resurrection, Jesus' followers understood and articulated the Christ Event through essentially Jewish categories drawn from Jewish tradition and liturgical practice. An appreciation of Judaism in Second Temple times is essential for an adequate understanding of Jesus' mission and teaching, and therefore that of the Church itself.

### Jewish Society in Jesus' Time

The Judaism into which Jesus was born and in which the early Church developed was characterized by a multiplicity of interpretation of the Scriptures and of Jewish tradition. These combined with external cultural and political pressures, such as the attractiveness of Hellenism and the heavy burden of Roman occupation, to lead to the formation of numerous sects and movements. Such groups included the *Sadducees,* who were closely associated with the Temple priesthood, held to a literal interpretation of the Bible and tended to cooperate with Roman rule; various groups of *Pharisees,* who developed a uniquely flexible mode of interpreting Scripture and held doctrines opposed by the Sadducees; *Essenes,* who strove for a life of abstinence and purity in a communal setting and viewed the established Temple priesthood as violating the Torah's sacrificial law (among the Essenes would seem to be the authors of the Dead Sea Scrolls); various other apocalyptic circles, who felt the End was near and the redemption of Israel from foreign oppression at hand; revolutionary movements such as the *Zealots,* who advocated violent rebellion against Rome; and various political groupings, such as the *Herodians,* who were supporters of the existing political situation and collaborators with Rome. Given the pressure of Roman occupation, these movements existed in a state of flux and tension rather than as neatly discrete groups.

## Pharisees and Sadducees

The Pharisees and Sadducees are the two groups perhaps most frequently mentioned in the gospels, often as Jesus' opponents in particular debates. Here, it is important to emphasize that these groups were quite often at odds with one another and, especially in the case of the Pharisees, often divided among themselves on key issues as well.

In Jesus' lifetime the Pharisees were a popularly based lay group, whose main concern was bringing the people as a whole to a level of sanctity and observance of the Torah then understood as being virtually equivalent to that expected of the Temple priesthood. The Sadducees, allied with the aristocracy and the Temple hierarchy, rejected the innovative interpretations of Scripture offered by the Pharisees and understood religious observance to be defined by literal adherence to the written text of the Bible.

The gospel portrayal of the Pharisees and Sadducees is influenced by the theological concerns of the Evangelists at the time the texts were set in writing some generations after Jesus' death. Many New Testament references hostile or less than favorable to Jews and Judaism actually have their historical context in conflicts between local Christian and Jewish communities in the last decades of the first century (*Notes*, IV). Gospel depictions of conflict between Jesus and groups such as the Pharisees often reflect the deterioration of Christian-Jewish relations in this later period, long after the time of Jesus. So it is at times difficult to ascertain Jesus' actual relations with these groups.

Still, some things are known which drastically change the traditional understanding of Jesus' relationship with the Pharisees. First, his teachings are closer to those of the Pharisees than to those of any other group of the period, and relatively distant from the biblical literalism that characterized the Sadducees. Secondly, the Pharisees were known to be divided among themselves on key issues, principally between the followers of Beth Hillel and those of Beth Shammai. The latter generally took a more strict interpretation of the law and the former a more lenient approach, from what we know of the two movements from later rabbinic materials. Jesus' interpretations, in the main, would appear to have been closer in spirit to those ascribed by later tradition to the "House" of Hillel. Certain of the conflicts between Jesus and "the Pharisees" as depicted in the New Testament then, may well reflect *internal* Pharisaic disputes, with Jesus siding with one "side" against the other.

*Jewish Roots of Christian Teaching and Worship*

Despite the difficulties of historical reconstruction, however, we can say with some degree of certainty that Jesus shared with the majority of Jews of his time a deep reverence for the Torah. Further, his teaching had much in common with teachings distinctive to the Pharisees in the period, for example belief in the resurrection of the dead, emphasis on the love of God and neighbor, expectation of the coming Kingdom of God and a final judgment, the importance of both humility before and trust in God, and the confidence to pray to God as a loving Father (*Notes* III). Likewise, the early Church organized its communal life and worship principally on Jewish liturgical models such as that of the synagogue (*Notes* V). Hence, Christian liturgy itself cannot be understood without reference to ongoing Jewish practice and tradition, both biblical and postbiblical (See *Sacramental Preparation* and *Catechesis and Liturgy* below).

## Catechetical Principles

*The Gospels and the Hebrew Scriptures*

It is essential to remember that the gospels represent theological reflections on the life and teaching of Jesus which, while historically based, were not intended by their authors to be eyewitness accounts. Indeed, the gospels were set down in final form some 40 to 70 years after Jesus' death. Thus they reflect a long and complex editorial process (*Notes* IV). In their final form they make use of a variety of literary genres, styles, and rhetorical devices common to the Jewish culture of the times.

Using methods familiar to us from contemporary Jewish apocalyptic and Essene writings (e.g., the Dead Sea Scrolls), as well as early rabbinic literature, the New Testament authors sought to explain their experience of Jesus in terms of their Jewish heritage, especially by using passages from the Hebrew Scriptures. When reading the prophets (e.g., Isaiah 7:14, 52-53; Hosea 11:1; Micah 5:1), the Evangelists interpreted Jewish hopes for deliverance as foretelling Jesus' coming. *Such post-Resurrection insights do not replace the original intentions of the prophets.* Nor does Christian affirmation of the validity of the Evangelists' insight preclude the validity of post-New Testament and present Jewish insight into the meaning of prophetic texts (*Notes* I, II). It can easily be seen, however, how use of the same symbols with different meanings can give rise to misunderstandings and even resentment between Jews and Christians today.

The Second Vatican Council clearly taught that God's covenant with and therefore presence among the Jewish people as God's own people has not been abrogated by the coming of Christ: "now as before, God holds the Jews most dear for the sake of their fathers; He does not repent of the gifts he makes or of the calls He issues" (*Nostra Aetate*, No. 4). Thus post-New Testament, rabbinic Jewish insight into the meaning of the Hebrew Scriptures, which Jews and Christians share, retains its own validity. With discerning respect for the differences between Jewish and Christian readings of the Bible, Christian catechesis can and should profit immeasurably from the traditions of Jewish biblical interpretation and spiritual insight.

## Jewish Religious Traditions

Since Jewish tradition provides the context not only for Jesus' message but also for the development of the early Church, an awareness of this ongoing heritage is essential for an adequate Christian catechesis. This heritage, it is important to emphasize, involves not simply biblical Judaism, but rabbinic and present day Jewish religious life as well. Just as each successive generation of Christians has reaffirmed and thereby "made its own" the Apostolic witness preserved in the New Testament, so each generation of Jews has continued to carry on Israel's ancient dialogue with God. Thus, in presenting the early Church's witness as a living reality pertinent to contemporary life, catechists do well to present also the living witness of the Jewish people to God's enduring fidelity to His covenant with them (*Notes*, VI). A tiny sampling of the spiritual riches pertinent to catechesis in ongoing Jewish tradition is given here in the hope of motivating further and deeper study of Judaism among Catholic religious educators.

*The Nature of God.* In Judaism, God is seen as the Lord of history, extending justice to all men and women, and as a loving, merciful parent fulfilling both paternal and maternal roles. Rabbinic commentary interprets God's Name in Exodus 34:6-7 as "thirteen names for mercy." God is both transcendent and immanent, King and Father, worshiped in awe yet close enough to "pitch his tent" with His people.

*Jewish Ethics.* Jewish ethics are marked by a sense of "imitation of God," from its understanding of Creation (Gen 1:27) to its understanding of Covenant ("Be holy as I the Lord your God am holy," Lev 19:2). The Jewish Law of Love, reaffirmed by Jesus, finds its source and fuller context in the Pentateuch (Deut 6:5; Lev 19:18, 33-34), as do the works of mercy (Lev 19; Deut 9:10-19), forgiveness of one who has wronged you and even the feeding of one's enemy (Exod 23:4; Prov 25:21-22). Rabbinic commentaries on these and similar biblical passages (e.g., on the need for repentance) can add depth of insight and a challenging concreteness to classroom discussion. On the basis of imitating God, for example, rabbinic commentary has expounded on the works of mercy: "He (God) clothes the naked. . . . You, too, should clothe the naked! The Holy One, praised be He, visited the sick. . . . You, too, should visit the sick!" (B. Sotah 14a). Rabbinic writings on the need to imitate God's forgiveness are numerous: "Rabbi Gamaliel said: Let this be a sign to you, that whenever you are compassionate, the Compassionate One will have compassion on you" (T. Bab. K. ix, 29, 30); "Be merciful on earth, as our Father in heaven is merciful" (Targ. Jerus. 1. Lev. 22.28).

Pope John Paul II, during his historic visit to the Rome Synagogue, stated that Jews and Christians are, together, "the trustees and witnesses of an ethic marked by the Ten Commandments, in the observance of which humanity finds truth and freedom. To promote a common reflection and collaboration on this point is one of the great duties of the hour."

*The Jewish Sense of Mission.* The Jewish sense of mission is expressed in the prophets Isaiah, Jeremiah, Ezekiel and in later prayers from medieval and modern times as "the hallowing of God's name" throughout the world. It is a call to see that God's Name is known, and praised by, all the nations of the earth. This belief that God should be honored by all humanity is developed in the rabbinic idea that God's Covenant with Noah (as distinct from the one with Abraham) is a universal covenant and a means by which all people can be brought to salvation. This universal concept underlies Judaism's vision of God's Kingdom as a time when all nations will come to worship on the holy mountain, and will gather from the East and from the West to sit down together at God's holy banquet (e.g., Isaiah, Micah, etc). The Jewish sense of mission has resulted in many martyrs, not only in biblical times, as reflected in the books of the Maccabees, but during Christian times as well, for example during the Crusades, when thousands of Jews died rather than abandon their faith. This "heroic witness" of the Jewish people through history (*Notes* VI) needs to be acknowledged and honored today. It is, finally, part of Jewish belief that when the divine Name is praised throughout the world, God's Kingdom will be fulfilled.

*Jewish Understanding of God's Reign.* The Jewish understanding of God's reign is of universal harmony and wholeness (*shalom*), in which all the peoples of the earth will gather to worship God. This understanding of the End toward which all human history is oriented provides a constant and present challenge to Christians and Jews (e.g., Isaiah 2:11; 25; 35; Micah 4:4).

*Jewish Prayer and Liturgy.* Jewish prayer—like Jewish ethics—is structured upon the idea of correspondence between heaven and earth. It is, accordingly, divided into two parts of ascending and descending blessings: the worshiper first offers praise to God, naming a special attribute, then asks for blessings which correspond to that quality. The great prayer of Jesus (the "Our Father") is characteristic of Jewish prayer not only in terms of its special phrasing (every line of the Our Father is paralleled in the Jewish prayer book, *Siddur*) but also in terms of structure. The first part of the prayer consists of ascending blessings in which God is praised as a Father. The worshiper expresses the missionary longing for the honoring of His Name and the coming of His Kingdom. In the second part of the prayer, the worshiper asks for those descending blessings appropriate for God as a Father to bestow: bread, forgiveness, deliverance. In between the two parts is a "hinge" line expressing the desire for correspondence between heaven and earth.

The desire for this correspondence between heaven and earth permeates the Sabbath liturgy, which invariably begins with the same motifs of praise of God and longing for His Kingdom. In rabbinic interpretation, the Sabbath laws are said to anticipate the Kingdom by freeing every creature from ordinary work (even beasts) and banning even the mention of sickness, death, and war. The harmony of the universe at the moment of Creation is recalled and extolled as God's purpose. The seventh day of peace (the Sabbath) is thus seen as the end of time as well as the beginning. The theme of this total peace (*shabbat shalom*) dominates the liturgy. This sense of wholeness and unity is intended to mark both the hearing of God's word in the synagogue and the festive Sabbath meal in the home. The Sabbath afternoon prayers recognize, however, that this perfect state has not yet arrived by concluding with the pilgrim psalms: an acknowledgment that humanity is not yet arrived at Jerusalem, is still on a journey to the holy society.

The great Jewish festivals underscore in different ways this constant journeying toward wholeness: Passover (*Pesach*), which celebrates the deliverance from bondage and the movement toward the Promised Land; Pentecost (*Shevuoth*), which celebrates the giving of the Torah, God's Word seen as the source of life, a bridge between His transcen-

.dent being and His indwelling presence; and *Succoth* or Tabernacles, which is a Festival of Thanksgiving, a Feast of Ingathering. The solemn feasts of New Year and Atonement (*Rosh Hashanah* and *Yom Kippur*) acknowledge this journeying as the human condition and express it in the realities of human sin and repentance, divine justice and forgiving love.

### Torah and Gospel

While the Jewish term, *Torah,* is usually rendered in English translations as "Law," a more accurate rendering of the Hebrew would be "Teaching" or "Instruction." In Judaism, *Torah* is the term used to identify the Pentateuch and by extension the whole of the Jewish "Way" of life in covenant with God (*Halakah*). Torah is thus understood as the revealed will of God, the response God expects of the people whom He has saved and with whom He has entered into an eternal, unbreakable covenant.

*Jesus and the Torah.* Jesus lived by this Torah and even entered into disputes concerning its meaning. The authority of Jesus' person and the uniqueness of his teaching are highlighted in the gospel texts, and certain of the gospel accounts of disputes between Jesus and his fellow Jews appear to revolve around the authority Jesus claimed for himself as *interpreter* of Torah.

Jesus accepted and observed the Law (cf. Gal 4:4; Lk 2:21-24), extolled respect for it, and invited obedience to it (Matt 5:17-20). Therefore, it can never be valid to place Jesus' teaching (gospel) in fundamental opposition to the Torah. The dynamic reality that is Jewish Law should never be depicted as "fossilized" or reduced to "legalism." This would be to misread and absolutize certain New Testament polemical passages apart from their particular context and intent. (See *Pharisees and Sadducees* and *The Gospels and the Hebrew Scriptures* above.)

*Saint Paul and the Law.* While Saint Paul argued that the Law was not binding on Gentiles who had been admitted to the covenant through what God had accomplished in Jesus, he never suggested that the Law (*Torah*) had ceased to be God's will for the Jewish people. In Romans 9–11, Paul reveals his deep love for his people (9:3), and insists that God has by no means rejected the Jews (11:1-2). Regarding the Jews and the Torah, Paul states that even after the founding of the Church, the relationship is enduring and valid, for "God's gifts and call are irrevocable" (11:29). Even though God has shown His Mercy in allowing Gentiles to become "the children of God" in Christ

(9:6-18), Paul's "kin according to the flesh, the Israelites," possess "the adoption, the glory, the covenants, the law-giving, the worship and the promises" (9:4; cf. 1975 NCCB Statement on Catholic-Jewish Relations).

*Catechetical Goal.* Catechesis should make clear the sense of "partnership" in God's plan that should prevail in all relations between Jews and Christians. The process of catechesis, in the words of the Vatican *Notes,* is to bring students to "a greater awareness that the people of God of the Old and the New Testament are tending toward a like end in the future: the coming or return of the Messiah—even if they start from two different points of view. Transmitted early enough by catechesis, such a conception will teach young Christians in a practical way to cooperate with Jews, going beyond even dialogue" (*Notes* II, 10–11).

### Presentation of Jesus' Passion

It is crucial for catechesis to provide a proper context for understanding the death of Jesus. Like the New Testament as a whole, the Passion narratives of the four gospels are not entirely eyewitness accounts of the historical events, but later, post-Resurrection reflections from different perspectives on the meaning of Jesus' death and resurrection. Common to all accounts is the core gospel message that Jesus died "because of the sins of all, so that all might attain salvation." (*Nostra Aetate,* No. 4). Any explanation which directly or implicity imputes collective responsibility on the Jewish people for Jesus' death not only obscures this central truth, but can also lead to antisemitism.

*Reconstructing the Events of Jesus' Death.* Biblical scholarship cannot at present reconstruct with full confidence all of the historical events surrounding Jesus' death. All four gospels, however, reveal a striking similarity in certain essentials: Last Supper with the disciples, betrayal by Judas, arrest in an outdoor area outside the city (because the authorities feared Jesus' popularity with his fellow Jews), interrogation before a high priest, appearance before and condemnation by Pontius Pilate, being led off to death at the hands of Roman soldiers, crucifixion, title on the cross ("King of the Jews"), death, burial, and resurrection. These details provide a level of agreement among the Evangelists practically unique in the Jesus story.

Certain differences of detail reflect the individual author's or redactor's own views from the time in which the narrative was set down. Comparison of the various gospel accounts of the Passion can help the teacher to understand what is particular to a given author and what pertains to the essence of the gospels' common understanding of Jesus' death and resurrection. For example, the phrase, "and all the people shouted back, his blood be on us and on our children," is cited only in Matthew 27:25, while both Mark and Luke distinguish between the "small crowd" before Pilate and "the people" who sympathize with Jesus (e.g., Luke 23:27).

Neither John nor Luke record a formal Sanhedrin "trial" of Jesus, making such a scene historically uncertain. Likewise there is a tendency from the earlier gospels (especially Mark) to the later (Matthew and John) to place more and more of the onus on "the Jews" and less on Pilate, who alone had the authority to order a crucifixion (John 18:31), a notion emphasized in Matthew's hand-washing scene (Mt. 27:24). The use of the general term, "the Jews" in the Passion narrative of the Gospel of John can lead to a sense of collective guilt if not carefully explained.

Such scenes, transmitted uncritically in the classroom, can lead to misunderstanding of the nature of New Testament narrative and even to anti-Jewish hostility among students, as history has shown all too well. Therefore, a careful attempt to contextualize passages describing conflict between Jesus and various Jewish groups is essential in catechesis today.

*The Pharisees and the Crucifixion.* The Pharisees should not be depicted as implacable opponents of Jesus. They shared with him much that was central to his teaching. Moreover, the Passion accounts do not mention the Pharisees as playing a significant role in Jesus' death. One passage, Luke 13:31, even tells us that Pharisees tried to warn Jesus of a Herodian plot against his life.

*The Role of Pilate.* Educators need to stress what is known from extrabiblical material about the oppressive nature of Roman rule in Judea and about Pilate's unsavory historical character. The Roman governor appointed the high priests of the Temple and could depose them at will. Thus, Pilate would have been in control of the situation throughout the events of Jesus' arrest and crucifixion. Pilate is known to have been a particularly strong and cruel procurator. He crucified hundreds of Jews without recourse to Jewish or Roman law. Among them, as we know from the gospels, was Jesus. Pilate was eventually recalled by Rome to account for his cruelties and the unrest in the Jewish population that they precipitated. The Creed, it should be recalled, mentions only Pilate in connection with Jesus' death, not Jews.

The modern experience of oppressed peoples under totalitarian occupation—from France under the Nazis to Afghanistan under the Soviets—may be utilized for an understanding of the tensions between collaborators and patriots.

*Catechetical Goal.* The central focus of catechesis should be on the theological significance of the events and on our own participation in it as sinners (Catechism of the Council of Trent). The above principles are especially important in catechesis preparing for Lent and Holy Week (*Notes* IV).

## Catechetical Practices

### Maturity in Faith as Catechetical Goal

Fostering maturity in faith is the central task of catechesis, at the earliest age and continuing through life in ways appropriate to the growth of the believer. Mature faith involves the fullest understanding of one's spiritual identity and the fullest respect for the spiritual identity of another. To understand their own identity, Christians need to know and appreciate their rootedness in Biblical Judaism. They need to recognize and accept the fact that Jesus was a devout Jew, and so cherish the Jewish traditions they have inherited through him. They also need to understand that Rabbinical Judaism developed at the same time as Christianity and that both modern religions are characterized by many similar responses to ancient teachings and customs. If their faith is mature, Christians will not be threatened by dialogue with modern Judaism, but rather, challenged and inspired by its spiritual riches. Mature Christian faith sees itself not as opposing Judaism, but as integrally bound with it in fulfilling God's redemptive plan for the world.

> "Attentive to the same God who has spoken, hanging on the same word, we have to witness to one same memory and one common hope in Him who is the master of history" (*Notes,* I, II).

### Sacramental Preparation

While the Catholic definition of a sacrament as "a sign instituted by Christ" might seem to make marginal any reference to Judaism, the reality is that here, as elsewhere in his teaching, Jesus and the early Church drew upon the riches of Jewish tradition. While Jews have never used the vocabulary of "sacrament" as developed in Christian liturgical tradition, the "sacramental view" of life—that Creation is holy and that God speaks and is present to us through material signs—is inherently Jewish.

*Signs of God's Presence.* A Jewish concept which profoundly implies this "sacramental" view is found in the rabbinic use the term *shekinah,* a feminine word signifying divine Presence. Numerous biblical stories describe ways in which God becomes present to the chosen people through concrete signs, e.g., the burning bush, the parting of the Red Sea, the cloud and pillar of fire in Exodus, the cloud which filled the Temple at its dedication (1 Kings 8), and the rush of the spirit upon David at the time of his anointing. Connected with such stories of liberation and empowerment are the Jewish rituals of washings (*mikveh*), and anointing. The Christian practice of baptism derives from the Hebrew *mikveh.* Christian practices of anointing reflect the Biblical practice of anointing kings and prophets. The Hebrew term "Messiah" means "the anointed one."

*Sacramental Theory.* In addition to the sacramental perspective and the Jewish origins of Christian ritual, Christian sacramental theory is rooted in Jewish concepts of the biblical and Second Temple periods: that human beings stand in constant need of repentance and atonement for sin; that the religious community may make use of the mediating ritual of priests; and that the commitment of married love is so holy that it can stand as a metaphor for the covenant between God and the people of God.

*The Eucharist.* The central action of Christian worship—the Eucharist—not only has its origins in the prayers and rituals of the Passover meal (e.g., the blessings over the bread and wine), but takes its essential significance from the Jewish understanding of *Zikkaron* ("memorial re-enactment"), i.e., the concept that God's saving presence is not only recalled but actually re-lived through a ritual meal. The Synoptic Gospels thus imply that Jesus instituted the Eucharist during a Passover *Seder* celebrated with his followers.

### Catechesis and Liturgy

A primary task of catechesis is preparation for the liturgy. Here, it can be stressed that both Jews and Christians find in the Bible the very substance of their communal worship: proclamation of and response to God's Word, prayers of praise to God and intercession for the living and the dead, recourse to the divine mercy.

*The Liturgical Cycle.* The Church's liturgical cycle of feasts parallels that of the Synagogue, and in great part draws its origins and continuing sustenance from it. Both Christians and Jews celebrate the Passover. Jews celebrate the historic *Passover* from slavery to freedom, and look forward to the fulfillment of human history in an age of universal justice and peace (*shalom*) for all humanity at the end of time. Christians celebrate the Passover Exodus accomplished in the death and resurrection of Jesus, likewise awaiting its final consummation at the end of time.

St. Luke describes Jews coming to Jerusalem for the feast of Pentecost, which celebrates the giving of the Torah. Christians celebrate the Jewish feast of Pentecost as the occasion of the giving of the Spirit to the apostles. Both traditions observe periods of fasting and repentance in their annual cycles. The liturgical spirit of Advent and Lent is paralleled by the equivalent (though in many ways profoundly distinct) spirit of *teshuvah* ("turning," repentance) and reconciliation evoked by the High Holy Days culminating in Yom Kippur, the Day of Atonement. Commentary on this feast in the Jewish Daily Prayer Book (the *Siddur*) spells out Jewish belief in free will and "the Evil Inclination," the different levels of sin, and the need for continual confession, remorse and a resolution of amendment.

*Spiritual Bonds.* Not only the great liturgical cycle but also innumerable details of prayer form and ritual exemplify the "spiritual bond" which the Church shares with the Jewish people in every age. The prayer of hours and other liturgical texts draw their inspiration from Synagogue Judaism and a common Bible (especially the Psalms), as do the formulas of the Church's most venerable prayers, such as the Our Father and other Eucharistic prayers. The offering of bread and wine, for example, is rooted in the Jewish *Berakah* ("Praising"): "Blessed are You, Lord our God, King of the Universe, who brings forth bread from the earth."

As Pope John Paul II stated: "The faith and religious life of the Jewish people, as they are professed and practiced still today, can greatly help us to understand certain aspects of the (liturgical) life of the Church."

### Catechist Formation

What is true of catechesis in general is of necessity all the more true of programs designed to prepare catechists. Fostering a positive and accurate appreciation of the Jews as God's people still today and of Judaism as a living witness to God's Name in the world should be an essential and not merely an occasional goal in all program planning (Notes, 1).

Catechists and all teachers of religion share in a special call to hand on the faith of the Church. Catholic faith and Jewish faith are, in the words of Pope John Paul II, "linked together at the very level of their identity" (Rome, March 6, 1982). It is vital that all programs of catechist formation and teacher training provide the elements of Jewish tradition, not only biblical but rabbinic and spiritual traditions and liturgical practice as well. In this way catechists will be better prepared to foster in the students a "full awareness of the heritage common to Jews and Christians" spoken of by the Pope (*ibid.*) and to share the richness of that heritage.

That this is a task for Catholic "diocesan and parochial organizations, schools, colleges, universities and especially seminaries" is made clear by the Second Vatican Council's Declaration on the Relationship of the Church to Non-Christians (*Nostra Aetate,* No. 4) and subsequent documents of the Holy See and our own National Conference of Catholic Bishops. It is a task "incumbent upon" teachers and theologians, in the words of the 1975 NCCB Statement on Catholic-Jewish Relations. A rich reservoir of resources for teachers and teacher trainers is already in existence (See *Resources for Teachers* below).

### Preparation and Evaluation of Textbooks

As Bishop Jorge Mejia, then of the Holy See's Commission for Religious Relations with the Jews, stated in announcing the promulgation of the Vatican *Notes,* "It is, in fact, a practical impossibility to present Christianity while abstracting from the Jews and Judaism, unless one were to suppress the Old Testament (Hebrew Scriptures), forget about the Jewishness of Jesus and the Apostles, and dismiss the vital cultural and religious context of the primitive Church" (*L'Osservatore Romano,* June 24, 1985). To be true to the task of presenting the Church's own "story" and message to the world, one must strive to present Judaism and the Jewish people accurately, fully and positively.

Publishers should be encouraged by the progress made in Christian-Jewish relations since the Council, and by the Council's own mandate, to grasp the opportunity given today to infuse their textbooks, teacher manuals and audio-visuals with materials drawn from the rich spiritual heritage of Judaism. The principles and practices listed briefly above will provide publishers with a handy check list of criteria to give to authors and evaluators of all teaching materials. School texts, prayerbooks and other media should, under competent auspices, continue to be examined in order to remove not only those materials that do not accord with the content and spirit of the Church's teaching, but also those that fail to show Judaism's continuing role in salvation history in a positive light.

Reclaiming the Jewish origins of Christianity, together with a sense of the continuing fruitfulness of the Church's spiritual links with the Jewish people today, can greatly enrich and deepen Christian education.

## Concluding Reflection

The stress in these guidelines, which are meant to complement rather than replace present Catholic religious education curricula, has been on the "common spiritual patrimony" shared by Christianity and Judaism. This is not meant to diminish the uniqueness of Jesus' message or that of the Church, but rather to deepen that message with an appreciation of its interrelatedness with the ongoing witness of the Jewish people.

Pope John Paul II, addressing the Jewish community in the great synagogue of Rome on April 13, 1986, expressed this vision:

> Jews and Christians are the trustees and witnesses of an ethic marked by the Ten Commandments, in the observance of which humanity finds its truth and freedom. To promote a common reflection and collaboration on this point is one of the great duties of the hour. . . . In doing this, we shall each be faithful to our most sacred commitments and also to that which most profoundly unites and gathers us together: faith in the one God who 'loves strangers' and 'renders justice to the orphan and the widow' (cf. Deut 10:18), commanding us too to love and help them (cf. Lev 19:18-34). Christians have learned this desire of the Lord from the Torah, which you here venerate, and from Jesus, who took to its extreme consequences the love demanded by the Torah. . . . The Jewish religion is not 'extrinsic' to us, but in a certain way 'intrinsic' to our own religion. With Judaism therefore we have a relationship which we do not have with any other religion. You are our dearly beloved brothers. . . . (Origins, April 24, 1986).

## Resources for Teachers

*Books*

Claire Huchet Bishop, *How Catholics Look at Jews* (Paulist Press, 1974). Studies of Italian, Spanish and French Catholic teaching materials.

Mary C. Boys, *Biblical Interpretation in Religious Education* (Religious Education Press, 1980). The problems and possibilities of the "salvation history" approach in catechetical theory and practice.

Douglas Charing, *The Jewish World* (Silver Burdett, 1985). Beautifully illustrated introduction for the late grade or high school.

Emil Bernhard Cohn, *The Immortal People* (Paulist, 1985). A short and dramatically told popular narrative of Jewish history for adults.

Helga Croner, ed., *Stepping Stones to Further Jewish-Christian Relations* (Stimulus, Anti-Defamation League of B'nai B'rith, 1977) and *More Stepping Stones* (Paulist Press, Stimulus Series, 1985). These two volumes include the major Catholic and Protestant statements on Christian-Jewish relations.

Philip A. Cunningham, *Jewish Apostle to the Gentiles: Paul as He Saw Himself* (Twenty-Third Publications, 1986). An excellent popular introduction to Paul's Epistles and their implications for Christian life today.

Annette Daum and Eugene J. Fisher, *The Challenge of Shalom for Catholics and Jews* (Union of American Hebrew Congregations/National Conference of Catholic Bishops, 1985). A dialogical discussion guide to the Catholic Bishops' 1983 Pastoral on Peace and War.

Eugene J. Fisher, *Faith Without Prejudice: Rebuilding Christian Attitudes Toward Judaism* (Crossroad, 1993). Written for Catholic elementary and secondary teachers, with practical suggestions for classroom use.

Eugene J. Fisher, *Homework for Christians Preparing for Jewish-Christian Dialogue* (National Conference of Christians and Jews, revised, 1986). A six-session program for high school and adult education programs.

Eugene J. Fisher, *Seminary Education and Christian-Jewish Relations* (National Catholic Educational Association, 1988). A curriculum and resource handbook for all teachers of theology.

Eugene J. Fisher and Leon Klenicki, *Root and Branches, Rabbinic Judaism and Christianity in Their Early Periods* (St. Mary's Press, *PACE* Monograph Series, 1986).

Eugene J. Fisher, James Rudin and Marc Tanenbaum, eds., *Twenty Years of Jewish-Catholic Relations* (Paulist, 1986). Essays by leading thinkers on the biblical, liturgical and educational implications of the dialogue since the Second Vatican Council.

Edward H. Flannery, *The Anguish of the Jews: Twenty-Three Centuries of Anti-Semitism* (Paulist Press, 1985). Father Flannery's classic text has been substantially revised and updated.

Leon Klenicki and Eugene J. Fisher, "Basic Jewish and Christian Beliefs in Dialogue," *PACE 13* (St. Mary's Press, 1983).

Leon Klenicki and Eugene J. Fisher, "Toward a Catholic High School Curriculum for Teaching the Holocaust," *PACE 10* (St. Mary's Press, 1979).

*Understanding the Jewish Experience* (ADL/USCC Department of Education, 1979). Models for parish teacher-training programs.

*From Death to Hope: Liturgical Reflections on the Holocaust* (Stimulus Foundation, 1983). A Christian-Jewish Holocaust Memorial Service.

Leon Klenicki and Gabe Huck, eds., *Spirituality and Prayer: Jewish and Christian Understandings* (Paulist Stimulus, 1983).

Leon Klenicki and Geoffrey Wigoder, eds., *A Dictionary of the Jewish-Christian Dialogue* (Paulist Stimulus 1984). Many terms Jews and Christians share have different meanings in the two traditions. The *Dictionary* explains from both viewpoints such key terms as after-life, church, election, eschatology, faith, justice, law, love, martyrdom, Messiah, repentance, sacrament, salvation, sin, and tradition.

John T. Pawlikowski, O.S.M., *Sinai and Calvary* (Benziger, 1976). Teacher background on Judaism and Christianity through history.

John T. Pawlikowski, O.S.M., *What Are They Saying About Christian-Jewish Relations* (Paulist, 1979). Survey of contemporary theological and scholarly biblical opinion for the general reader.

John Pawlikowski, O.S.M., and James Wilde, *When Catholics Speak About Jews: Notes for Homilists and Catechists* (Archdiocese of Chicago, Liturgy Training Publications, 1987). Guidelines and ideas on the proper presentation of Judaism by catechists and homilists.

A. James Rudin, *Israel for Christians* (Fortress Press, 1983). A rabbi discusses Zionism and the modern state of Israel for Christian readers.

Anthony J. Saldarini, *Jesus and Passover* (Paulist, 1984). Popularly written exposition of the Passover and its relationship with Christian liturgy.

Lawrence H. Schiffman, *Judaism: A Primer* (Anti-Defamation League of B'nai B'rith, 1986). A basic introduction to Jewish beliefs, practices, and history.

F. M. Schweitzer, *A History of the Jews* (Macmillan/ADL, 1971). By a Catholic author for the general reader.

F. E. Talmage, *Disputation and Dialogue* (KTAV/ADL, 1975). Key readings from Christian and Jewish masters over the centuries on topics such as Messiah and Christ, Law and Grace, Letter and Spirit.

Rose Thering, O.P., *Documentary Survey Report of Catholic Institutions' Implementation of Official Church Teaching Since the Second Vatican*

*Council* (Seton Hall University, 1985). A study of educational programming concerning Jews and Judaism on the elementary, secondary,
college, and university levels.

Norma Thompson and Bruce Cole, eds., *The Future of Jewish-
Christian Relations* (ADL/Character Research Press, 1982). Essays on
the prophets, the Holocaust, mission, liturgy, and education.

Edward Zerin, *What Catholics And Other Christians Should Know
About Jews* (Wm. C. Brown, 1980). High school level introduction to
Judaism for Christians.

*Abraham, Our Father in Faith* (Superintendent of Schools Office,
Archdiocese of Philadelphia, 1979). A curriculum guide for religion
teachers on the primary and secondary levels.

## Journals

*Face to Face* (Anti-Defamation League of B'nai B'rith, 823 United
Nations Plaza, New York, NY 10017). An interreligious bulletin of
Christian-Jewish relations. Quarterly.

*SIDIC* (Via del Plebescito, 112, 00186, Rome, Italy). Published by
the Sisters of Sion in Rome, each issue (three times a year) is devoted
to a special subject of interest to educators, such as catechesis, the
family, the chosen people, prophetic texts, and liturgy.

## Audiovisuals

*Christians and Jews: A Troubled Brotherhood,* a filmstrip created by
Sister Suzanne Noffke, O.P., presenting through images of art and
sound the history of the relationship over the centuries.

*Heritage: Civilization and the Jews.* A nine-part public television series with text by Abba Eban and viewer's guide with discussion group
activities available from Heritage Education Division (WNET/THIR-
TEEN, 356 W. 58th Street, New York, NY 10019). A Christian-Jewish
Study guide has been prepared by the Interreligious Affairs Department of the American Jewish Committee (165 E. 56th St., New York,
NY 10022).

*A Moment in History.* Visit of Pope John Paul II to the Rome Synagogue. Catholic Telecommunications Network (3211 Fourth St. N.E.,
Washington, D.C. 20017).

*The Courage to Care.* Rescuers of Jews during the Holocaust, with
text ed. by Carol Rittner, R.S.M., and Sandra Myers (ADL).

## Contributors

*Mary C. Boys*, S.N.J.M., is associate professor of theology and religious education at Boston College and former chair of the Catholic-Jewish Committee of metropolitan Boston. Her most recent book is *Educating in Faith: Maps and Visions* (Harper & Row, 1989).

*Terrance Callan* holds a doctorate in religious studies (New Testament) from Yale University. He is dean and professor of biblical studies at the Athenaeum of Ohio, a Roman Catholic seminary and ministry training center located in Cincinnati. He is author of *Forgetting the Root: The Emergence of Christianity from Judaism* (Paulist, 1986) and *Psychological Perspectives on the Life of Paul* (Mellen, 1990).

*Philip A. Cunningham* is associate professor of theology and director of the ministry institute at Notre Dame College in Manchester, New Hampshire. He holds a doctorate in religion and education from Boston College, and is the author of *Jesus and the Evangelists* (Paulist, 1988) and *Jewish Apostle to the Gentiles* (Twenty-Third, 1986). He has completed a content analysis of the presentation of Jews and Judaism in current Roman Catholic religion textbooks.

*David P. Efroymson's* doctorate, from Temple University, was written on anti-Judaism in the theology of Tertullian. He is professor of religion and former chair of the department at La Salle University in Philadelphia. His "The Patristic Connection" appeared in Alan T. Davies' *Anti-Judaism and the Foundations of Christianity* (Paulist, 1991).

*Eugene J. Fisher* holds a doctorate in Hebrew culture and education from New York University. He is director for Catholic-Jewish Relations for the National Conference of Catholic Bishops in Washington, and a Consultor to the Holy See's Commission on Religious Relations with the Jews. His latest publications, both in 1990 for Paulist Press, are: *The Jewish Roots of Christian Liturgy* and *In Our Time: The Flowering of Jewish-Catholic Dialogue* (with Leon Klenicki).

*Anthony J. Saldarini* is a professor of theology at Boston College, specializing in Biblical studies and Judaism. He holds a Ph.D. from Yale University and is an associate editor of the *Catholic Biblical Quarterly.* His books include *Pharisees, Scribes and Sadducees in Palestinian Society: A Sociological Approach; Jesus and Passover;* and *Scholastic Rabbinism.*

*Urban C. von Wahlde* holds a doctorate in New Testament from Marquette University. He is currently professor of New Testament Studies and chairperson of the theology department at Loyola University, Chicago. He is associate editor of the *Catholic Biblical Quar-*

*terly.* His most recent publications are *The Earliest Version of John's Gospel* (Wilmington: Michael Glazier, 1989) and *The Johannine Commandments: 1 John and the Struggle for the Johannine Tradition* (New York: Paulist, 1990).